L.F.

George Herbert is regarded as a metaphysical, and at times solely as a religious poet. In this book Marion Singleton focuses on the relation between Herbert's poetry and the cultural background of his life. Singleton examines the style, structure, and thematic basis of *The Temple* in the context of the Renaissance ideal of aristocratic courtliness. She provides the first detailed study of Herbert's association with the literary tradition of the courtier and his strategic use of it in *The Temple*.

The book includes discussions of several important topics: the definition of the courtly ideal and its place in English and French humanism; the increasing distance between the ideal and the actual versions of courtliness in the early seventeenth century; and linguistic srategies and structural innovations devised by courtier poets from Wyatt and Sidney to Herbert's contemporaries. The conclusion examines Herbert's transformation of the secular ideal of service at the king's court into a sacred ideal of service in God's temple.

God's Courtier touches upon issues of relevance not only to its nominal subject, but also to the courtier poet tradition in general. Thus, it will interest literary historians as well as scholars of sixteenth and seventeenth century literature.

God's Courtier

God's Courtier

Configuring a Different Grace in George Herbert's *Temple*

Marion White Singleton

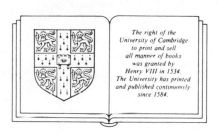

The right of the
University of Cambridge
to print and sell
all manner of books
was granted by
Henry VIII in 1534.
The University has printed
and published continuously
since 1584.

CAMBRIDGE UNIVERSITY PRESS

Cambridge   New York   New Rochelle
Melbourne   Sydney

Published by the Press Syndicate of the University of Cambridge
The Pitt Building, Trumpington Street, Cambridge CB2 1RP
32 East 57th Street, New York, NY 10022, USA
10 Stamford Road, Oakleigh, Melbourne 3166, Australia

© Cambridge University Press 1987

First published 1987

Printed in the United States of America

Library of Congress Cataloging in Publication Data

Singleton, Marion White.
God's courtier.

Bibliography: p.
1. Herbert, George, 1593–1633. Temple.
2. Christian poetry, English—History and
criticism.   3. Courts and courtiers in
literature.   I. Title.
PR3507.T43S56   1987   821'.3   87-10976

British Library Cataloguing in Publication Data
Singleton, Marion White
God's courtier : configuring a different
grace in George Herbert's Temple.
1. Herbert, George, *1593-1633*
Temple, The
I. Title
821'.3   PR3507.T43
ISBN 0-521-33473-X

For my children:
Pamela, Peter, Nancy,
Gordon, Lisa, Martin

Contents

Acknowledgments

First here I wish to thank those teachers who set me on the way to this book. Harvey Birenbaum, Catherine Blecki, and Nils Peterson initially taught me to read Renaissance literature and to interrogate the authorial voices transmitted in those texts. William O. Harris, Milton Miller, and John M. Steadman oversaw the earliest version of *God's Courtier* with the exemplary patience, encouragement, and guidance that all those blessed, as I was, with such wise teachers will remember with affection and admiration. I am also grateful for the support provided by the Patent Fund of the University of California, Riverside, and especially for the assistance so willingly and frequently given by the library staff at Riverside.

Later stages of the manuscript benefited greatly from the suggestions, criticisms, and generous readings of Alan Gaylord, David Kastan, Peter Saccio, Peter Travis, and the anonymous readers of Cambridge University Press. The Faculty Research Committee of Dartmouth College provided welcome support in preparing the manuscript. Thanks also to my editor at Cambridge, Elizabeth Maguire, who saw me through the long period of revision, and to Jim Woods, who worked with me faithfully through the production of the book.

My deepest debt - which no printed acknowledgment could ever discharge - is recorded in the dedication. These are my primary exemplars of faith, will, and grace.

Introduction

The Temple is a curious and wonderful structure. Its three oddly assorted parts, *The Church-porch, The Church,* and *The Church Militant,* invite but finally resist interpretations of coherence: the spatial movement from exterior to interior of the first two parts gives way in the third to a design both spatial and temporal, while their formal diversity disunites, rather than links, the second-person didacticism of *The Church-porch*'s uniform stanzas, the first-person immediacy of *The Church*'s endlessly varied lyrics, and the sweeping history and prophecy contained by the regular couplets of *The Church Militant. The Church,* whose 160 separate poems detail continually shifting relations between a speaker and his God,[1] functions as centerpiece for *The Temple* as a whole but rejects the conventions of narrative sequence even as it seems to offer the story of a spiritual progress. Yet the two manuscripts of the work, W and B,[2] reveal two stages of writing at least: the poet both reordered and augmented the structural "parts" of *The Church.* Individual lyrics echo and re-echo each other in such interwoven complexity that no unitary explanation of their design can fully articulate the generative possibilities Herbert has succeeded in building into his *Temple.*[3]

The problem of narrative structure is compounded further by the enigma of the voice which speaks throughout *The Temple:* the Verser who addresses a "sweet youth" with "early hopes" in *The Church-porch,* the "I" who addresses God, the self, the world in the *Church* lyrics and who offers to God his own vision of church history in *The Church Militant.* Herbert's twentieth-century critics name that voice "the speaker" or "the Christian," consider the "I" persona rather than person, identify multiple personae changing from poem to poem. The speaking of spiritual experience in the first-person lyrics of *The Church* is now rarely read as a single voice recognizable as the

1

author of *The Temple,* deliberately incorporating his own biography
and history throughout the entire structure.

These two interpretive challenges – the nature of *The Temple*'s
structure and the identification of its speaker – govern my study of
Herbert's poem(s) and determine both the form and the title of this
book. I read *The Temple* as a relational, rather than a narrative,
structure, one in which possibilities of sequence, progress, and defined movement from beginning to middle to end give place to fluid,
continually shifting connections: from poem to poem in creatively
disjunctive juxtaposition, across groups of poems, and especially between parts of poems, images, phrases, and situations call
both forward and back in virtually inexhaustible repetition and vari-
ation. Each poem of *The Temple* (as well as each poem's parts) demands to be read in relation to other poems and parts. No single
pattern of relations can ever finally and fully inform our reading;
each relationship that we discover yields new connections and
new meaning.

In "The H. Scriptures. II" Herbert describes just such a relational
structure:

> Oh that I knew how all thy lights combine,
> And the configurations of their glorie!
> Seeing not onely how each verse doth shine,
> But all the constellations of the storie.
> This verse marks that, and both do make a motion
> Unto a third, that ten leaves off doth lie:
> Then as dispersed herbs do watch a potion,
> These three make up some Christians destinie. . . .[4]
>
> (1–8)

The "configurations" and "constellations" that Herbert seeks to
interpret in scripture provide a model for my reading of *The Temple*
and offer a justification for my procedure.[5] Herbert might well have
modeled his construction of a poetic Temple on his configurative
reading of the Bible. Like his, my reading will attend to the marking
and motion of "verses" – parts, as well as wholes – by juxtaposing
parts of two poems ("both do make a motion") to others "that ten
leaves off doth lie." Herbert's analogy – "as dispersed herbs do
watch a potion, / These three make up some Christians destinie" –
claims interpretive value for parts, in the reader's effort to reassemble

meaning out of dispersal, just as the strange passivity of the figure[6] implies that meaning "awaits" – thus depends upon – the reader's act of assemblage.

Scripture, then, exacts from each of its readers an individual interpretation, the discovery of the parallels that, Herbert says, "finde me out" and "make me understood." I would reverse the terms and attempt instead to find out the "I" who speaks in *The Temple,* to make that voice understood by tracing the configuration I call "God's courtier."[7] For if "The H. Scriptures. II" offers a model for interpreting the structure of *The Temple,* it may also provide a clue to the voice heard in its poems. Scripture, to Herbert, generates multiple configurations; any cluster of three (or more) verses, set into relationship by the reader, makes up "some" Christian's destiny. But it is the configuration of "my life" that this speaker wants to read out of his text; and it is Herbert's life that I wish to discover in the "I" who addresses us in *The Temple,* who offers "each part / Of my hard heart" ("The Altar") to God in that frame, and whose "particularities of . . . condition and disposition" Nicholas Ferrar, in his preface to the work, discloses to its readers "for the clearing of some passages."[8]

Ferrar's claim that Herbert is "a pattern or more for the age he lived in" suggests that seventeenth-century readers *did* interpret the voice in *The Temple* as Herbert's and raises the question of life-as-pattern: how can such a discontinuous and unconventional "narrative" reveal an intelligible pattern to its readers? There is no clear precedent in Renaissance texts for the form of *The Temple,* nor is there an apparent source in any earlier work of spiritual autobiography for the formal and topical profusion creating that pattern.[9] Although I take as my critical task the articulation of Herbert's "pattern . . . for the age he lived in," I do not claim to offer a "definitive" interpretation of the structure of *The Temple,* nor would I argue that other readings of the voice in the poem are no longer valid. Herbert's recent critics have enabled us to hear many voices in *The Church.* All readers of Herbert have experienced the delight and renewed insight of recognizing Stanley Fish's wily catechist, Richard Strier's subtle exponent of the doctrine of justification by faith, and Barbara Harman's narrator who so finely weighs the costs of self-representation.[10] Each of these readers of *The Temple* has configured a distinct pattern of utterance and emphasis and persuaded us of its validity. But as Fish points out in his conclusion to *The Living*

Temple, "the shape of both the problem and its solution was a function of the interested perception that I brought to the tasks of scholarship and criticism" (p. 171). If "the past is always a structure seen in the context of the interests of the present and cannot otherwise be seen," if each interpretation depends upon the particular "categories of understanding" (p. 172) that enable us, as critics, to see texts in new ways,[11] my endeavor is to make visible the configuration of a Renaissance courtier which I perceive in Herbert's text. I hope through this perspective to enable other readers of *The Temple* in our time to see how that figure might have constituted a meaningful pattern for readers in Herbert's age.

Biographical readings in our age are, with depressing frequency, discounted as critical naiveté. The validity of my approach must depend on my readers' judgement. I hope they will recognize the extent to which biography and history are configured within the image of God's courtier in *The Temple* once my evidence is set forth, and acknowledge my argument that Herbert deliberately incorporated his life into the poetic design in order to authorize his account of spiritual experience.[12] This kind of configuration, of course, does not exclude either selective use of biographical data or the retrospective patterning by which, necessarily, any artist gives shape to biographical material.

My configuration begins with hearing, rather than seeing. The voice of the "I" in *The Temple* sounds, from time to time, a cool and worldly note rather alien to the sweet singer of Bemerton whom we so often like to hear. He remarks on his relation to God in "The Priesthood": "The distance of the meek / Doth flatter power." In "Affliction" (I), he confesses, "I was entangled in the world of strife, / Before I had the power to change my life." Searching his soul, the speaker of "The Sinner" finds "quarries of pil'd vanities, / But shreds of holinesse." He offers a bargain to God in "Submission":

> Were it not better to bestow
>   Some place and power on me?
> Then should thy praises with me grow,
>   And share in my degree.
>
>   (5–8)

This speaker has imagined that serving God might incorporate the advantages of great place: "and not onely I, / But all my wealth and familie might combine / To set thy honour up, as our designe" ("The Crosse"). Yet in self-admonishment he warns: "do not spread thy robe / In hope of great things" ("The Size").

We recognize how explicitly courtliness is patterned not only in tone, but image as well: the thickly piled velvet of "vanities" in "The Sinner" dresses a courtier no less than the "glorie and gay weeds" that prick the speaker's eyes in "Frailtie." Only a courtier would think to exchange his flower for Christ's thorns, his posy for Christ's rod, his bower for Christ's cross ("The Thanksgiving"). And the vignette of "brave Glorie puffing by / In silks that whistled" in "The Quip" is juxtaposed in telling particularity to the self-reference of the following stanza:

> Then came quick Wit and Conversation,
> And he would needs a comfort be,
> And, to be short, make an Oration.
> *But thou shalt answer, Lord, for me.*
> (17–20)

This speaker's words, tone, images begin to figure a worldly self whose language betrays attachment to courtly values and courtly aspirations, who seeks to join earthly and heavenly dignities,[13] whose desire to gain place in the world in giving himself to God recurs throughout the *Church* sequence as a dilemma never quite, never wholly mastered.

Critics have often acknowledged the presence of courtly style in Herbert and sometimes read his sequence as "sacred parody" of secular love lyrics.[14] If we trace the configurations of courtliness in *The Temple*, however, we discover the power of the pattern as well as its persistence. God's courtier is wracked by contradictions, unvoiced by anxiety, tainted with pride, plagued by inner wranglers ("attendants," as Herbert puts it in "Affliction" (IV), who plot against him), obsessed by delay and inutility, longing for an unimaginable flowering. Herbert was criticized in his own time, Barnabas Oley tells us, for not having "managed his brave parts to advantage"; to these critics, he "lost himself in a humble way."[15] The courtier patterned in *The Temple* does struggle against the loss of great place and the loss of the self which desires such place; this longing stands in the way of his equally urgent wish to give himself to God. As the ground of his dilemma, it shapes his complaints in a familiar contemporary form.

I suggest that it is Herbert, not Walton,[16] who first configures the courtier who must transfer his allegiance from the worldly court to the court of heaven. Walton's idealized image of his subject is far more unitary than the far-from-ideal representation Herbert has given us in *The Temple*. The absolute transformation Walton wants to show robs Herbert's text of its power to *exemplify*, a term that comprises both "being an exemplar," a model of striving toward goodness, and "being an example," sharing with one's readers insufficiency, limitation, fallibility – speaking, that is, for human imperfection. Herbert incorporates courtly ambition and earthly attachment into his first-person lyrics because they do re-present his life experience, because they can present an intelligible pattern to other worldly aspirers of his own age. He patterns a rejection of the court of this world: a rejection that takes years to make, that demands relinquishing much of what has constituted the "self," that exacts the replacement of worldly values and perspective with those of the court and the king of heaven.

Even critics who multiply the "I" of the *Church* lyrics into changing personae must come to terms with the self-perception of division and multiplicity within individual poems. Thomas Greene and Stephen Greenblatt have amply demonstrated how problematic the concept of self was for Renaissance writers;[17] my interpretation of Herbert's "I" as person suggests that Herbert both recognizes and *raises* the question of self-identity by recording his experience of "divisions" and "partitions." In *The Church*, the self is divided by conflicting desires, continually redefining or attempting to transform its identity.

Harman's introductory chapter to *Costly Monuments*, "The Critical Controversy," traces a dialectic of "self" and "culture" (meaning, primarily, theology) among Herbert's major critics. She argues that

> cultural ideas exert a force on persons – sometimes an extremely visible one, sometimes a less apparent and less easily describable one – and they shape the self's power to write itself up, out of, or as Herbert says in "Jordan (II)," into the sense (1. 14). What we need, therefore, is not a description of the way persons determine cultures, or culture determines persons, but rather an analysis of the dialectic relationship between the two. (p. 30)

My configuration of God's courtier in *The Temple* could be described as the tracing of a dialectic between Herbert and the culture of courtiership; but by "configuration" I mean to suggest that the self continually reshapes its role in that dialectic by the process of *refiguring* from poem to poem. The courtier within *The Temple* rewrites the culture whose power to define him he both acknowledges and resists. In *Self-Consuming Artifacts,* Stanley Fish sets the self in dialectic with God in order to suggest the power of dissolving distinctions as the self attempts to lose itself in God. But in Chapter 6, I shall try to show how a poem like "Discipline" enacts a reconstructed relationship to God: here the self maintains identity because God's courtier has rewritten his speech to God and thereby revised the roles both God and the self are to play.

Furthermore, the "I" of Herbert's *Temple* is contextualized by history as well as biography. When Nicholas Ferrar claims Herbert as a pattern or more for his age, he is stressing a particular relation to a historical moment in which courtliness as an ideal maintained its power over the imagination, while actualizing that ideal, as England moved toward civil war and a rejection of court and king altogether, seemed ever less possible. The ideal courtier figured by sixteenth-century humanists, in theory, served both God and the prince and took both for his model.[18] That these two exemplars might exert irreconcilable demands upon actual courtiers, the problem Herbert confronts in the *Church* lyrics, breaks into full consciousness only as the seventeenth-century courts of James and Charles begin to betray an ideal to which earlier courtiers had given assent, toward which it had still been possible to, at least, aspire.[19] In this sense, I argue that Herbert speaks directly to the consciousness of his age: in his poetry, kings dissolve into heaps of decaying flesh no less than peasants, only God's higher court can control his own inner wranglers, the braveries of the world are fictive delusions opposing the "simplenesse, and sad events" of God's "Regiment."[20] He is telling his age that the courtly ideal is played out, deeply corrupt, riddled with contradictory demands, unactualizable. He is configuring himself as courtier in order to reconstruct the pattern of courtliness as a recovery of whatever ideal *potentia* it might still possess.

The reconstruction transforms the idea of the worldly courtier into the ideal of God's courtier. The transformation is enacted in *The Church* by what Herbert depicts as a continuous "mending and making," rewriting the pattern of self in poem after poem – and more, from one poem to another – in an attempt to lose his worldly desire for great place by taking up the humble way. As I shall try to show in Part Two of this book, the reconstruction is never complete.

The courtier in Herbert's design will become God's servant, but the courtly self is never fully abandoned. The hard realism of the courtier still speaks in politic flattery to a very kingly God in "The Priest-hood"; it is a marred and mortal lover of this world's goods – not a miraculously transformed "holy Mr. Herbert" – who sits to eat at Christ's feast in "Love" (III). The resolved serenity of Walton's simple, finally unitary figure lacks the complex authority of Herbert's courtier, in whom the elements of earth and heaven commingle with both honesty and authenticity. He gains the right to be an exemplar by participating in – as well as by denouncing – the ills of his time.

My configuration of God's courtier attempts, initially, to refigure the model of courtliness so equivocal, yet still so powerful, in Herbert's age. Part One, "The Court," establishes the courtly contexts out of which Herbert's text constructs a figure mingling piled vanities and shreds of holiness. Chapter 1 traces the structure of contradiction inherent to the courtly ideal. Courtesy books reveal how uneasily the makers of the pattern struggled to harmonize its "parts" – the dual claims of earth and heaven. These contradictions provide a ground for Herbert's pattern because, as Chapter 2 will show, would-be actualizers of the ideal could not avoid the irreconcilable demands of the two realms which had been built into its configuration. Chapter 2 also constructs a link between two major forms of exemplary biography: those like Walton's, designed to attest the holiness of their subjects, and those like the lives of Sidney by Thomas Moffet and Fulke Greville, intended to affirm an ideal of courtliness. These biographies are selective assemblages of events in their subjects' lives which articulate an ideal aspired to by these actual persons – or so it is claimed – in order to create a model for others to follow. They reveal, and confirm, that spiritual values inform the courtly ideal and that courtly values – service to the state, leading the ruler toward virtue – continue to inform the desire for an exemplary mode of vocation expressed by such seventeenth-century figures as Bishop John Williams, Henry Wotton, and George Herbert.

This chapter works out the configuration of entanglement. Ideal aspirations are enmeshed in the actual "world of strife" that all would-be exemplars must inhabit. Its center is Herbert himself, entangled in relationships with friends, family, patrons which offer conflicting models of service; entangled in a historical moment of increasing religious and political strife; entangled for at least seven years (from 1623 to 1630) by a delay in settling upon a vocation, for which none of the scanty biographical evidence quite accounts.

Chapter 3 completes my configuration of the courtly contexts which inform Herbert's construction of God's courtier in *The Temple*. We so customarily read Herbert as a devotional poet that, with the exception of Louis Martz's brilliant insights on Herbert and Sidney in *The Poetry of Meditation* and on Herbert and Carew in *The Wit of Love*,[21] we seldom read his courtly voice in the context of other poets who take the uneasy equilibrium between ideal and actual versions of courtliness as their subject. Yet such poets as Wyatt, Gascoigne, Sidney, Carew, and Suckling offer a promising "category of understanding" for Herbert. They utilize linguistic strategies very like Herbert's, figure themselves as courtiers caught in nets of false and true speaking, respond to the continuing power of courtly ideality by continual attempts to reshape the model for their own time.[22]

Part Two, "The Temple," then brings together the problems of structure and figure which I have proposed as my primary concern, and traces the transformations that redefine a building, a Temple, as a person, God's courtier. Chapter 4 examines Herbert's disintegration of the courtly world and the courtly self because, I argue, this act of unmaking is a necessary preliminary in Herbert's text to the remaking of the self. In "An Offering," Herbert proposes that, could he recover the "divisions" of lust and "partitions" of passion that have "parcell[ed] out" his heart, he might offer to God "many gifts in one." The wholeness he hopes to recover depends upon an initial *un*covering, a self-disclosure of the hard heart's divisions and partitions. If we read individual poems in *The Church* as discrete entities, we shall find many recoveries of wholeness, transformative reconstructions of the divided self, and redirections of service to the king of heaven. Yet *The Church*, like *The Temple*, is a configuration of parts. Any given poem's validity of statement is simultaneously complete in itself *and* contingent upon its multiple relations with other poems, adjoining or "ten leaves off." Chapter 4 therefore studies those acts of fragmentation and attempts to recover wholeness which begin to configure a revised courtliness but cannot complete the task. We shall discover how pervasively the courtly world is subjected to dissolution in *The Church*, how fragmented language enacts such dissolutions, and how linguistic reconstructions stand as recoveries of what has been lost only within the framework of individual poems.

Chapter 5 will break through these self-enclosures to show how the configuration of God's courtier requires a continually rewritten text.[23] *The Church* contains a fragmented "plot," a sequence which repeatedly reverses sequential movement, a progress of choices that both advances and retreats, a structure of delays concerning the problem of vocation, one whose resolutions are broken by doubt and whose momentary assurances give way to renewed anxiety. These configurations reveal a far more difficult process of constructing an exemplary self than the resolved conclusions of individual poems might suggest; yet it is the courtly image refigured from poem to poem that enacts the *experience* of self-construction. I take the problem of vocation as my center in Chapter 5 because the transformation of the worldly courtier into God's courtier is centered in that search and grounded in Herbert's ultimate choice.

But as Chapter 6 will show, *The Temple* as a three-part structure rewrites, and asks us to reinterpret, even the apparent resolution of Herbert's search for vocation within *The Church*. The remade self joyously taking on the garments of priesthood in "Aaron" would seem to have completed its transformations. But *The Church* does not close with "Aaron," nor does the euphoria of that poem govern all the lyrics which follow it. Furthermore, *The Church* is not *The Temple*. Herbert has framed his chronicle of interior experience with two very different accounts: the advice to a sweet youth in *The Church-porch* that configures the society of contemporary England and the paired, but unequal, progresses of the Church and Sin through all times and places in *The Church Militant*. One might, in fact, wonder why *The Church* is not entitled *The Temple* and vice versa, since the lyric center of Herbert's work details the spiritual struggles of an individual "hard heart" trying to transform itself into a Temple fit for Christ to inhabit.

"Temple," in this sense, must mean "person." Neither the world of English society so dubiously placed outside the church in *The Church-porch* nor the institution so inexorably overtaken by Sin in *The Church Militant* can constitute a temple within the human heart. The exemplary pattern Herbert is creating, the image of God's courtier as Christ's temple, must be reinterpreted – once again, and continually – in the light of the world presented in the first and final poems of *The Temple*. This world constitutes the ground of spiritual experience, the place of action, the condition of being. Herbert shows that no transformation can be complete, given this ground and these conditions.

God's courtier is a pattern for his age because he enacts continuous mending and making; because his world, the place of his service, never can be transformed into a Temple. Herbert's very courtly will and grace exemplify effort, not achievement. He speaks to his age by modeling struggle as well as serenity. God's will and God's grace might help him to "mend his rhyme," but as Herbert points out in "The Elixir," all is conditional: *if* God's courtier will learn "In all things thee to see, / And what I do in any thing, / To do it as for thee," he *may* become a Temple. Only a thoroughly worldly courtier of the late Renaissance could so sharply model a pattern of loyal service that fully incorporates the interior and exterior limits to "perfect freedom."

Although in some ways I shall defend Walton's fictional design for Herbert's life as a myth that discovers a truth, his "holy Mr. Herbert" is, finally, the image which, I think, most exaggerates and thus oversimplifies the evident piety so often revealed in the poetry. In trying to reconstruct the worldly voice in Herbert's poems, I don't mean to deny his devotion to God but instead to recover a perspective that may be obscured if we attend primarily or exclusively to his Christian piety. The world is the context which sharpens, enlivens, and even, I believe, empowers the spirituality of Herbert's text.

I hope that the idea of God's courtier will offer new categories of understanding for readers of *The Temple*. In joining structure and figure in this pattern, I will try to create an image of the historical George Herbert whose poem inscribes both the disintegrations and the reconstructions of his age. My method, configuration, works by assembling fragments rather than by articulating a whole and unitary figure. Like Herbert in "The Altar," my endeavor is to "join" the parts of his "hard heart" within a frame that might articulate a pattern and a perspective, and perhaps begin to recover the figure which attempted to pattern, and thereby to encompass, his age within the frame of a self continually undergoing the work of mending and making.

Part One

The Court

Chapter One

The Ideal of the Courtier

The Renaissance idea of the courtier, still a potent source of ideal (if not actual) virtue as *The Temple* is written, provides a conceptual basis for Herbert's self-figuration as courtier. He simultaneously affirms and challenges the value of the courtly ideal, which retains its potency in his work only by undergoing a radically transforming redirection from secular to sacred realms. Herbert draws upon humanist sources, not to validate the ideal in familiar sixteenth-century terms, but to set it in opposition to seventeenth-century actuality. The courtier in *The Temple* confronts his tradition by rewriting it. Figured into Herbert's courtly poems – and exerting powerful demands upon the self who attempts to construct an exemplary pattern – are those contradictions that were inscribed in the initial formulations of the humanists but seldom acknowledged directly. Although the humanists conceived of an ideal uniting spiritual and worldly values, even their imaginary courtiers, we find, could not harmonize service to both realms into a single exemplary mode.

I derive the courtly ideal from sixteenth- and early-seventeenth-century courtesy books, English, Italian, and French: Castiglione and Elyot, Guazzo and La Primaudaye, Cleland and James 1.[1] My procedure is both selective and synthetic; its basis, the extraordinary variety of versions but also the continuing thread of "ideality" that creates the synthesis I propose here. Herbert's depiction of his efforts to emulate Christ as well as to serve Him embodies the essential concepts governing the courtly ideal: a generative source – the exemplar; a primary action – service; a means of personal development – the virtues.

These principles prescribe the conduct of courtly lives and the patterns of courtly vocation. They are conceived in ideal form but are

meant as guides to real courtiers. Although I have learned much from
several recent studies of Castiglione – in particular, Daniel Javitch's
Poetry and Courtliness in Renaissance England and Wayne
Rebhorn's *Courtly Performances*,[2] my definition of the ideal and my
perception of its inherent contradictions differ from theirs precisely
because I do not focus exclusively on Castiglione. As my citations of
The Boke Named the Governour and *The French Academie* (notes 3
and 5, respectively) suggest, the ideal model of courtliness developed
not only as an elaborate game at the court of Urbino but also as an
educational program for young aristocrats and as a philosophy of
service to the common good. That is to say, courtiers were not simply
inhabitants of the court or followers of the prince; they became
government officials, diplomats, members of the Privy Council.
The books prescribing their training and defining their roles established a model of excellence for generations of young aspirants to
great place. This model, as I shall show, raises problems of the exemplar to be followed, the nature of service, and the attainment of
virtue rather different from those encountered by Castiglione's noble
role-players.

The idea of the courtier comprises a rich cluster of relationships
and values, but an even richer source of potential contradiction and
conflict. Although Javitch's brilliant study of oppositions between
Castiglione's ideal and the classical ideal of the orator is surely
convincing with respect to *Il Cortegiano,* that opposition does not
hold for such humanist texts as Elyot's or La Primaudaye's, where
the classical model is incorporated rather than rejected. Yet both
kinds of source for the ideal are available to Herbert, and elements of
both figure in the courtier depicted in *The Temple*.

By the seventeenth century, courtesy books betray a growing
uneasiness occasioned by the difficulties of reconciling two ideal
models, one earthly and one heavenly; two levels of virtue, one willed
and one infused; two modes of action, one active and one passive;
two concepts of nobility, one attainable by instruction and exercise,
one achievable only by the will of God. These contradictory elements
of the ideal paradoxically provide Herbert with a means of restoring
value to courtliness in the sacred realm even as he denies its value in
secular terms. The courtier-self figured by Herbert in *The Temple*
gives full poetic weight to the stress of a resolution that endures
contradiction instead of glossing over it.

i

The idea of the ruler as the perfect pattern of nobility lies at the heart of the courtly ideal as the sixteenth-century humanists present it in their books on the courtier. The exemplary quality of the ruler derives from his function as "God's vicegerent" on earth; his role as intermediary between God and man, anointed by God to carry out His commands as secular shepherd of His people; and his embodiment of the virtues that nobility is commonly supposed to possess. As Sir Thomas Elyot reminds his readers in *The Boke Named the Governour,* "from god only procedeth all honour."[3] The spiritual basis of honor therefore controlled the conception of both ideal king and ideal courtier.

In the *Basilicon Doron,* King James I instructs his son Henry, for whom this *speculum principi* was written, that God "made you a little God to sit on his Throne, & rule over other men." Consequently, James says, the king must provide his people with a pattern of virtue, though his somewhat presumptuous term – "little God" – might suggest a rather more self-exalting perception than does "vicegerent."[4] La Primaudaye's definition of "the duty and office of a Prince" in *The French Academie* far more moderately stresses God's rule rather than the king's:

> first, he must have the lawe of God continually before his eies: he must engrave it in his soule, and meditate upon the words and ordinances thereof, all the dayes of his life, desiring of God to graunt him the spirite of understanding to conceive them well, and according to that divine rule to direct all his intents and actions to the glorie of that great, eternall, and Almightye Kinge of Kinges: aswell for the salvation of his own soule, which he ought to preferre before the rule of the whole world: as for the good of those that are committed to his charge to governe, teach and judge them.[5]

The exemplar of exemplars, the most perfect pattern of nobility, was not the earthly king, but Christ himself.[6] As John Cleland puts it at the close of *The Scottish Academy:*

> hee who is A and Ω, the beginning and ending, the party and resting place of our whole Pilgrimage in this world, shal be my

first and last advise unto you al; and to everie on of you, that you
honour, feare, and serve him with a pure, free, and devout hart
for ever, at home and abroad. . . .[7]

The apparently smooth continuum between rulers of heaven and
rulers of earth in La Primaudaye and Cleland extends downward to
the exemplary courtier. Just as the earthly king, a pattern of perfection, is modeled on the heavenly ruler, so the courtier is expected to
take his sovereign for a pattern of virtue. Though nobility, like
royalty, is conferred by birth, the courtier must be educated to
become a wise counselor just as the prince must learn to become a
wise ruler. As even James I advises Henry, kings – no less than their
courtly servants – must develop moral virtue in order to execute their
function.

Sir Thomas Elyot's traditional account of nobility's historical
development emphasizes that virtue is the foundation of nobility, but
proper education and the emulation of virtuous models are nobility's
means of propagation. Gentlemen, he says, were originally so called
"more for the remembraunce of their vertue and benefite, than for
discrepance of astates."[8] His conclusion equates nobility unequivocally with virtue: "nobilitie is not after the vulgare opinion of
men, but is only the prayse and surname of vertue" (II, 37–8). The
first book of this primary English text claims to set forth "the best
fourme of education of bringing up of noble children from their
nativitie, in suche maner as they may be found worthy, and also able
to be governours of a publike weale" (I, 24). Elyot argues that
the "education and vertue in maners" of "inferior governours"
must parallel the education and virtue of princes "in as moche as
therby they shall, as well by example as by authoritie, ordre
well them, whiche by theyr capitall governour shall be to their rule
committed" (I, 26).

Elyot's version of the ideal, like La Primaudaye's, stresses the
ruler's subordination to God on the one hand and his service to the
common good on the other. Yet, as we've noted, James's image of
the ruler as a "little God" in *Basilicon Doron* betrays potential
dangers in an actual king's interpretation of his role. It is all the more
interesting, then, that George Meriton, preaching his *Sermon of
Nobilitie* before James in 1607, sets forth four levels in order of
increasing value: nobility of birth or fortune, moral and divine

nobility.[9] Here Meriton makes explicit what had been largely implicit in earlier assertions of the spiritual end to which courtiers and kings must ultimately aspire. The courtier, like the ruler, must exemplify virtue if he is to realize the potential for nobility provided by his birth and developed by his education. But his virtuous deeds must culminate in that higher level and superior end that Meriton calls "Divine Nobility":

> It is an elevation of our degree, or nature unto GOD, a comming unto him, a conformity with him: the top of this kindred is GOD himselfe, and then doth it most appeare in us, when neglecting mortall things we aspire unto heavenly, imitating herein our holy predecessors the spirites and soules of the righteous, striving to live as they do, fearing to degenerate from them, and ever remembering . . . [that] our conversation be in heaven.
>
> (sigs. C3^r–C3^v)

To be sure, Meriton as a clergyman may be considered a special pleader in arguing that "Onely *Christian Nobility* is best which admits of noe exception: in regarde whereof all the rest are but shadowes, and shapes of noblenes . . ." (sig. D1^r), but the disjunction between this statement and James's idea of the king points out an increasing equivocality in seventeenth-century depictions of the ideal. Meriton may only be carrying to its ultimate conclusion that insistence upon the heavenly end of the courtier's final aspirations which Pietro Bembo had articulated so eloquently in the Fourth Book of Castiglione. Bembo's smooth chronological progress from the worldliness of youth to the spirituality of age does resemble Meriton's definition of divine nobility as an "elevation of our degree" in establishing the possibility of a continuum from the one form of nobility to the other. But we remember also how, in Castiglione, Bembo's peroration is gently mocked by his hearers.[10]

ii

The problem of the exemplar as generator of the ideal is compounded further by the problematic status of courtly service. Service is measured by the effective demonstration of "justice, liberality, magnanimity, gentleness and . . . other virtues" that, as Castiglione points out, "befit a good prince" as well as his courtly servant.[11] According to La Primaudaye, the cardinal virtues complete the ruler's qualifications and define his exemplary role: "If he be prudent in his enterprises, bold in his exploits, modest in prosperitie, constant in adversitie, stedfast in word, wise in counsail, . . . all his subjects may have what to imitate" (sig. Uu 5^r).

The virtues appear most explicitly and surprisingly in Herbert's work, not in *The Temple,* but in that work which (unlike *The Temple*) we can be sure was written after he took up his office at Bemerton: *A Priest to the Temple, or, the Country Parson.*[12] Herbert's definition of the ideal parson in Chapter III opens with a remarkable – and remarkably traditional – list:

> The Countrey Parson is exceeding exact in his Life, being holy, just, prudent, temperate, bold, grave in all his wayes. (p. 227)

This confluence of theological and cardinal virtues is commonly found in the courtesy books as well. "Bold" is only another term for the collocation of qualities included in fortitude, here united with the other three cardinal virtues – justice, prudence, and temperance – and in turn framed by the theological values of holiness and gravity, now associated with the cardinal virtues to provide a definition which had, in the courtesy books, been applied equally to the ideal ruler and to the ideal courtier emulating his lord. As Castiglione puts it, a king of "noble progenie" will,

> yf he be helped forwarde with the instructions, bringinge up, and art of the Courtier, whom these Lordes have facioned so wise and good, . . . be moste wise, moste continent, moste temperate, moste manlye, and moste juste, full of liberalitie, majestie, holynesse, and mercye. . . .   (pp. 313–14)

We find further evidence that Herbert is applying traditional terms in his claim that the country parson is Christ's "Vicegerent" – the term customarily applied to the earthly ruler in books of the courtier.[13] Of course, the same idea of the pastor as Christ's vicegerent is found in the theological context to which Herbert's poetry also belongs. What is essential to realize, if we are to appreciate the complexity with which Herbert interweaves secular and sacred traditions, is that a similar conception of the ideal, founded upon the same assemblage of characteristic virtues, dominated both traditions and could "figure" either a courtier or a parson.

Although the courtesy books apply both classical and Christian standards of aspiration toward the good, they perhaps too facilely pass over the difficulties of enacting such standards in actual courtly service. As Rosemond Tuve and William O. Harris have shown, the four cardinal virtues of classical tradition and the three principal virtues of Christian tradition have become completely intermingled in sixteenth-century models of behavior.[14] Harris points out that by the early sixteenth century "the cardinal virtues had indeed come . . . to be thought of as the kingly virtues, the proper means of training rulers and of honoring them, as well as the standard of judging their conduct. . . ." (p. 145). The standard applied to the courtier as well as to his prince: "So trained, the renaissance nobility, certainly in Tudor England, was expected to exemplify these ideals" (p. 152).

Yet, even as courtesy books conjoined classical and Christian values, their analyses of the virtues once more reveal disjunction. Traditional interpretations distinguished two modes, or levels, of virtue: acquired — the virtues of *habitus* — and infused. La Primaudaye, for instance, identifies the difference between what the courtier can achieve by his own efforts and what he can attain only by patiently awaiting God's action:

> And truely, the reason of man, naturally ingraffed in his hart, which so farre foorth as he is man, and according to his habilitie and maner of life he imitateth and followeth, is divers from that which by speciall grace from above commeth to the elect, accompanieth them, and helpeth them in all their actions. (sig. B vii^v)

His warning against man's "pride and trust in himselfe, and in his owne vertue, which in the end cannot but be the cause of his utter undoing" (sig. B viii^v), reveals a potential conflict between the unquestionable need to develop the virtues of *habitus* and their ultimate insufficiency to achieve the end toward which they are directed.

This concept of dual levels of virtue rests on the commentary of St. Thomas in the *Summa Theologiae*, which separates man's ability to achieve virtue by the exercise of his own will from his need finally to await the infused virtue exercised by God's grace — which cannot be willed, striven for, commanded, or developed, only received.[15] In the courtesy books, these two levels of virtue are scarcely perceived as problematic. Yet contradiction inheres in the concept. On the one hand, effort is encouraged; on the other, passivity is validated.

Traditional interpretations of fortitude reflect still another implicit contradiction in measures of the courtier's virtuous service. Through its division into "parts" by Macrobius, Aquinas, and later commentators, as in its earlier definition by Cicero, fortitude entails two fundamental attitudes: contempt for the goods of worldly prosperity and patience in the face of worldly adversity.[16] Neither the earthly ruler nor the worldly courtier serving him could be a perfect pattern of nobility if he were overly attached to those very goods of Fortune that properly belonged to his worldly position; at the same time, however, he must learn to develop patience in adversity.

Although Herbert's courtier figure finds both aspects of fortitude problematic, the second is stressed particularly in poem after poem. The development of patience in adversity, of course, has frequently been recognized as a central theme throughout *The Temple*, but its relation to other problems built into the courtly ideal has not previously been examined.[17] The dual pattern of fortitude can be seen as analogous to the dual levels of acquired and infused virtue; in both cases two contrary modes of behavior, one active and the other passive, are required. It is possible for man, once he is instructed by his education in virtue, to understand the ultimate worthlessness of earthly goods and, by the exercise of his own will, to develop a wise contempt toward them; what is required is his active rejection of their delusive attraction. But in the state of adversity, he can only adopt a passive stance of patience and submission, simply accept and endure that adversity as sent by God for his own moral growth.[18] Human and divine will are by such definitions set up for tension, opposition – an interplay that Herbert presents as both disturbing and dynamic.

These patterns of virtuous behavior can also be associated with the dual levels in the doctrine of nobility promulgated by La Primaudaye and Meriton. The value of a concept like divine nobility for Herbert, as well as its disjunctive relation to nobilities of birth or fortune and even to "moral nobility," should be apparent. Gifted with the goods of birth and education, striving for that moral nobility attainable by the right exercise of virtue as far as it can be instilled by education and demonstrated by practice, Herbert aspires beyond these levels to the higher mode of divine nobility. But like the reception of virtue infused by God's grace or the patience acquired only by enduring the testing period of adversity, this form of nobility can be realized solely through a spiritual quietude which rests in dependence upon God's will.

iii

I do not wish to imply that contradictions in the courtly ideal were never recognized in sixteenth-century treatises but rather to identify the increasing pressure of the problem in later texts. Even the earliest statements bear witness to a less than ideal actuality: the Lord Julian in Castiglione remarks that the Count and Sir Frederick "with their eloquence have shaped suche a Courtier as never was, nor I beleave ever shalbe" (p. 207), while Elyot laments that "gentilmen in this present tyme be not equall in doctryne to the auncient noble men" (I, 98). By the seventeenth century, consonant with changing historical conditions,[19] the courtesy books undergo not only a multiplication of subject matter but a "disintegration" of ideal content, as Hoby's translation of *The Book of the Courtier* in 1561 gives place to Peacham's *Compleat Gentleman* of 1622.[20]

The shift in terms depicts a widening audience, but it also hints at a thinned-out concept. Now, all too often, only the idea of virtuous behavior remains, rather than the carefully prescribed training in specific virtues typical of the sixteenth-century texts. Two representative seventeenth-century treatises give lip service to the old ideal, but their pages are filled with quite different advice: Daniel Tuvill advocates judicious flattery and praises dissembling while Henry Peacham is concerned with the minutiae of surface manners and the semblance of reputation. For Peacham, even learning – in Elyot, the main path for development of the virtues – is now valued because by its means, the gentleman "winneth to himself both love and admiration, heigthing with skill his Image to the life. . . ."[21]

The nature of pressures on courtly tradition by the time *The Temple* is written is suggested by John E. Mason's finding that seventeenth-century "books of policy" – those courtesy books devoted especially to statecraft – show an increasing Machiavellianism in contrast to the rather more idealistic English treatises of the sixteenth century.[22] This affirmation of expediency bears some relation to the conscious creation of an admirable image in Peacham. And the divergence from the humanist ideal stressed by Elyot and La

Primaudaye in the preceding century helps to explain the new emphasis in English texts. The increasingly "politic" nature of worldly service and a growing concern with "heigthing the image" measure out the distance of the Jacobean court world from the earlier humanist idea. Machiavellian accommodation to the self-interested motives of actual governors leads to abandonment of striving for virtue and even of belief in the validity of such efforts.

The seventeenth-century courtesy books seldom contrast the state of earthly kings so unfavorably and directly with that of the heavenly ruler as we shall find Herbert doing in *The Temple*. But with growing intensity, they do acknowledge the distance of actual courtly behavior from the ideal pattern of virtue.[23] In the darkening climate of the Jacobean court, Daniel Tuvill's comments (1614) remind us more of Webster or Tourneur than of Elyot and Castiglione: "The times are dangerous and deceitful in which we live. The World affoords us almost nothing now which is not personated and disguised. . . ." Tuvill warns further that many men now have "honie in their mouthes, but a Razour at their girdles" (p. 7). This perception of courtly reality goes far to explain the evident Machiavellianism of his advice to courtiers, in spite of his perfunctory denunciations of Machiavellian practices. Tuvill justifies his recommendations in his comment on persons at court: "Some that having drunke of Machiavel's impure and troubled streames, care not so much for virtue it self as for the outward shewe and appearance thereof, because they are perswaded, that the credite of it is a helpe, but the use of it a hinderance" (p. 31).

iv

The increasing concern for self-interest and expediency rather than virtue in the Jacobean treatises suggests that when, as Herbert notes in *The Church-porch*, "worth and service fail," the courtly vocation may not be as clear a choice for the typical young aristocrat of Herbert's time, or for Herbert himself, as it might have seemed to the Elizabethans. For Castiglione, the courtier's service is unquestionably devoted to the prince, whereas the English humanists emphasize, more broadly, the concept of service to "the common good."[24] A young nobleman might carry out that service through the exercise of arms, the practice of diplomacy abroad, or the function of counselor at court; but each of these callings entails an active life in the political and social world of great place, and that life is validated by its fulfillment of the measures of virtue spelling out the ideal.

Furthermore, the choice of vocation depended on a calling by God. La Primaudaye's definition illuminates the intensity of Herbert's anxiety concerning the matter in *The Temple:*

> . . . every one of us must take his vocation and calling for a principle and ground, & for a station assigned of God, unto which we must direct our levell, withdrawing our mindes from the yoke and bondage of those naturall perturbations that are in us. Wee must not be led with ambition and desire to take hold of many sundry matters at once, being assured, that every worke done according to our calling, however contemptible soever it be among men, shineth before God and shall be rewarded by him, beyng accounted very precious in his sight.   (sig. Eee vi^v)

Aegremont Ratcliffe's *Politique Discourses* also emphasizes the crucial leading of God:

> There is not one, who (beside his apparent calling made by man's meanes) is not secretly by the unspeakable providence of God, called to some vocation: that is to say, to one manner of living, or other. And who hath not his particular distinct talent assigned him, to be employed to God's glorie, & the common utilitie of ye society of al men?   (sig. A ii^r)

This recognition of a spiritual as well as a worldly source and end for vocation gives rise to still another implicit contradiction that appears in the courtesy literature as the debate between active and contemplative lives. If the end of man's earthly work is to serve "God's glorie," and if, as John Cleland says, "Prince and people, Noble and ignoble, if they be Christs, are al spiritual, and must walk in the spirit, and performe the works of the spirit, which are love, joy, peace, long suffering, gentlenes, goodnesse, faith, meeknesse, temperance, flying from the works of flesh" (p. 108), then would it not be better to reject absolutely those delusive works of the flesh? The debate, of course, is an old one; but the courtly setting for service gives a new edge to the difficulty. Service to the common good now conflicts with the claims of a spiritual vocation, even as both ideals maintain their power as potential life patterns.

Even such a worldly treatise as Stefano Guazzo's *Civile Conversation* commences with argument and counterargument for the two paths.[25] Guazzo's brother, withdrawn in contemplative melancholy, is visited by a physician who presents the case for the active life and moreover denies that his patient is in truth pursuing a spiritual calling. His patient claims that the true end of his life is

> to clime to the true service of God, and the enjoying of those heavenly incomprehensible and eternall benefites which he hath promised to his faithfull, the desartes, al by places and solitarie, are the right ladders. And contrariwise, companies are nought els but hookes and tonges, which withdrawing us by force out of the course of our good thoughts, set us in the way of destruction.
> . . .
> (I, 24)

The physician, in rebuttal, insists upon his patient's obligation to his fellow man:

> And though you alledge unto me, of these which have refused promotions, and publike offices, thinking it a thing blame-worthy to bring their free mind into bondage, and to intangle it with the affaires of the worlde, yet there have been other excellent Philosophers, who . . . have reprooved the opinion of those aforesaide, and that not without great reason: for giving themselves wholy to the studie of the sciences and contemplation, they altogether abandoned those persons, to whom by the Lawe of nature they were bounde to give succour, and considered not that (man being borne not onely for himselfe, but for his Countrie, parents, and friends) hee seemeth either too farre in love with him selfe, or too farre out of love with others, which followeth not his proper nature to benefite others, being borne therunto . . . [a]ll the prayse of vertue consist[s] in doing. . . .
> (I, 31–2)

This opening section of *The Civile Conversation* is entirely typical of the way in which courtesy books weigh the spiritual value of contemplating final ends against the worldly (yet, it is often claimed, God-sanctioned) value of serving society. Herbert chooses the same image of entanglement in "the world of strife" in one of his most explicitly biographical poems, "Affliction" (I).[26] His poetic handling of conflicting claims between action and contemplation, no less than the possibility that he did consider a *vita contemplativa* seriously at one period, reflects a representative problem of his time. One solution to the active-contemplative debate was traditionally the "mixed life" – an initial withdrawal into contemplation to develop self-knowledge, followed by a dedication to active service. Herbert's preoccupation with delay may reflect a version of this pattern. The problem recurrently troubles him, just as it did the young Milton in somewhat comparable circumstances, though we should remember that Milton's preparatory period of delay came in his twenties, whereas Herbert was approaching his late thirties and still not settled upon a calling. Yet the anxiety Herbert feels about his long delay in taking up his ultimate vocation, and his critical attitude toward his own preoccupation with self-knowledge, reflect a similar pair of contrasting emphases in English and Italian courtesy books, described by Ruth Kelso as a striving for "personal perfection" by the Italians versus an ideal of "service to the commonwealth" on the part of the English (p. 39). Though Kelso tends to overstate the contrast, as a matter of relative emphasis it clearly carries weight and, as Guazzo's criticism of the "self-absorbed" nature of the contemplative life would suggest, it may also be associated with the debate between active and contemplative lives.[27]

The question of whether divinity was a suitable calling for the aristocracy posed an even more specialized form of the problem of vocation. In the light of Christ's role as perfect exemplar for the ruler and the ruler's role as exemplar for the courtier – each assumed to be devoted ultimately to God – such a question would seem at least inappropriate, if not perverse. Actual conditions of service in the Anglican church in sixteenth- and seventeenth-century England show why the issue was debated at all. The ministry was poorly paid and relatively low in social status; if "service" is defined primarily as service to the state or to the ruler, the possession of a small living in a country parish hardly meets this exalted image of the aristocrat's proper function.

Some courtesy writers do assert the suitability and even the superiority of divinity as a calling. Ratcliffe, for example, weighs the respective merits of "politique" and "spirituall" vocations, describing the first as concerned with "corporall and temporall things, which appertaine to the policie, rule, & government of this present life among men" and the second as promoting "the government and inwarde peace of conscience, and reformation of the minde, which is the cheefe and principall part of man . . ." (sig. 44^r). Unlike the young Herbert, Ratcliffe concludes that the two forms of vocation should

not be mixed. The ecclesiastic, like the political man, is in fact an
active servant of humanity: "there is no action so excellent, as that
which instructeth and informeth the interior, which is the principall
part of man, where hence all the good or evil of the exterior pro-
ceedeth" (sig. 57ᵛ).[28]

Not all courtesy books solve the question of divinity as a suitable
vocation so easily. As Kelso remarks, "Divinity, though sometimes
piously mentioned as a calling for gentlemen, drew forth even less
enthusiasm than medicine," citing Lyly's rebuke in *Euphues* to those
who "thinke it a blemish to their auncestours, and blot to their own
gentrie, to read or practize Divinitie."[29] Such attitudes give added
point to Barnabas Oley's report that some of Herbert's contemporaries considered his choice of a calling a waste of his noble birth, his
talents, and his training:

> And for our Authour (The sweet singer of the Temple) though he
> was one of the most prudent and accomplish'd men of his time, I
> have heard sober men censure him as a man that did not manage
> his brave parts to his best advantage and preferment, but lost
> himself *in a humble way:* That was the phrase, I well remember
> it.[30]

"[Losing] himself in a humble way" helps to define Herbert's role
as courtier in *The Temple*. The figure who is entangled in the contradictions of the ideal confronts directly what the courtesy books
could only obliquely acknowledge. The worldly king, in actuality,
may *not* take Christ as his model: who, then, shall be the courtier's
exemplar? If service to the common good enmeshes the courtier in a
world of men with "honey in their mouthes, but a Razour at their
girdles," how, then, can one's vocation "shine before God" as La
Primaudaye prescribes? Although Herbert's Country Parson seems to
unite the classical and Christian virtues without equivocation, the
courtly "I" of *The Temple* finds in himself "quarries of pil'd vanities" so great that his "shreds of holinesse . . . dare not venture / To
shew their face" ("The Sinner" 5–7). The humble loss of self reported by Barnabas Oley empowers the country parson with virtue
even as it disempowers the courtly aspirant who laments, in "Affliction" (I), his entanglement in the world of strife, but it also subjects the traditional courtly ideal to the unsparing light of courtly
actuality.

Chapter Two

Actualizing the Ideal

The sparse facts of Herbert's life, as we know them, are in this chapter surrounded by the network of relationships in which he was entangled and out of which he wove a dramatic design for the first-person lyrics of *The Church*. My reading of the "I" in Herbert's text as person, not *persona*, grows out of the context discussed in this chapter: the condition of courtly actuality in Herbert's decade of choice – the 1620s – and the biographical circumstances which, transformed by his art, enabled him to become "a pattern or more for the age he lived in."[1]

An aspiring courtier entangled in the strife-filled world of the 1620s is a representative figure of his age. His accommodations and resistances not only test the sixteenth-century model of courtesy but begin to envision new patterns of courtly ideality. Disintegration of the ideal may entail its dissolution; yet that process may also lead to redirection, reconstruction, and reintegration. If the ideal simply dissolved in the seventeenth century, we could scarcely speak of the pressure of actuality; we should cease altogether to be concerned with this peculiar construct of the idealistic humanists. That pressure *depends upon* the persistence of the ideal. Contemporary biographers and historians can teach us how powerfully the desire for a "pattern or more" for the age confronted a no less forceful and painfully evident momentum for change.

This is why my account of Herbert's entanglement begins with what I term "exemplary biography" – denoting that special literary development of the seventeenth century which, searching for an ideal pattern in actual lives, must recreate it in new forms. The biographers' insistence on ideality is countered by the historians' laments over actuality. The testimony of contemporary history gives poignant weight to Herbert's entanglements and begins to suggest the direction of change. I define that change as a gradual unfolding of dual possibilities. The seventeenth-century courtier could adopt a "path of descent," accepting the degraded actuality attacked by the historians and defiantly celebrating what Peacham called "heigthing the image," thus creating a new courtly model or, alternatively, a "path of ascent," responding to actual conditions by abandoning the worldly court altogether in an attempt to revivify the spiritual basis of the old ideal. My examples of each of these paths are potential exemplars for Herbert. Although they are historical figures in this chapter, all of them will be recognized once more in the chapters of Part Two as aspects of the "I" in Herbert's lyrics, troubled and troubling voices within the self-consciousness struggling with its entanglements in a world of strife.

i

Walton's life of Herbert depicts a figure as courtly as it is holy. As David Novarr points out, Walton structures his biography on the transformation of the "brilliant and worldly courtier" into the "holy country parson."[2] Like Nicholas Ferrar in his prefatory address to the reader of *The Temple,* and like Barnabas Oley in his introductory memoir to Herbert's *Remains,*[3] Walton defines Herbert's relinquishment of "laudible ambition" for worldly preferment in order to enter God's service as precisely the action that makes him an exemplar for his class and his time. In Walton's myth or truth, Herbert intended *The Temple* to portray *"the many spiritual conflicts that have past betwixt God and my soul, before I could subject mine to the will of* Jesus my Master: *in whose service I have now found perfect freedom."*[4] Even though Novarr has amply documented Walton's often irresponsible use of evidence in order to create this exemplary image,[5] Walton's claim for the significance of Herbert's vocational choice gains credibility because it so closely resembles the viewpoints of Herbert's "dear brother" Ferrar and his near-contemporary Oley.[6]

If it is Herbert's choice of sacred over secular service as well as his saintly character which makes him a pattern for his age in the eyes of his contemporaries, it is all the more interesting that Walton's biography should credit him with the same exemplary characteristics that constitute the courtly ideal to define an earlier model of virtue, Sir Philip Sidney, represented as an ideal courtier in the biographies of Thomas Moffet and Fulke Greville, as well as a virtuous model of Herbert's own time (and, incidentally, patron of Herbert), Bishop Williams, depicted as ideal statesman and churchman in the biography of John Hacket.

Unlike Herbert, Sidney and Williams each fulfill the expectations of service to king and country that we have followed in courtesy books since Elyot's *Boke Named the Governour*. Herbert, born of equally aristocratic stock, educated to the same expectations and for some years apparently harboring similar aspirations, eventually chooses a different course, neither the complete integration of courtly virtues with service to the ruler adopted by Sidney, nor the dual role of service to church and state chosen by Williams. The value placed by Walton on Herbert's rejection of secular service carries greater weight when we recognize how closely his construction of a model life resembles the exemplary models created by the biographers of Sidney and Williams. Each of these writers figures accurately the aspirations of his age. It is still more important that their subjects seem to have deliberately "figured" themselves in shaping their life choices. To recognize Sidney *and* Williams *and* Herbert as mirrors of the ideal courtier is to realize how important such idealized images were in both sixteenth and seventeenth centuries and, moreover, to recognize their power as motivating forces for actual behavior. Of course the actual life did not always correspond to the ideal image. Nonetheless, the pattern, as the exemplary biographers perceive it, should be given more attention, and perhaps more credence, than we customarily allow today.

My term "exemplary biography" links the "ecclesiastical" biographies of Walton and Hacket with the "courtly" biographies of Moffet and Greville, in contrast to the usual practice. Donald Stauffer and Richard Altick both distinguish the ecclesiastical biography as an independent seventeenth-century form in order to point out not only the vocation common to their subjects, but also a common concern of their authors with an exemplary devotion to God proper to ecclesiastical office.[7] In this respect, their term usefully describes Walton's claims for Herbert's saintliness and Hacket's insistence on the piety of Williams. But it cannot explain either the structural importance of Herbert's transition from secular to sacred service in Walton, or Hacket's concern to justify Williams' dual service to the King as Lord Keeper of the Great Seal and to God as Bishop of Lincoln. And it obscures the close resemblance of these works, like many other seventeenth-century biographies,[8] to the "courtly" biographies of Sidney written by Moffet and Greville.

The term "exemplary biography" reveals the common basis shared by all these works: the virtuous pattern of nobility formulated in the sixteenth century and incorporating both sacred and secular values.[9] Not only do they assert the traditional courtly virtues of their subjects, but they also give dramatic prominence to the fall from worldly prosperity, as in the case of Williams, and the rejection of worldly prospects, as in the case of Herbert. Walton's account of Herbert's life up to the point of his taking orders at Bemerton emphasizes both the courtly virtue that confirmed Herbert's worthiness for great place in the court of the world and the lack of virtue in that court which justified Herbert's rejection of worldly employment.

Sidney's biographers, however, view the matter differently. He is a pattern for his age not only because of his virtue but also because of his service to the state.[10] Although the similarity of the first criterion to Walton's claims for Herbert demonstrates the continuing basis of the ideal, the second shows a discontinuous shift in the manner of service chosen by these two exemplars. The sixteenth-century formulation of the ideal courtier was not really fully formed in biography per se until after the death of Sidney, who perhaps can be viewed as the first "ideal" model of the English courtier and whose qualities can therefore be perceived as paradigmatic for the form. The full title of Nobilis – The Noble Man: or a View of Sidney's Life and Death in Praise of that Great Knight Sir Philip Sidney, compiled by Thomas Moffet of London and sent by way of an example to Sidney's most honorable nephew William Herbert, heir of the very illustrious Earl of Pembroke – the earliest biography of Sidney, could serve as a compact description of the genre and its purpose. Moreover, its recipient places it within the network of courtly relationships to which George Herbert himself belongs. The motto that follows the title – "The best of gifts is the spirit of them" – explains the occasion; this little book was a New Year's gift from Moffet to the young William Herbert, kinsman and later patron of George, at about the time he entered New College, Oxford.[11]

The concept of a life which is exemplary because of its virtue dominates the courtly image of Sidney in Nobilis just as it dominates the saintly image of Herbert in Walton's Lives. Sidney's education is designed to instruct him "in the veneration of God, then in literature, and finally in public affairs and virtuous action" (p. 71); the basis of his love of learning is his "zeal for virtue." Although Sidney represents an ideal of secular service, his fusion of classical and Christian virtues is nevertheless essential to his potency as an exemplar. He pursues his university career "within the boundaries of duty and virtue; and in his eyes, his speech, and his manners he presented a certain pattern of modesty and of antique integrity" (p. 76). He is, however at ease with the world, not overly attached to it: "one did not know whether the spirit he had, was rather elevated, sublime, and looking away from the world, or courteous, retiring, and humble" (p. 78).

Walton depicts Herbert in remarkably similar terms:

> And in *Cambridge* we may find our *George Herberts* behaviour
> to be such that we may conclude, he consecrated the first-fruits
> of his early age to vertue, and a serious study of learning. (p. 267)

Just as Sidney's "antique integrity" receives early notice from his elders, so Herbert's gravity even in youth attracts the attention of the learned, although instead of the spirituality that Moffet wishes to emphasize in Sidney's retiring nature, Walton's description of Herbert's aristocratic reserve evokes the courtly vanity that Herbert himself acknowledges in the poetry:

> if during this time he exprest any Error, it was, that he kept
> himself too much retir'd, and at too great a distance with all his
> inferiours; and his cloaths seem'd to prove, that he put too great
> a value on his parts and Parentage.   (pp. 267–8)

This image of Herbert would seem, in fact, more appropriate for a young Sidney. But it enhances Walton's construction of the would-be courtier and suggests how internal as well as external pressures weigh on those aspiring to actualize an ideal pattern.

Moffet does acknowledge the pressure of the actual in recounting Sidney's entrance into court service and his parents' fears for his ability to maintain virtue in that setting:

> For the courts are, as it were, common inns of kingdoms, in
> which live a great many of the base along with the upright. By no
> discipline can it be avoided that day by day a foison of delights
> and desires newly abound, and variously transform men into

women, women into men, men into beasts, the scrupulous and
devout into sodomites and gallants. Wherefore, lest he should
engage in something which would be grievous to the minds and
eyes of his parents, though from his very arrival he had adopted
the manners of courtiers, straightway he carefully withdrew
himself (so far as is permitted one) from association with evil-
doers; yet he never separated himself from the side of his uncles
or the eyes of the Queen.   (pp. 68–9)

The point is that Sidney, as exemplary courtier, *can* maintain virtue
at court. Moffet assumes that in the 1580s the upright still reside
there along with the base.

In Walton's account, the negative image of "painted Court-
pleasures" is not introduced until he has made clear that Herbert is
eminently suited for high worldly position.[12] In early passages of
the *Life*, Walton evokes a courtier worthy of preferment, rather
than a humble and holy country parson, with no trace of nega-
tivity. He points out Herbert's "love of a Court-conversation" and
endows him with characteristics equally appropriate to Moffet's
Sidney or to Castiglione's courtier: "He had acquir'd great Learning, and was blest with a high fancy, a civil and sharp wit, and
with a natural elegance, both in his behaviour, his tongue, and his
pen" (p. 270).

Walton further remarks that during the early years of his Oratorship, Herbert was "very high in the Kings favour; and not meanly
valued and lov'd by the most eminent and most powerful of the
Court-Nobility" (p. 274). Unsupported by independent evidence, the
claim is of little biographical value. However, it demonstrates how
strongly Walton was concerned to present his ideal churchman as
one who might easily have become a courtier instead. The double
potentiality makes Herbert's eventual choice all the more admirable.
Since Walton's ultimate purpose is to eulogize his subject as a saintly
Anglican minister, his reference to Herbert's "laudible ambition to be
something more then he was" (p. 274) stands in puzzling contrast to
the dismissal of "painted court-pleasures" (p. 277) that he will later
attribute to Herbert. These two passages suggest that ambiguity of
attitude toward court service which persists in a Royalist churchman
like Walton even after the Restoration; yet the ambiguity is already
implicit, over half a century before Walton writes his life of Herbert,
in Moffet's description of Sidney's exemplary behavior in spite of the
temptations to vice at court.

Fulke Greville, writing his *Life of Sidney* after Elizabeth's death and by then himself tasting the sour fruits of princely disfavor, presents Sidney as no less exemplary, but the court as a somewhat more chancy and capricious locale for virtuous service. Greville begins his *Life of Sidney* by deploring the vicissitudes of changing times. His explanation for choosing Sidney rather than a more recent subject is almost elegiac in its suggestion that we shall never see his like again. In Sidney, he says, "the life it self of true worth, did (by way of example) far exceed the pictures of it in any moral Precepts. . . . he himself hath left such an instance in the too short scene of his life, as I fear many Ages will not draw a line out of any other mans sphere to parallel with it."[13]

Walton's purpose, too, is to offer a virtuous pattern for emulation to an age desperately in need of it. His address to the reader of his collected *Lives* echoes Greville's estimation of Sidney's "reall vertue":

> *many of his particular acts and vertues might have been neglected, or lost, if I had not collected and presented them to the Imitation of those that shall succeed us: for I humbly conceive writing to be both a safer and truer perserver of mens Vertuous actions, then tradition, especially as 'tis manag'd in this age.*
>
> (p. 6)

Herbert's entire life, like Sidney's, reveals the design of an unfolding virtue from youth to full adulthood:

> as he grew older, so he grew in learning, and more and more in favour both with God and man: insomuch, that in this morning of that short day of his life, he seem'd to be mark'd out for vertue, and to become the care of Heaven; for God still kept his soul in so holy a frame, that he may, and ought to be a pattern of vertue to all posterity. . . .   (p. 269)

This design exemplifies the workings of divinity, for it is "the God of Constancy, who intended him for a great example of vertue" (p. 277).

Walton commends Herbert "especially to his Brethren of the Clergy," in accordance with his ultimate choice of a calling. On the other hand, Greville offers Sidney as a model not only to young noblemen and "many Gentlemen excellently learned" but to rulers, thus praising his service to the secular realm and echoing Castiglione's prescription that the principal function of the courtier is to lead his prince toward virtue: "This one mans example" serves as "a nourisher of vertue" to the court.

Nevertheless, for Greville as well as for Moffet, who emphasizes Sidney's "Christian and heroic spirit," it is Sidney's devotion to God that finally validates his exemplary power: "Above all, he made the Religion he professed, the firm basis of his life." His "religious Zeal" on his deathbed confirms the pattern of his earlier life. In Greville's account, Sidney approaches that holy death eulogized by the biographers of such Anglican saints as Herbert and Nicholas Ferrar:

> yet had the wound whereof he died made rather an addition, than diminution to his spirits. So that he shewed the world, in a short progress to a long home, passing fair, and weldrawn lines; by the guide of which, all pilgrims of this life, may conduct themselves humbly into the haven of everlasting rest.   (p. 95)

Walton's account of Herbert's death makes a comparable claim:

> Thus he liv'd, and thus he dy'd like a Saint, unspotted of the World, full of Alms-deeds, full of Humility, and all the examples of a vertuous life. . . .   (p. 319)

The difference between Sidney's life progress, "passing fair, and weldrawn lines" and Herbert's end "unspotted of the World" and "full of Alms-deeds" shows how substantially Herbert's choice of a calling has altered the model of ideal virtue. Yet the two exemplars share above all the fundamental Christian virtue of humility.

These comparisons help us to recognize both the essential courtliness of Herbert's idealized image constructed by Walton and the essential spirituality underlying Sidney's representation in the biographies of Moffet and Greville. In its blending of sacred and secular service, John Hacket's memoir of Bishop Williams postulates an ideal probably much closer to Herbert's aspiration than to Sidney's. Whereas Sidney was content with a purely secular role, John Williams served his God as Bishop of Lincoln and his King as Keeper of the Great Seal. By amply detailing the difficulties of fulfilling this double role in either of the Stuart courts in the early seventeenth century, Hacket provides, implicitly, a rationale for Herbert's exemplary choice of humble service far from the center of power.

Scrinia Reserata is important, not because we can rely on its accuracy, but because it offers further confirmation that the courtly ideal persists in the seventeenth century while also revealing significant changes in its direction and emphasis. Hacket's prefatory remarks apply the same terms to his purpose that we have noted in Moffet, Greville, and Walton:

> I repeat it, that my Labours may have a right Construction, that I cast out this Matter into the Figure of a Moral Example; else I had been far more Compendious. Yet it is the true Image of his Life, whom I describe, and not a *Cyrus*, or feigned Idea of Wit. . . . A right History is a System of Exemplary, or Practick Philosophy. . . . [It may not please] those who are delighted with Romances, and like to have Shadows commended that were never extant, rather than such as lived among us, did us good, and deserv'd Glory; who are no wiser than they, that had rather have Felicity in a Dream, then Waking.[14]

This collocation of exemplary figure and "true Image of his Life" is alien to our conceptions of truth and fiction in biography. But Hacket's language suggests the basis of selectivity common to all the biographers discussed here, including Walton. They choose those details from their subjects' lives that most clearly point toward their exemplary embodiment of virtue and most concretely deserve to be emulated; they suppress, ignore, or at least underplay those aspects of the lives that are neither worthy of emulation nor, in the construction of a moral figure, deserving of notice. This process resembles the affirmation of the virtues of the ruler or noble person so apparent in contemporary panegyric and should be understood in similar terms.[15] The purpose is not to provide an objective assessment of the subject's merits and defaults but to depict his capacity for virtue *as well as* his actual virtuous accomplishments, on the assumption that, as Sidney himself recommended in the *Apology,*

> any understanding knoweth the skill of the artificer standeth in that *Idea* or fore-conceit of the work, and not in the work itself. And that the poet hath that *Idea* is manifest, by delivering them forth in such excellency as he hath imagined them. Which delivering forth also is not wholly imaginative, as we are wont to say by them that build castles in the air; but so far substantially it worketh, not only to make a Cyrus, which had been but a

particular excellency as Nature might have done, but to bestow a
Cyrus upon the world to make many Cyruses, if they will learn
aright why and how that maker made him.[16]

The difference, underlined by Hacket's clear reference to the *Apology*
in his preface to *Scrinia Reserata,* is that Sidney's models are drawn
from the "artificer's" idea of virtue, on the supposition that actual
persons cannot be as excellent as we can imagine a person to be,
whereas Hacket follows the practice established by Sidney's own
biographers of demonstrating that exemplary virtue can indeed be
embodied in real persons. This concern with the "true image" drawn
from actual life rather than from "Romances" indicates a new – and
not exclusively Puritan – emphasis upon the individual as exemplar
in, and for, his own time. It provides a new impetus in the seventeenth century not only for biography but for autobiography: both in
the exemplary mode, searching out the pattern of a life hidden within
contingency.

Models from life continue, nevertheless, to exhibit the same
virtues bestowed upon the feigned Cyruses whose excellency is not
limited by Nature. Hacket's explanation of Williams' exemplary
industry in learning parallels the claims of Sidney's and Herbert's
biographers for their subjects and in turn echoes the ideal of courtly
virtue, source for these living models:

> He was the Pattern of a most diligent Student to all that did
> emulate him then, or would imitate him hereafter. . . . No doubt
> he look'd far afore him, upon the hope of a great Recompence in
> Church or Commonwealth: that contented him, and confirmed
> him. . . . They are much mistaken, that think to piece together
> two Things so different, the Pleasure of Ease, and the Guerdon
> of Virtue. (I, 7–8)

Like Walton's approval of Herbert's worldly ambition and Moffet's
claim that Sidney's "zeal for virtue" is the basis of his interest in
learning, Hacket's polarity between ease and virtue,[17] contrasting
duty to the state with the pleasure of self-development, reflects the
crucial difference between English and Italian versions of the courtly
ideal suggested by Kelso and the conflicting pulls upon Sidney un-
mentioned by Moffet and Greville but evidenced in Sidney's correspondence with Languet.[18] Williams chooses the guerdon of virtue in

proper exemplary fashion. According to Hacket, Williams studies "history both sacred and secular of all states in Europe" as preparation for serving the state – just as Sidney and Herbert, according to their biographers, also fit themselves to serve the common good:

> The issue of his life bewrayed his End therein; for he discirned his own Abilities to be fit for Public Employment; therefore he search'd into the notable Particularities of all Kingdoms, Republicks, and their Churches, with all the Importances that hung upon them. And he guessed right, that King James would give all he could ask for such a Minister.   (I, 14)

I have suggested that the exemplary subjects themselves aspired to the ideal retrospectively affirmed by their biographers, thus attesting to the influence of the virtuous pattern even though the life may not have conformed so perfectly to that ideal as their biographers claim. Hacket's long and close association with his subject, together with his use of actual documents rather than reported, and possibly spurious, conversations – as in the case of Walton's biography of Herbert – offers some evidence of Williams' own conception of his role. His speech on the first day he sits as Lord Chancellor in the Court of Chancery echoes the traditional ideal of service to the ruler: "I hold by my Place the Custody not of mine own, but of the King's conscience." His commitment to this ideal is further supported by his justification for accepting the post even though he is untrained in the law.[19] He urges the importance of "Moral and Intellectual Endowments" for a judge in a court of equity, arguing that his "Sincere, Upright, and well-meaning Heart" might "cover Thousands of other Imperfections." Service to the king is linked with a calling by both earthly and heavenly rulers, since his appointment is "the immediate work of God and the King: And their Actions are no ordinary Effects, but extraordinary Miracles." He will, therefore, "endeavour, as much as I can, to make my self fit, and put my whole confidence in his Grace and Mercy, *Qui neminem dignum Eligit, sed eligendo facit,* as S. Austin speaks" (I, 73; see also I, 34–6).

It is clear that the dual exercise of power in ecclesiastical and civil realms does require some justification; Williams draws upon the authority of Cicero, quoting his approbation of Demetrius Valerius as "a full scholar fit for the Sacred, and for the Civil Gown" (I, 39). Hacket supports his subject's view of the matter: "The King's Services in a righteous way is not opposite to Christ's Evangelical Administrations, but coincident" (I, 56). And, he claims, Williams "pretended to make no more requital then to serve God in his Calling, to be true to the King, and no Exactor upon his People" (I, 60).

The defensive tone of these comments shows that Hacket could not assume that all of his readers would immediately and un-questioningly accept his judgment that Williams was "a man as like Vertue it self, as could be pattern'd in Flesh and Blood" (I, 74). If we believe Hacket, Williams served both his God and his King with eminent success and exemplary virtue. But if we turn to such contem-porary historians as Anthony Weldon and Arthur Wilson, Williams' service to church and state was marked by Machiavellian self-advancement and conspicuous absence of virtue – so great that he richly deserved the political downfall which Hacket attributes to intrigues by other members of the corrupt Caroline court.[20] Hacket's memoir is, to a considerable degree, an attempt to justify his subject's career in answer to the vehement attacks of Wilson and Weldon.[21] Yet both the exemplary biographers and the debunking historians share a significant common ground. Though they differ with respect to Williams himself, they are united in deploring a loss of the virtuous ideal at the courts of James and Charles and in perceiving an inevitable progress toward dissolution of the court altogether in the "tumults" of civil war.

Hacket's model subject serves in a world extraordinarily differ-ent from Sidney's world, where both the upright and the base reside at court but the virtuous courtier can avoid the one group and cultivate the other.[22] In Hacket's view, the courtly world finally rejects the service Williams would offer because it is no longer able either to recognize or to value exemplary virtue. It is this world in which Herbert is enmeshed once he accepts the Public Oratorship in 1619, like Williams claiming that it "hath no such earthiness in it, but it may very well be joined with Heaven,"[23] and in which he perhaps entertains "Court-hopes" as Walton alleges; it is this same world that he finally rejects when he takes up the cure of souls at Bemerton at the close of the decade, not long after Williams' fall from grace.[24] Walton's praise of Herbert's ambitions, like Hacket's approval of Williams' dedication to virtue, amply confirms that the ideal maintains its force.

ii

The changing climate in which the ideal must be exercised is best traced in the work of historians such as Weldon and Wilson, who are concerned primarily with the actual decline of virtue rather than with its continuing power to influence individual lives that are acknowledged, even by their biographers, to be exceptional in their exemplary excellence. These writers, whom Hacket takes such pains to refute, depict a court so corrupt, degenerate, and moved by greed for power, wealth, and influence that we cannot conceive how any young courtier could maintain an ideal of virtuous service in such a setting. The corruption extends to the ecclesiastical realm as well. Wilson reflects without surprise on the willingness of the bishops to serve at the nullity trial of the Countess of Essex in 1613: "Kings will never want fit *Ministers* in Corrupted Times, both in *Church* and *Common-wealth,* as long as there are *Degrees,* and *Places* of *Ascent* to clime to" (p. 69). Weldon, too, uses this occasion to execrate the bishops: "I know not in what bad action they would not be lookers on . . ." (p. 71). For both writers, the time's "abounding iniquity" has drawn God's entirely just punishment upon England in the form of civil war. But it is the loss of ancient virtue in the nobility and the crown that has spread corruption throughout the kingdom. According to Weldon, honor has been "so prodigally wasted, as we are utterly bankrupt, having spent our old Stock, and have not bravery enough to erect a new" (p. 24). Both Wilson and Weldon, to be sure, were violently attacked for their "infamous libels" by some of their fellow-historians, and it is worth noting that Weldon, as an ex-courtier dismissed from service, might have a particular bias (DNB). Yet even Bishop Goodman, who says of him, "I have never read a more malicious-minded author, nor any who had such poor and mean observations," acknowledges that in King James' time the kingdom "fell to luxury and riot."[25] The most ironic sign of the temper of the times, however, is surely Mrs. Turner's outcry on the scaffold, as she awaits hanging for her part in the poisoning of Overbury:

> O the Court, the Court! God bless the King and send him better servants about him, for there is no religion in most of them but malice, pride, whoredom, swearing and rejoicing in the fall of

others. It is so wicked a place as I wonder the earth did not open
and swallow it up. Mr. Sherif, put none of your children thither.
                                          (cited in Stone, p. 394)

Contemporary historians like Wilson and Weldon, writing after
war has broken out, would argue that in fact God did cause the earth
to "open and swallow it up," since they attribute the fall of the
monarchy to the loss of moral value attending the Stuart reigns. This
loss was to produce remarkably varied responses among the members of Herbert's generation. The examples of his own older brother
Edward, Thomas Carew, and Sir John Suckling illustrate what I have
called a path of descent, an acquiescence in the sapping of moral
authority that betrays the virtuous ideal by settling for its show
rather than seeking its substance. The life choices of Nicholas Ferrar
and Sir Henry Wotton, on the other hand, represent a path of ascent.
These exemplars continue to strive toward virtue and indeed, to raise
it to a higher level than the secular by rejecting the possibilities of
worldly great place in the active life and moving instead toward
the contemplative life. These contrasting paths figure polarized
possibilities of service to earth and heaven that exert their pull on
Herbert in life and find representation in the conflicting tensions
experienced by Herbert-as-courtier in the vocation poems of *The
Temple*.

Lord Herbert of Cherbury is as representative of his time as his
younger brother. His autobiography is a most interesting transitional
document because it reveals – unconsciously – such contradictions
between the ideal pattern of virtue and an actual courtier's behavior.
His perception of the courtly ideal in many ways resembles that set
forth in the courtesy books and in the biographies of Sidney, yet it
also demonstrates how much the ideal has changed under the impact
of a new ruler and new hazards of service to the crown. Lord
Herbert's commitment to courtly values includes considerable attention to duels, ladies' favors, and his own appearance in a shift of
focus which we can suppose neither Moffet nor Greville would
admire, while his preoccupation with the loss of honor entailed by
his recall as King James' ambassador to Paris confirms the pernicious
effect of the increasingly unstable conditions of courtly service so
deplored by Wilson and Weldon.

The autobiography is, in intent at least, as exemplary as the
biographies considered earlier in this chapter. Like Moffet and Greville, Lord Herbert considers his account valuable as "instruction" to

posterity. Although his *Life* is a means to examine "what hath been done well or will, to the intent I may both reform that which was amiss, and so make my peace with God," Edward Herbert also wishes to "comfort my self in those things which through Gods great grace and favour, have been done according to the Rules of Conscience, Vertue, and Honor."[26] Without irony, he figures himself as the exemplary courtier.

This very worldly self-assessment opens with an almost sermon-like assertion that man's faculties must be directed to "God onely" because no "worldly felicity," no "Transitory or perishing Object in this world," can satisfy man's hopes. These are probably not just the pious exclamations one might expect of even the most rakish courtier once he has reached his sixties, since Lord Herbert repeats them in his digression on the proper education of the young. This section of the autobiography, corresponding in detail to the educational program found throughout the courtesy books, suggests the persistence of its author's belief in the virtuous ideal even in a work that shows how little his life actually conforms to it. Because of youth's "fraile nature," "theire Manners [must] bee well guided and themselves by degrees habituated in Vertue"; the young must also "keepe the company of grave learned men who are of good Reputation and heare rather what they say and imitate what they doe then follow the example of young wilde and rash persons."[27] His prescriptions recall Greville's praise of Sidney's association with "grave and learned men." Lord Herbert's warning against becoming "Insolent and vayne glorious" by too great an attention to "puft knowledge" rather than "goodness and vertuous manners," however, resembles the faint dispraise in Walton of George Herbert's tendency at Cambridge to maintain "too great a distance with all his inferiours" and "put too great a value on his parts and Parentage."

But Lord Herbert's lively, and entirely unrepentant, accounts of his frequent duels associate him with the wild and rash rather than with the grave and learned. He justifies this behavior by an appeal to

> how strictly I held my selfe to my Oath of Knighthood. For the rest I can truly say That though I have lived in the Armyes and Courts of the greatest Princes in Christendome yet I never had quarrell with man for my owne sake, noe not although in my owne Nature I was ever Chollerique and hasty yet I never without occasion quarrelled with any body.[28]

These attempts to justify his motives for dueling not only betray the increasing emptiness of the courtly code, but stand in ironic contrast to his brother's comments on the practice in *The Church-porch:*

> Catch not at quarrels. He that dares not speak
> Plainly and home, is coward of the two.
> Think not thy fame at ev'ry twitch will break:
> By great deeds shew, that thou canst little do:
>   And do them not: that shall thy wisdom be;
>   And change thy temperance into braverie.
>
> (stanza 37)

The self-justification evident in Edward Herbert's response to his fall from royal favor reveals a far more serious concern with the loss of honor. He stresses his devotion to the king's service throughout his autobiography, assuring his readers that his ambassadorship was indeed carried out "according to the Rules of Conscience, Vertue, and Honor." In his letters to James and Charles after his removal from the post, he repeatedly complains of the dishonor that has been done to his name since the recall has not been followed by a compensating reward. Above all, he is concerned that others might think his worth has been disvalued by his sovereign. Two years after the recall from Paris, he writes Charles to complain that "no man in the memory of man ever return'd from the charge I had in that cuntrey that had not some place of honor and preferment given him" (Lee, p. 258). Clearly, what matters is the "publique disgrace" he has suffered – the mere reputation of honor, not the virtuous substance of honorable service. Edward Herbert fails to achieve that patient acceptance of adversity required by the virtue of fortitude which Hacket claims for Bishop Williams in a similar fall from favor also in the late 1620s and that Walton claims for George Herbert in the same period. In his obsession with the outward form of honor, Lord Herbert figures the shift from the virtuous model of an Elizabethan courtier exemplified by Sidney to a distinctly different Caroline model of courtliness in which "heigthing the image" takes precedence.

Sir John Suckling and Thomas Carew, notorious rakes nevertheless full of "grace and gallantry" in the mode of Buckingham,[29] represent even more perfectly than Edward Herbert the Caroline idea of a courtier, in a descent to the actual signified by their disillusioned and disillusioning responses to the court world of intrigue, favoritism, and devaluation of traditional virtues. Suckling is a particularly interesting case, since he serves his ruler well but ceases to either accept or exemplify the virtues as the primary basis of service. He can mix "earthly" and "heavenly" things enough to write religious poems bearing a considerable resemblance to George Herbert's artful simplicity and even a treatise on religion that is certainly serious in intent, though scarcely a major piece of theology. And he writes a letter of advice to Henry Jermyn, to be passed on to Henrietta Maria, that is soundly conceived in the best tradition of a counselor's advice to his prince.[30]

But Suckling gained notoriety, rather than honorable fame, from his lavishly clothed troops that accompanied Charles to war on the Scots in 1639: "100 very handsome young proper men, whom he clad in white doubletts and scarlett breeches, and scarlet coates, hatts, and . . . feathers, well horsed, and armed."[31] This attention to "heigthing the image" to create a glittering surface is further compromised by recurrent attributions of cowardice. As one lampoon puts it:

> Sir *John* got him on an Ambling Nag,
>   To *Scotland* for to ride a,
> With a hundred horse more, all his own he swore,
>   To guard him on every side a.
>
> No Errant Knight ever went to fight
>   With halfe so gay a Bravado;
> Had you seen but his look, you'ld have sworn on a book
>   Hee'ld have conquer'd a whole Armado.[32]

The example of Suckling suggests how complex is the interweaving of a decline in "moral authority of the monarchy" with the persistence of "renaissance ideas of nobility as the hallmark of both personal merit and ancient lineage" noted by Lawrence Stone. Carew is a still more typical example of what Stone calls a "distinct culture group" of courtiers in the 1620s and 1630s.[33] The Royalist courtier was, in theory, devoutly Anglican, but could be remarkably "prophane" in his moral behavior, as Carew himself admits in his commendation of Sandys' psalm translations while asserting his own unworthiness to write sacred poetry.[34] Indeed, the popular lore of Carew's life creates an image of both descent and ascent in the often-repeated tale that in his last years he rejected those "temptations . . . [that] had led him too far from the paths of virtue" so that now "love-songs were exchanged for penitential psalms; his muse abandoned the service of Venus, and was employed in pouring forth passionate strains of sorrow and prayer."[35] Rhodes Dunlap has shown how inaccurate is this model of a rake's progress and reform. Yet as in the case of Suckling, the vices and follies, superficialities and shows attributed to these Caroline figures arise from the same debasement of courtly actuality (and, simultaneously, fascination with its excesses) that we have noticed in the testimony of the historians.

As the quintessential courtier of the 1620s and 1630s, Carew serves as our final measure of the distance the image has traveled from Sidney in the 1580s. The "ideal" represented by Carew may help to show why Bishop Williams suffered such a notable fall from grace once he ran afoul of a favorite like Buckingham but also why his virtue – exemplary of an older ideal – required so much justification from Hacket. Who would believe it? As in the case of Bacon, if Williams *was* virtuous, the court world no longer valued that virtue sufficiently; and if either of these men were as unprincipled as their attackers argued, that fact in itself would attest to the emptying of substance from the traditional ideal of the courtier. If conduct books in the seventeenth century begin to reveal diffusion and disintegration of the ideal, actual courtly lives in the period far more intensely confirm the process.

By polarizing earthly and heavenly values, the direction of change during these years makes such an integration as Herbert seems to have envisioned in 1619 far less possible of realization. The increasingly worldly image figured by the lives of Edward Herbert, Suckling, and Carew traces a path of descent because their aspirations are linked primarily to external appearance and secular accomplishment. The path of ascent offers an alternative to this acquiescence to the loss of virtue in the court world by moving toward spiritual goals and by denying personal ambition. This refusal to participate in the business of a world denuded of virtue is exemplified in its purest, most extreme form by Nicholas Ferrar's choice of withdrawal to the contemplative life at Little Gidding; Sir Henry Wotton's post as Provost of Eton represents a more traditional balance of active service and contemplative retirement.

Ferrar's choice of a calling stands absolutely opposed to the acceptance of worldly "realities" exemplified by such new courtly models as Carew and Suckling. It also constitutes a kind of reply to

the equivocalities encountered by Bishop Williams, in the same period still trying to integrate the claims of both worlds. Like his "dear
brother" Herbert, Ferrar as a young man moved close to the center of
power. With Herbert, he was a member of Parliament in 1624, and
with Herbert's stepfather, served as a major official of the Virginia
Company. But he, too, renounced his aspirations to worldly service
and devoted himself to God's service in the mid-1620s, though unlike
Herbert he remained a lay-servant, a deacon but never a priest.[36]

According to Alan Maycock, Ferrar told his tutor before becoming deacon that "he would never take priest's orders – 'he durst not
advance one step higher' – nor did he ever alter that resolve."
Ferrar's decision served his plans to embark upon the contemplative
life at Little Gidding. As deacon, he "would be able to lead the
family's devotions in their daily offices, but it was not his purpose to
constitute himself their chaplain." The phrase "durst not advance
one step higher" does have a remarkably Herbertian ring. Herbert
might not have shared this view, but his poems about the priesthood
express even more intensely his sense of unworthiness for the office.

Ferrar's action is important because of his close friendship with
Herbert and because of the implications of this move away from the
center of worldly power.[37] In the mid-1620s, their searches for a
calling take a similar direction in the decision to enter the diaconate –
a movement toward divinity but not a commitment to the cure of
souls – that postulates a turn toward spirituality in response to the
pressures of the age. As Chapter 1 has shown, the choice between
active and contemplative lives constituted one of the major dilemmas
and principal subjects of the courtesy books; but by the seventeenth
century the pull toward a life of retirement, whether secular or
religious, began to exert ever greater force in the light of conditions
at court.

In 1626 Sir Henry Wotton – claimed by Walton to be a close
friend of Herbert's, and certainly close to Donne and to Edward
Herbert – took a similar step. His letter to King Charles explains his
intention in terms that recall Ferrar's comment that he "durst not
advance one step higher." He is anxious to serve – "shall I sit and do
nothing in the Porch of Gods House whereinto I am entered?" – but
fears to take up the office of priest: "so, God knows, the nearer I
approach to contemplate his greatness, the more I tremble to assume
any cure of souls even in the lowest degree." Yet he comforts himself
with a "Christian hope, That Gentlemen and Knights sons, who are

trained up with us in a Seminary of Church-men . . . will by my example (without vanity be it spoken) not be ashamed, after the sight of Courtly Weeds, to put on a Surplice." And he hopes "to compose some Hymnes unto his endless glory, who hath called me, (for which his Name be ever blessed) though late to his Service, yet early to the knowledge of his truth, and sense of his mercy."[38]

This long letter to Charles almost perfectly configures the alternatives to devalued court life that were sought in the 1620s by men of such worldly capabilities as Herbert and Ferrar, as well as those of such worldly stature among the older generation as Wotton. Although he had held high secular office, in this letter Wotton declines even the possibility of high office in the church. As his description of the diaconate as "the Porch of Gods House" suggests, he is imaging a pattern of ascent, rejecting the realm of the Court and approaching the realm of the Temple. He is as preoccupied with use and service as Herbert is in the vocation poems of *The Temple*. In hoping that the students of Eton will not be ashamed, "after the sight of Courtly Weeds, to put on a Surplice" in emulation of his example, he prefigures the contrast between courtier and churchman so central to Walton's construction of an exemplar out of the materials of Herbert's life. Though Wotton does not make the decision Herbert announces in his address to the "Blest Order" in "The Priesthood" – "fain would I draw nigh, / Fain put thee on, exchanging my lay-sword / For that of th' holy Word" – Wotton's "trembl[ing] to assume the cure of souls" does reflect the fear expressed by Herbert in that poem:

> I am both foul and brittle; much unfit
>   To deal in holy Writ.
>
>   .   .   .   .
>
> Wherefore I dare not, I, put forth my hand
> To hold the Ark. . . .
>   (11–12, 31–2)

Moreover, Wotton's desire to serve God's glory by composing holy hymns resembles Herbert's dedication of his poetic abilities to God. In contrast to the ideal images constructed in exemplary biographies, however, Wotton is figuring *himself,* in as conscious and deliberate a creation, still addressing an ideal both courtly and Christian.

Wotton's letter outlines an alternative far closer to Herbert's than to Ferrar's, yet a common necessity to choose between the worlds of Court and Temple dominates all three lives in the same decade. The devalued courtly image represented by Edward Herbert, Carew, and Suckling enables us to appreciate the counterforce exerted by the exemplary figures of Ferrar, Wotton, and George Herbert. But the differing responses of Ferrar and Wotton also point out that Herbert's particular choice of a calling may not have seemed as inevitable to him as it now appears to us, viewing the completed pattern of his life.

These figures, like those of Williams and Sidney, are all potential exemplars of Herbert's life and his poetry. Deeply implicated in the conflicting drives and shifting ideals of his own time, Herbert makes his vocational choice a structural center for the transformations enacted in *The Temple*. The hesitancies, doubts, and delays that mark his developing awareness of God's will for him in the personal lyrics of *The Church* confess that he shares a biographical dilemma with others of his time. The dramatic structure that transforms courtier into churchman is not simply the artistic fiction of either Herbert or his biographers but rather a representation of polarities central to his age, experienced as conflicting patterns of life choice by many of his contemporaries and instrumental in devising new versions – reconstructions, recreations – of the old ideal of virtuous service.

iii

Herbert's biographical entanglements can now be examined. They are contextually essential to his art because they are the source of potential patterns: model paths of life change, exemplary images fashioned by selves or biographers and exerting their force upon Herbert in life. There is not just a humble Christian but also a worldly courtier within *The Temple*, attempting to unweave his entanglements, to make sense of his experience by perceiving design, in order to bequeath the possibility of transformation to others through the exemplary power of his poems. Herbert's deliberate use of his own experience in the *Church* lyrics articulates the pressures of actuality that surround him in life and aligns him with the self-conscious exemplars we have been concerned with thus far.

We know few facts of his biography and even fewer firm dates for his poems. Yet these slight materials give clear evidence for the pervasive and troubling presence of hesitation, doubt, delay concerning the choice of a calling. Though his poems have been assigned to years as early as 1614 and as late as 1630–3, nearly all the positively dated poems are from the 1620s. This decade frames Herbert's two major vocational choices – his assumption of the office of Public Orator of Cambridge and his entrance into the priesthood at Bemerton – thus identifying these years as the crucial period of transformation.[39]

Born in 1593, Herbert entered Westminster School in 1605 and Trinity College, Cambridge, in 1609, having been appointed King's Scholar a few months before together with John Hacket, the future biographer of Bishop Williams. In 1612 Herbert took his B.A. degree; in 1614 he was appointed Minor Fellow at Cambridge; in 1616 he took the M.A. degree and was appointed Major Fellow. He received the post of Public Orator in 1619.[40] In 1624 he requested and received a six-month leave of absence from the position. There is no evidence of his acting as Orator after 1623 except, possibly, speaking at the installation of Buckingham as Chancellor of the University in July 1626.[41]

In 1624 and perhaps 1625, Herbert represented his native place, Montgomery, Wales, in Parliament.[42] Amy Charles has discovered that late in 1624 the archbishop of Canterbury granted a dispensation allowing Herbert to be ordained deacon "at any time by Bishop Williams, without letters dimissory from the bishop of his own diocese"; shortly thereafter, Herbert became comportioner of a rectory at Landinam presented by Williams. This lay position does not constitute firm evidence that Herbert was in fact ordained deacon at this time. That date is still not known.[43] In 1626 Herbert was appointed, again by Williams, Prebendary of Lincoln Cathedral and installed – by proxy – on July 5 into the prebend of Leighton Ecclesia. The record of installation describes him as deacon and, as Amy Charles points out, "The responsibilities he assumed with the office did not include the cure of souls. . . ."[44]

In 1627 Herbert resigned the Oratorship; we do not know when he resigned his fellowship at Cambridge, in spite of Walton's suggestion that he did so following his mother's death, also in 1627.[45] In the same year, Herbert, his brother Edward, and their cousin Thomas Lawley received a joint grant from the crown of a manor at Ribbesford, which was sold to Sir Henry Herbert later in the same year for £3,000.[46] In 1628, according to Walton, he spent "about Twelve Months" at Woodford, Essex, the home of his brother Henry, to recover from illness and, in search of better air, went on to the home of his stepfather's brother, Lord Danvers Earl of Danby, at Dauntsey in Wiltshire. On March 5, 1629, he married Jane Danvers, a cousin of the Danvers brothers. On April 26, 1630, he was instituted at Bemerton, and on September 19 ordained a priest. Herbert died on March 1, 1633; in that same year the first edition of *The Temple* was published.

The chronology of his literary activity is even more sketchy. His first published verse, two Latin poems on the death of Prince Henry, appeared in *Epicedium Cantabrigiense* . . . in 1612, and in 1613 two Latin poems on the marriage of Princess Elizabeth to the Elector Palatine were included in an anthology given to the Elector on the occasion of a visit to Cambridge.[47] A poem on the death of Queen Anne appeared in *Lacrymae Cantabrigienses* . . . in 1619. The *Musae Responsoriae,* a reply to Andrew Melville's *Anti-Tami-Categoriae,* probably dates between 1620 and 1622. The two collections of Latin poems, *Passio discerpta* and *Lucus,* although not published during Herbert's lifetime, are usually on internal evidence assigned a date no earlier than 1623.[48] Herbert's epigram, *In Natales et Pascha Concurrentes,* was probably composed in 1618, and the most important of his three Latin epigrams to Bacon most likely dates from early 1621. The English poems to the Queen of Bohemia may be dated in the early 1620s, since they refer to Elizabeth's exile in Holland,[49] while the *Memoriae Matris Sacrum* was entered with Donne's funeral sermon on Herbert's mother in 1627.

This sparse outline of dates is really all we know with certainty about Herbert's life, and two of these events – the extended visits to Sir Henry Herbert and the Earl of Danby – are reports from Walton unsupported by independent evidence. We have no solid basis upon which to date the writing of *The Temple* or to determine his vocational intentions in the 1620s beyond the information summarized here. Herbert's biographers, editors, and critics have erected an enormous superstructure of speculation upon these scant foundations. While the process is necessary in considering relationships between Herbert's life and his art, there is considerable danger in forcing the few known facts to fit a given interpretation of his behavior. My concern here is the matter of vocation: what little we do know about these crucial years suggests that Herbert is caught in conflicting desires and hesitancies about his proper mode of service.

We notice first the multiplicity of directions implied by Herbert's various offices. His earliest Cambridge appointments and the M.A. degree suggest that at this time he intended to become a University Fellow, combining a life of scholarship with divinity: a respectable choice for the younger son of an aristocratic family, though not one proposed by Walton. The office of Public Orator is somewhat more ambiguous in intent. Most later commentators remind us that Herbert's two predecessors, Sir Robert Naunton and Sir Francis Nethersole, found the post "a steppingstone to a career as a secretary of state"; on the other hand, as Hutchinson notes, Herbert's successor, Robert Creighton, "had no political ambitions and ended his exemplary life as bishop of Bath and Wells" (p. xxviii).

There is no direct evidence that Herbert ever gave up his early plans to "set foot in Divinity," but his activities in the early 1620s certainly suggest that his conception of service to the church may have included some form of service to the state as well. Walton's claim that Herbert "followed the court" and cultivated the attention of King James are partly supported by the panegyric and worldly tone of his public letters and speeches as Orator – for instance, he praises James' collected works as "a library in itself" to rival the Bodleian – and his membership in Parliament is, of course, not only secular but political, another worldly entanglement.[50]

Yet at the same time that Herbert was serving in Parliament, Amy Charles' evidence shows that he was considering a move away from "secular employment." His ordination as deacon is usually taken as his decisive turn toward the priesthood, since such a position precluded most forms of civil employment unless, as Charles points out, "like Williams, he could find a way of combining the sacred and the secular" ("George Herbert, Deacon," p. 273). Walton reports a response by Herbert to an unnamed "Court-friend's" expostulation that sacred orders were "too mean an employment, and too much below his birth, and the excellent abilities and endowments of his mind," but Herbert's response, as reported by Walton, perhaps too neatly coincides with his biographer's desire to exalt the choice of divinity for the aristocracy:

It hath been formerly judged that the Domestick Servants of the King of Heaven, should be of the noblest Families on Earth: and, though the Iniquity of the late Times have made Clergy-men meanly valued, and the sacred name of *Priest* contemptible; yet I will labour to make it honourable, by consecrating all my learning, and all my poor abilities, to advance the glory of that God that gave them. . . . (p. 277)

Walton's reported "conversations" derive from many sources, often, as here, unnamed and distant in time from their origin; consequently, recent critics tend to treat those which fit Walton's thesis especially well as somewhat dubious in the absence of supporting evidence. In this case, there is simply no way to determine whether such a conversation took place at all or whether it – or something like it – occurred in 1625, as Walton alleges, or closer to 1630, when Herbert finally did enter holy orders.

The complexity of Herbert's attitude toward various forms of service to God is nowhere better expressed than in his comment to Nicholas Ferrar's cousin, Arthur Woodnoth (executor of Herbert's will), in respect to Woodnoth's own choice of a calling. Woodnoth reports to Ferrar that Herbert "told me we were much troubled about words for the Name of a Divine would satisfy all when in truth, I might doo the office tho I wanted the tytle" (cited in Novarr, p. 305). Herbert's ordination as deacon might indeed have been a further step toward the ultimate goal of divinity; but it might also have been a *via media*, another possible version of joining earthly and heavenly things. The diaconate might have been followed by withdrawal to the contemplative life, on the model of the Ferrar family at Little Gidding or even with them; it could equally have led to just such a retirement to the country as Herbert seems to have made – residing at a nobleman's house, directing his efforts toward restoration of the derelict church he served as prebend by raising funds among his wealthy connections, marrying a rich man's daughter, and perhaps devoting himself to the writing of poetry, as many country gentlemen of large and small estate did in this period.[51]

In the context of the lives of other men in positions similar to Herbert's, the diaconate represents not necessarily a decisive stage in a smooth progress toward a determined end, but an alternative: another step in that extended search for a calling which gives such intensity to his outcries against time in the *Church* lyrics. The decision to take holy orders in 1630 *was* final; but that decision cannot be unquestionably dated any earlier in Herbert's life than his thirty-seventh year.

The problem of delays and hesitations during the 1620s should also be related to the network of noble families and influential connections in which Herbert was enmeshed by virtue of his birth, his training, and his talents. The Herbert family "held office from generation to generation without a break" (Stone, p. 469); these connections with great place tend to support Walton's account of Herbert's "Court-hopes" and provide at least a conjectural basis for those ambitions that Walton can still perceive as "laudible." Herbert's kinsman William Herbert, recipient of Thomas Moffet's New Year's gift in the 1590s, had become Earl of Pembroke and Montgomery by the 1620s and was one of the most powerful men in the kingdom.[52] King James, according to Walton, admired the "excellent Latin" and "expressions so suted to the genius of the King" in Herbert's letter thanking him for the gift of his *Opera Latina* to Cambridge. When James asked the name of the Orator, William Herbert commended his young relative by replying "That he knew him very well; and that he was his Kinsman, but he lov'd him more for his learning and vertue, than for that he was of his name and family" (pp. 271, 273). This praise of Herbert's worldly abilities is repeated in Edward Herbert's autobiography, long after Herbert's death and, interestingly, given there as much emphasis as the exemplary holiness of his later life:

> My Brother George was so excellent a Scholar, that he was made the publick Orator of the University in Cambridge, some of whose English Works are extant which, though they be rare in their kind, yet are far short of expressing those perfections he had in the Greek and Latin Tongue, and all divine and human Literature. . . .   (p. 8)

Herbert was even more closely linked to the world of the court through Edward, James' ambassador to France in the early 1620s, and their younger brother Henry, who became Master of the Revels in 1623. His cousin Sir Robert Harley was still an influential figure at court in these years, critical of the Crown's policies but not yet fully committed to the Parliamentarianism and Presbyterianism that he and his wife would later espouse after his dismissal as Master of the Mint. Sir John Danvers was close enough to the dispensers of great place to be the recipient of his stepson's appeal to use his good offices to help secure the Oratorship. Herbert was also connected with other high officials of James' court through acquaintanceship and, perhaps, patronage. Although there is no independent evidence to support Walton's claim that James' kinsmen Lodowick Stuart, Duke of Lennox and Richmond, and James, Marquis of Hamilton, were "two of [Herbert's] . . . most powerful friends," there is no particular reason to doubt this sort of statement from Walton, especially since these two noblemen were undoubtedly close to Edward Herbert. We have reliable evidence from Herbert's own letter to Danvers that he considers his predecessor in the Oratorship, Sir Francis Nethersole, his "ancient acquaintance"; in reference to his "working the heads" to obtain the office, Herbert remarks: "I have a strong opinion of him, that if he can do me a courtesie, he will of himself . . ." (cited in Hutchinson, p. 369).

Herbert's relationship with Bacon associates him in another way with the world of great place, and may also measure a significant change in his attitudes. His contribution to the volume of epigrams on Bacon's death argues that his attachments were not to be influenced by opportunistic ambition – a marked contrast to his comments about Nethersole in the letter to Danvers a few years earlier. Walton's claim that the Lord Chancellor "put such a value on [Herbert's] judgment, that he usually desir'd his approbation, before he would expose any of his Books to be printed" (p. 273) is perhaps exaggerated, but Bacon was friend and admirer of Herbert and patron as well, since Herbert assisted with the Latin translation of the *Advancement of Learning* (1623). Bacon dedicated his psalm translations to "his very good friend, Mr. George Herbert" because "in respect of divinity and poesy met . . . I could not make better choice."

Herbert's praise of the *Novum Organum* suggests still another way in which he conceived the possibility of uniting earthly and heavenly things. Far from castigating Bacon for his insistence that man concentrate his intellectual efforts upon knowledge of phenomena in this world, Herbert praises Bacon's priestly role in the study of *"mundique et animarum"* – the universe and souls together.[53] This viewpoint does not fit our customary twentieth-century idea of Bacon's contribution to thought any more than it conforms to our usual perception of Herbert as the pious Anglican singer of Bemerton. Nor does our usual view of Herbert fit the sophistication implied by Edward Herbert's dedication of *De Veritate* to his brother George and William Boswell, submitting the manuscript to their judgment and approval.[54] Marchette Chute, commenting on the "alien" quality of Edward Herbert's deism to his brother's mind and on Herbert's somewhat surprising connections with Bacon, suggests that "There must have been a courtesy in his mind that made him welcome a vision he could not share, so that he could sympathize with high purpose even when it led to a conclusion very different from his own" (p. 67). Chute's insight is valuable in calling attention to the way Herbert managed to move in both worlds, of Court and Temple, for the greater part of his life, though I would stress, as she does not, that these very characteristics may have been a source of conflict when Herbert faced his choice of a calling.

Since Herbert's connections are with worldly and powerful men and women of his time, it is not surprising that Oley should remember him criticized for having "lost himself in a humble way." Herbert's three letters to Danvers during his effort to secure the Orator's post show a very conscious worldliness, even as they betray a barely mastered doubt over the choice of a calling. They attest Herbert's attraction to the position and the efficiency and enthusiasm with which he set out obtaining it. They also reveal doubts on the part of those close to him concerning the implications of his desire for the office:

> I understand by Sir *Francis Nethersols* Letter, that he fears I have not fully resolved of the matter, since this place being civil may divert me too much from Divinity, at which, not without cause, he thinks, I aim; but, I have wrote him back, that this dignity, hath no such earthiness in it, but it may very well be joined with Heaven; or if it had to others, yet to me it should not, for ought I yet knew; and therefore I desire him to send me a direct answer in his next Letter.[55]

By January 19, [i.e., 1619–20], when the position is almost his, Herbert writes Danvers a brief note inquiring about his "dear sick Sister" and adds,

Concerning the Orators place all goes well yet, the next Friday it is tryed, and accordingly you shall hear. I have forty businesses in my hands, your Courtesie will pardon the haste of

Your humblest Servant,
GEORGE HERBERT

The phrase "forty businesses" has plenty of earthly concern in it, as do all of Herbert's letters from these years. Two letters from the previous year, when he was still "setting foot into Divinity to lay the platforme of my future life," demonstrate his interest in the courtly art of civil conversation. He writes his younger brother Henry, at Paris in 1619, in terms remarkably like those of the courtesy books. He now has leisure, he says,

> to impart unto you some of those observations which I have framed to myself in conversation; and whereof I would not have you ignorant. . . . You live in a brave nation, where except you wink you cannot but see many brave examples. Bee covetous, then, of all good which you see in Frenchmen, whether it be in knowledge, or in fashion, or in words; for I would have you, even in speeches, to observe so much, as when you meet with a witty French speech, try to speak the like in English: so shall you play a good marchant, by transporting French commodities to your own country. . . . have a good conceit of your wit, mark what I say, have a good conceit of your wit; that is, be proud, not with a foolish vanting of yourself when there is no caus, but by setting a just price of your qualities. . . . (Hutchinson, p. 366)

Some years later, the author of "The Quidditie" holds no such favorable view of the good in Frenchmen, but rather remarks that the true verse which brings him into God's presence "never was in *France* or *Spain*." Herbert's advice to Henry aligns him with the court world and the values espoused by those raised to great expectations. Yet in urging Henry to develop a "good conceit" of his wit he foreshadows a most central problem faced in "Jordan" (II), where weaving himself into the sense becomes a sign of that lack of humility which "setting a just price on your qualities" would seem to represent.

In the same year, Herbert writes Sir Robert Harley – signing himself "Your most indebted kinsman" – such "passages of newes which this time affords" with all the chatty, free-ranging wit concerning the affairs of the great that we find in similar letters of court gossip written by more familiar courtiers of the period. There is wry comment on Buckingham's sudden access of apparent devotion, since he now arrives an hour early for prayers; gossip about marital troubles between Sir Charles Howard and his wife; and discussion of a Frenchman whose poem to King James was not suitably rewarded (Hutchinson, pp. 367–9). The urbane, witty, entirely superficial tone of the letter brings us closest to a George Herbert implicated in the same world as the Jacobean and Caroline courtiers who embody the courtly ideal of the period for us today.

Herbert's worldliness in these years contrasts sharply with both his retirement in the later 1620s and his service at Bemerton from 1630 to 1633. Joseph Summers, arguing that Herbert's rejection of worldly ambitions reflects his despairing judgment upon the course of events, is particularly helpful in tracing the equivocal relations between Herbert's family and the court in the mid-twenties – a further source of entanglement. The Virginia Company was under attack by the Crown, and Sir John Danvers and Nicholas Ferrar, as officers of the Company, were vehemently opposing that attack. Edward Herbert was recalled from France in 1624. And as Summers also reminds us, George Herbert's denunciation of war in his Cambridge oration upon the prince's return from Spain could hardly have met with Charles' approval once he ascended the throne and began to reverse his father's peace policy. Although Summers does not mention Herbert's cousin, Sir Robert Harley, in this connection, both G. E. Aylmer and Perez Zagorin have shown that his opposition to the Crown began as early as the mid-twenties.[56]

Summers' point of view is supported by Nicholas Ferrar's emphatic claim in his preface to *The Temple:*

> Quitting both his deserts and all the opportunities that he had for worldly preferment, he betook himself to the Sanctuarie and Temple of God, choosing rather to serve at Gods Altar, then to seek the honour of State-employments. As for those inward enforcements to this course (for outward there was none) which many of these ensuing verses bear witnesse of, they detract not from the freedome, but adde to the honour of this resolution in him.
>
> (p. 3)

Ferrar's statement counters Walton's claim that Herbert abandoned court-hopes after the deaths of his patrons King James, the Duke of Lennox and Richmond, and the Marquis of Hamilton. Still a third view, closer to Ferrar's stress on "inward enforcements," is proposed by Charles Cotton in his commendatory poem prefixed to Walton's collected *Lives* of 1675:

> And Herbert: he whose education,
> Manners, and parts, by high applauses blown,
> Was deeply tainted with Ambition;
>
> And fitted for a Court, made that his aim;
> At last, without regard to Birth or Name,
> For a poor Country-Cure does all disclaim. . . .

Ferrar's view of the matter ought to carry more weight than either Walton's or Cotton's. Yet it is also true that the "taint" of ambition serves as problem and pretext in many of the *Church* lyrics. Each of these interpretations argues for the presence of a powerful inner drama in Herbert's life during the 1620s, and is figured within the courtly self-representation of Herbert's poetry.

In still another respect, the network of relationships to which Herbert belonged may have contributed to his doubts about great place in a world where the crown could no longer command the loyalties of its formerly most faithful subjects. The later years of Herbert's own family, after war broke out, finally culminate the stresses that even in the 1620s were beginning to separate Anglican devotion from Royalist loyalism. Little more than a decade after *The Temple* was published, Edward Herbert gives over Montgomery Castle to Parliamentary forces, declaring in letter after letter his loyalty to the king's opponents; Sir Robert Harley and his wife become major supporters of the Parliamentary cause; and Herbert's stepfather becomes one of the regicides who in 1649 sit in judgment upon the ruler who was once thought to be God's anointed vicegerent upon earth.[57]

These later developments are directly relevant to Herbert's perception of the world surrounding him in the 1620s. *The Temple*'s vision of worldly flaws extends to the spiritual condition of society as well as speaking of the poet's own spiritual state. We think of Herbert as the pre-eminent spokesman for Anglican values and for the church as an institution linked indissolubly to the state; but we should also remember his denunciation of divisive controversy in "Church-rents and schismes" and the initial refusal of the Cambridge licensers to accept two key lines in *The Church Militant*: "Religion stands on tip-toe in our land, / Readie to passe to the *American* strand" (ll. 235–36). According to Walton, the licensers were persuaded to accept the lines only because Ferrar refused to alter the text and, furthermore, in deference to Herbert's saintly reputation (p. 315), but Puritan admirers of Herbert later in the century liked to quote these lines as evidence for his prophetic recognition of what lay ahead.[58]

Herbert is staunchly Anglican in such poems celebrating the via media as "The British Church." When, as Cambridge Orator, he lauded James' eloquent rhetoric and deep learning, he surely spoke as a loyal subject of the crown. In his choice of vocation, however, he rejected the ideal of public service in the great world, whether exclusively secular after the model of Sidney or directed to both church and state after the examples of Bishop Williams and Lancelot Andrewes. He also rejected the purely contemplative model provided by Nicholas Ferrar and the combined academic service and devotion to writing "holy hymns" elected by Sir Henry Wotton. As country parson in a tiny rural parish, Herbert served the mixed life of action and contemplation that had been recommended in some traditional sources. But his life differed from those sources in extending the grace and courtesy of the courtier to the humblest of his parishioners as well as to God.

The language of his poetry confirms the denial of worldly values implied by such a choice and separates him in another way from the high Anglicans of his time. If earlier in his life he might have considered Lancelot Andrewes as a model of service to both God and King, his advice on sermon style in *The Country Parson* decisively rejects Andrewes' "crumbling" of the text as a rhetorical model.[59] This stance echoes his continual struggle in *The Temple* to dispense with worldly wit and develop the plainness appropriate to speaking truth to God. Like the prophetic statement in *The Church Militant* that so worried the Cambridge licensers, Herbert's ideal for his country parson in some ways seems closer to the Puritans than to the Anglicans – at least to those Anglican elegancies and Royalist pieties which a few years after his death would finally be emptied of the virtuous image they had maintained for the last hundred years.

It is not surprising that Herbert's poetry appealed to the Puritan

Richard Baxter as much as to the last truly courtly Royalist, King Charles, who on the eve of his execution echoes the language of Herbert's supposed message to Ferrar on his deathbed concerning "the service of Jesus my Master, in whom I have now found perfect freedom."[60] If Charles indeed studied Herbert devotedly during his imprisonment,[61] he read this poet once his own worldly hopes were thoroughly defeated and could only have found in *The Temple* lessons in turning toward God's mercy in a state of humility. It is pleasant to think that finally, through his poetry, Herbert did succeed in fulfilling the cardinal function of the ideal courtier: leading his prince toward virtue.

I have packed this chapter with names, tensions, equivocalities. Yet the network of relationships in which Herbert is enmeshed by circumstance is informed continually by the idea of pattern: the shape of a life which gains meaning, and can be perceived *as* shape, because it constitutes a fully conscious response, if not a resolution, to the conflicting forces of ideal and actual. Tradition and history intersect in the lives of courtly figures during the 1620s, and these figures themselves seek a pattern for their strivings. So, I argue, does Herbert. *The Temple* is essentially – though by no means solely – Herbert's record of his attempt to make of his life a "pattern or more for the age he lived in."

Exemplary biographies show how much that seventeenth-century model resembled the courtly ideal developed in the sixteenth century. That ideal continued to exert its power. Contemporary histories, on the other hand, show how much the shape of courtliness changed once actual courtiers in the Stuart period no longer even claimed to exemplify the virtues they were still supposed – ideally – to represent. Herbert's life reveals the extent of his entanglement in a shifting and treacherous actuality. The courtly self figured in *The Temple* represents both that actuality and a persistent desire to embody the traditional ideal. The choice of a calling traced by that figure creates a structure of tensions and a perilous progress for the *Church* sequence because vocation means for Herbert, as for others of his time, identification: the self is defined, discovered, finally *real*ized, in a mode of service. Herbert, in the lyrics to be discussed in Chapter 5, creates a self-as-pattern. This creation weaves, out of the entanglements of context, a meaning that only the text of a life, or a body of poetry, can articulate.

Chapter Three

A Failing Equilibrium

The distance between courtly ideal and actuality becomes a central poetic subject even as the sixteenth-century humanists formulate the idea of the courtier. Seventeenth-century poets show an increasing disequilibrium between the two poles as belief in the possibility of realizing the ideal begins to disintegrate under the pressures of historical change. Many of the *Temple* lyrics reflect Herbert's debt to his courtly predecessors but reveal an extraordinary transformation. Earlier poets poise the virtuous ideal that ought to prevail in the worldly court against its failure in actuality. Herbert, however, weighs the actual court world in still greater imbalance against the ideal court of heaven. While sixteenth-century poets can still, in desire if not in fact, associate the virtuous ideal with the secular court, for Herbert the decay of virtue requires a radical redirection of the courtier's service to the King and Court of heaven.

It is as if Herbert begins where his predecessors end. He is unique in reshaping the traditional ideal of secular virtue and service by transferring it to the sacred realm. In this sense his poetry is both courtly and holy. His poetic solution to the loss of virtue in his age culminates but also reintegrates the historical process of disintegrating values traced in Chapter 2. While there I showed Herbert's biographical entanglements, here I link his poetic figure of the courtier to earlier examples of the image and trace the linguistic strategies devised by his predecessors as they articulate the courtier's difficult balances. Thomas Wyatt and George Gascoigne deserve brief notice at the outset since their courtier figures record an imbalance between the ideal being formed even as they write and the actualities confronted by early Tudor courtiers. Sidney, near the close of the century, serves as transition and pivot, modeling two radically contrasted forms of imbalance in his revisions of the *Arcadia* and in *Astrophil and Stella*. Thomas Carew and Sir John Suckling provide my final context for Herbert's courtier because they speak to his time: they, too, depict disequilibrium and undercut traditional ideals. I shall argue that they perceive the disintegration of the ideal as powerfully as Herbert but envision an opposite direction for transforming it: the descent to the actual they modeled in life counters Herbert's path of ascent.

i

When courtly poets deplore the widening distance between actual and ideal, they are adopting an appropriate role of urging their readers toward virtue, much like that other role of leading the prince to virtue enacted by many of them in life.[1] Though these poets adhere to a common ideal, they share an acute awareness of the equivocalities involved in actually conducting one's life according to the model set by courtesy books. They discover disequilibrium rather than consonance. By lamenting the actual loss of virtue and calling for its restoration, by weighing conflicting claims of experience and aspiration, they show the pressure of "what is" outweighing the ideal of "what ought to be." Wyatt is a useful beginning point since he depicts imbalance between ideal and actual in his poetry, yet in life aspired still to realize the humanist idea.[2] Like Herbert, he implicates himself in the vices he castigates in order to exemplify the struggle toward virtue.

His moral emphasis signifies the familiar English concern with the courtier's virtue rather than his skills and graces.[3] His satires repeatedly evoke the literature of courtesy, the norms whose moral force he measures by their distance from the behavior of actual servants to the king. The epistle to Brian, "A spending hand," is designed, like Herbert's Church-porch, to rhyme its reader to good: "I thowght forthwith to write, / Brian, to the, who knows how great a grace / In writing is to cownsell man the right."[4] The poem's ironic counsel images a debased courtly actuality:

> Use vertue as it goeth now a dayes:
> In word alone to make thy langage swete,
> And of the dede yet do not as thou sayse;
> Elles be thou sure thou shalt be farre unmyt
> To get thy bred, eche thing is now so skant.
>
> (37–41)

The image anticipates Herbert's observation, nearly a century later: "They that by pleading clothes / Do fortunes seek, when worth and service fail, / Would have their tale beleeved for their oathes." Wyatt divides "word" and "dede" to expose the effects of linguistic duplicity. Speech masks the courtier's real motives; at court, fictions of self-presentation prevail over the plain speaking of true virtue.

Wyatt closes his counsel by administering the lesson of the second part of fortitude, the development of patience in adversity. His reply to Brian's remonstrance invokes the spiritual testing which ought to measure and moderate courtly ambition:

> Laughst thou at me? Why do I speke in vayne?
>   'No, not at the, but at thy thrifty gest.
>   Wouldest thou I should for any losse or gayne
> Chaunge that for gold that I have tan for best,
>   Next godly thinges, to have an honest name?
>   Should I leve that? then take me for a best?'
> Nay, then, farewell, and if you care for shame
>   Content the then with honest povertie
>   With fre tong what the myslikes to blame
> And for thy trouth sumtyme adversitie:
>   And therewithall this thing I shall the gyve –
>   And in this worould now litle prosperite,
> And coyne to kepe as water in a syve.
>
> (79–91)

Just as Herbert reminds himself in "The Size" that "Thy Saviour sentenc'd joy / And in the flesh condemn'd it as unfit," so Wyatt's argument for adversity to Brian declares that worldly prosperity is no proper end for the courtier in a Christian universe. Still Wyatt does not fully confront the contradictions entailed by serving both God and King which lead to Herbert's conclusion in "The Size": "do not spread thy robe / In hope of great things."

Gascoigne begins to exploit the disequilibrium of ideal and actual as a structural principle. "Gascoignes woodmanship" traces the failing fortunes of a would-be courtier in a corrupt courtly world through a repeated sequence of oppositions. Like Wyatt ironically advising Brian, Gascoigne catalogues the courtly vices he attempts – and fails – to emulate sufficiently. While truth-speaking is requisite for the ideal courtier, Gascoigne shows language distorting and deceiving:

> He thought the flattring face which fleareth still,
> Had bene full fraught with all fidelitie,
> And that such wordes as courtiers use at will
> Could not have varied from the veritie.[5]

What has been lost weighs heavily against the precepts Gascoigne claims to have brought to his worldly career:

> In *Aristotle* somewhat did I learne,
> To guyde my manners all by comelynesse,
> And *Tullie* taught me somewhat to discerne
> Between sweete speeche and barbarous rudenesse.
> (p. 350)

In spite of these precepts, "The craftie Courtiers with their guylefull lookes / Must needes put some experience in my mawe" (p. 351). Here, as in so many anti-courtly poems, "experience" denotes the distance of actuality from the ideal. The power of these inversions arises from the reminder of what ought to be:[6]

> Who can nor speake, nor write in pleasant wise,
> Nor leade their life by *Aristotles* rule,
> Nor argue well on questions that arise,
> Nor pleade a case more than my Lord Mairs mule,
> Yet can they hit the marks that I do misse,
> And winne the meane which may the man mainteyne. . . .
> (p. 351)

Gascoigne's most brilliant analysis of courtly ideal and actuality is *The Steele Glas*, where his figure of the transforming crystal serves, on the one hand, "such as love, to seme but not to be" and, on the other, shows "Not what I would, but what I am, or should."[7] The entire structure of the poem articulates disequilibrium. Courtly actuality is subjected to a terrible indictment:

> O blinde desire: oh high aspiring harts.
> The country Squire, doth covet to be Knight,
> The Knight a Lord, the Lord an Erle or a Duke,
> The Duke a King, the King would Monarke be,
> And none content, with that which is his own.

Yet none of these, can see in Christal glasse
(Which glistereth bright, & bleares their gasing eyes)
How every life, beares with him his disease.
But in my glasse, which is of trustie steele,
I can perceive, how kingdomes breede but care,
How Lordship lives, with lots of lesse delight,
(Though cappe and knee, do seeme a reverence,
And courtlike life, is thought an other heaven)
Than common people finde in every coast.

(pp. 153–4)

That indictment outweighs the ideal that should govern these lives:

O Knights, O Squires, O Gentle blouds yborne,
You were not borne, al onely for your selves:
Your countrie claymes, some part of al your paines.
There should you live, and therin should you toyle,
To hold up right, and banish cruel wrong,
To helpe the pore, to bridle backe the riche,
To punish vice, and vertue to advaunce,
To see God servde, and *Belzebub* supprest.
You should not trust, lieftenaunts in your rome,
And let them sway, the scepter of your charge,
Whiles you (meane while) know scarcely what is don,
Nor yet can yeld, accōpt if you were callde.

(p. 154)

These contrasts prefigure the imbalances that structure many of the *Temple* lyrics, as for example "Dotage," where the "false glozing pleasures" and "guilded emptinesse" of the worldly court are outweighed by the true delights of the clear court of heaven. *The Steele Glas,* while placing the world of courtly virtue unmistakably in the past – "kings decline, from princely government" and "Lords do lacke, their auncestors good wil" – still invokes the possibility of restoring virtue to earthly courts. Yet Gascoigne's ideal image of a "world, of worthy government" is a dream of seeming envisioned only in the poet's "glasing christal glasse." He does not, like Herbert, remove virtue absolutely to the Court and King of heaven.

Gascoigne's vision of actuality does, however, anticipate Herbert's image of empty show replacing virtuous substance as the way things are now in *The Church-porch:*

our curious yeares can finde
The christal glas, which glimseth brave & bright,
And shewes the thing, much better than it is,
Beguylde with foyles, of sundry subtil sights,
So that they seeme and covet not to be.

(p. 148)

This empty but glittering surface which remains when the core of
virtue is gone reflects the actuality of an increasingly brilliant court
world with corruption at its heart that both literature and history
show to mark the Stuart reigns. As Gascoigne's use of the figure
makes clear, the condition does not newly arise in the seventeenth
century; but as its growing frequency of appearance in the later
period attests, the decay of virtue that led to the fall of the monarchy
obsessed courtly poets as well as Puritan moralists.

ii

Wyatt and Gascoigne represent two relatively early measures of
the distance between the courtly ideal and the actual lives which
ought to embody it. They associate the secular ideal with spiritual
values and enjoin their courtly readers to follow the precepts of
religion. As Gascoigne remarks, "fewe regard, their needy neigh-
bours lacke, / And fewe beholde, by contemplation, / The joyes of
heaven, ne yet the paines of hel" (p. 152). Yet their courtier figures
remain enmeshed in the worldly court, still trying to recall it to
virtue. Sidney's revisions of the Arcadia, however, begin to assert
more explicitly a disjunction between spiritual values and the courtly
ideal. Although I now consider a prose work by a courtly poet, the
revised Arcadia is particularly useful as prologue to Herbert's figuration
of God's courtier. Sidney seems to be working toward a model of
Christian courtiership that does not make a quantum jump beyond the
world of great place absolutely, as does Herbert, but nonetheless begins
to redefine courtly virtue in distinctively Christian terms.

Sidney's Protestantism may have influenced his developing concept of the courtly ideal. His concern with statecraft as a means of
advancing religion is to a degree a call for greater spirituality governing the secular ideal of service.[8] In the Arcadia Puritana, however,
Franco Marenco traces Sidney's debt to Puritan thought and con-

cludes that even in the *Old Arcadia* Sidney begins to question the active ideal.[9] Marenco reads the *Arcadia* as a Puritan and moralistic reaction to courtly tradition, naming La Primaudaye the "moral spirit" of the work.[10] Although I feel that Marenco overstates the degree to which Sidney questions the ideal of active heroic virtue in the *Old Arcadia*, his analysis tends to support my argument that in the revised *Arcadia* Christian, "passive" virtues of humility and patient endurance of adversity begin to predominate over the concept of heroic action that can shape the world to one's wishes.[11]

The essential precedence of Christian virtues is suggested by the parallel circumstances in which Sidney's two ideal courtiers, Pyrocles and Musidorus, find themselves in the revised Book Three. Outside the castle of Amphialus, Musidorus is embroiled in a succession of brutal and bloody slaughters. Though all the requisite heroic virtues are exercised in the endless sequence of individual encounters and battles *en masse,* Sidney depicts the results in terms that reduce the victims to an anonymous heap of scattered fragments:

> In one place lay disinherited heades, dispossessed of their natu-
> rall seignories: in an other, whole bodies to see to, but that their
> harts wont to be bound all over so close, were nowe with deadly
> violence opened: in others, fowler deaths had ouglily displayed
> their trayling guttes. There lay armes, whose fingers yet mooved,
> as if they woulde feele for him that made them feele: and legges,
> which contrarie to common nature, by being discharged of their
> burthen, were growne heavier.[12]

In a passing irony, Sidney comments that the horses ran "scattered about the field, abashed with the madnesse of mankinde." The succession of slaughters is inconclusive – though of course the epi-sode is unfinished – and has no effect upon the fortunes of the princesses imprisoned by Cecropia. All of Musidorus' undeniable active heroic virtue throughout the first two books has led only to a weary round of destructive carnage in which the virtue of the partici-pants is chiefly celebrated in their funerals.

Within the castle, Pyrocles' heroic virtue is no more useful in extricating Pamela and Philoclea from their captivity. The effective source of virtue is rather the model of patient endurance provided by the princesses, not their would-be rescuer's immoderate zeal for action. Pyrocles (here in his role as Zelmane) foolishly relies upon the accouterments of war:

> *Zelmane* . . . desired no more, but to have armour and weapons brought into her chamber, not doubting, therewith to perfourm any thing, how impossible soever, which longing Love can perswade, and invincible Valour dare promise. (III.14.4, p. 437)

This dependence upon the power of a merely physical courage leads to a submission of the will that overturns the proper government of the faculties. Unable to endure Cecropia's cruelty to her captives, Zelmane

> Was so confused withall (her courage still rebelling against her wit, desiring still with force to do impossible matters) that as her desire was stopped with power, so her conceit was darkned with a mist of desire. For blind Love, & invincible valure stil would cry out, that it could not be, *Philoclea* should be in so miserable estate, and she not relieve her: and so while she haled her wit to her courage, she drew it from his owne limits.
>
> (III.22.2, pp. 479–80)

Unable to endure the supposition that Philoclea has been killed by Cecropia, Pyrocles bursts out in accusation against providence: "O tyraunt heaven, traytor earth, blinde providence; no justice, how is this done? how is this suffered? hath this world a government?" (p. 483). His "desperate agonie" leads to his attempted suicide and his continued longing for death, from which he is dissuaded by Pamela's Christian argument condemning his "weake waylings" as a lack of heroic endurance and a shameful repining against the mortal condition: "if she be dead, was she not borne to die? what then do you crie out for? not for her, who must have died one time or other; but for some fewe years: so as it is time, & this world that seeme so lovely things, and not *Philoclea* unto you" (p. 486).

This dissuasion from suicide echoes the very similar passage in the *Old Arcadia*, although the later version suggests a greatly expanded notion of inadequacies in the active heroic ideal. Whereas in the *Old Arcadia* Pyrocles is driven to despair as a consequence of his own abandonment of reason to passion, here his helpless position is entirely blameless. His inability to aid the princesses by exercising his undoubted valor is a condition of the world he inhabits. In this world the heroic ideal is entirely ineffective. The Christian virtues of patience and endurance are the essential lessons to be learned; indeed, they constitute the ideal represented by Pamela and Philoclea.

Sidney's revision begins to shadow forth Herbert's pattern. An initial assumption that the secular ideal can no longer be realized in a world where heroic virtues bear the taint of mortality leads to a transvaluing recognition that the virtues exemplified by Christ alone signify true courtiership – the divine nobility recommended in La Primaudaye's courtesy book and in Meriton's sermon on nobility. Sidney is approaching a spiritualized ideal which, in his revised Arcadian world, accomplishes what even the most exemplary courtly virtue of the secular kind cannot achieve.

As the balance between ideal and actual shifts toward Christian values, we approach Herbert's reshaping of the courtly ideal and begin to recognize how he is indebted to his predecessors. These poets envision a world of inverted values, indict a court in which show has supplanted substance, and declare that Christian values ought to define the true courtier. These premises are central to Herbert's conception of God's courtier. In "Jordan" (I), he dismisses the "fictions onely and false hair" and the winding structures of courtly pastoral, poising the duty their lines offer "Not to a true, but painted chair" against his plain statement of allegiance to "*My God, My King.*" "Jordan" (II) contrasts his own earlier attempts to weave himself into his lines, "Curling with metaphors a plain intention, / Decking the sense as if it were to sell," with the "*sweetnesse readie penn'd*" of divine love that he might simply "copie out." In "The Forerunners," the elegancies of courtly versifying – "sweet phrases . . . lovely metaphors . . . enchanting language . . . sugar-cane . . . hony or roses" – are relegated to "foolish lovers" who ought, "if they will love dung, / With Canvas, not with arras, clothe their shame"; this is the native tongue of folly, while God's poet speaks his love plainly – "*Thou art still my God.*" "The Forerunners" links courtly style to a debased courtliness. Herbert figures "lovely enchanting language" as a courtier in a "broider'd coat," clothing his shame in arras when it belongs properly to the world of stews and brothels, in sharp contrast to the "bleak paleness" reflecting the true beauty that "dwells on high." Just as God's courtier must relinquish his worldly aspirations for great place to follow Christ's example of humble service, so also he must abandon the curled metaphors of secular love if he is to speak the plain truths of sacred love.

Sidney's refiguration of the courtly ideal in his *Arcadia* revisions anticipates the turn toward distinctively Christian values that will lead to Herbert's construction of a figure both courtly and holy. But it is Sidney's "principle of contrasts"[13] in *Astrophil and Stella* which provides a linguistic model for Herbert's transformative oppositions in *The Temple*. Herbert reverses Sidney's pattern. Astrophil's plain language at the close of a poem asserts his actual experience of human limits over against his aspiration toward the ideal expressed in the elevated language of earlier lines. Herbert's contrasts weigh a debased though elegant courtly diction against an elevated yet plain-spoken ideal. Sidney's contrasts, as Louis Martz has pointed out, reflect Astrophil's "search for simplicity."[14] Astrophil's simplicity, however, is directed to earthly love:

> For nothing from my wit or will doth flow,
>   Since all my words thy beauty doth endite,
>   And love doth hold my hand, and makes me write.[15]

Herbert asks Immortal Love in "Love I": "Who sings thy praise? onely a skarf or glove / Doth warm our hands, and make them write of love," thus rewriting Sidney's text and redressing the imbalance. In "A true Hymne," he depends on God's hand to finish his poem, "enditing" a spiritual ideal and uniting it to his natural feeling:

> Whereas if th' heart be moved,
> Although the verse be somewhat scant,
>   God doth supplie the want.
> As when th' heart sayes (sighing to be approved)
> O, *could I love!* and stops: God writeth, *Loved*.
>   (16–20)

In spite of the powerful difference between secular and sacred love which Herbert underlines by echoing Sidney's sonnets, *Astrophil and Stella* does begin to raise those questions concerning the proper *locus* of virtue that Herbert answers by definitively rejecting courtly love as either means to virtue or fit subject for poetry. Moreover, much of Sidney's rejection of courtly values in *Astrophil* (insofar as he does reject them) rests upon his recognition that "What had begun as an ideal of conduct had ended as an imperative of courtly affectation."[16] Sidney is concerned not only with the "decay of a poetic idea" but with the degeneration of a poetic style that all too frequently betrays its loss of value – "daintie wits" flaunting their "phrases fine" in sonnet 3, searchers for the purling spring of Parnas-

sus and imitators of "Dictionarie's methode" in sonnet 15. As an
antidote to that language, and to the diminished courtliness that lies
behind it, Sidney proposes the plain speaking of Astrophil – a pose
perhaps in its too-conscious self-awareness, but still an affirmative
counterpoise to the limits he uncovers.

He is still courtly. Astrophil's plainness is thoroughly worldly; in
insisting upon immediate psychological actualities, he withdraws
authority from the ideal, rather than reasserting or transvaluing it.[17]
Yet it is his ability to deploy the courtier's language which empowers
him to deny its value. Herbert empowers his rejections, too, in "The
Forerunners" by displaying his sweet phrases and lovely metaphors
before attempting to bring them to church "well drest and clad" and
washed with his tears. He recalls Sidney most notably, however, in
those dramatic endings that both poets employ so brilliantly. Sidney
opposes "fit words" and "inventions fine" in sonnet 1 of *Astrophil* to
the plain talk of its close – " 'Foole,' said my Muse to me, 'looke in
thy heart, and write' "; in sonnet 71, the "sweetest soveraigntie / Of
reason" is overthrown in an instant by line 14 – " 'But ah,' Desire
still cries, 'give me some food.' " A parallel strategy governs Herbert's sententious catalogue of man's sins in "Miserie," which descends abruptly from righteous attack to honest admission – "My
God, I mean my self" – in the last line, and he deliberately echoes and
reverses Sidney's sonnet 1 at the close of "Jordan" (II):[18]

> As flames do work and winde, when they ascend,
> So did I weave my self into the sense.
> But while I bustled, I might heare a friend
> Whisper, *How wide is all this long pretence!*
> *There is in love a sweetnesse readie penn'd:*
> *Copie out onely that, and save expense.*
>
> (13–18)

These lines also glance back to sonnet 19, " 'Scholler,' saith *Love,*
'bend hitherward your wit,' " and to sonnet 90, "And love doth hold
my hand, and makes me write." As Martz has noted, the conclusion
of "Jordan" (II) most nearly echoes sonnet 3 of *Astrophil:* ". . . in
Stella's face I reed, / What Love and Beautie is, then all my deed, /
But Copying is, what in her Nature writes." But earthly nature is the
source of Astrophil's love and the inspirer of his invention, while
Herbert's transforming echo points out the difference when God's

hand is in the design: freedom from pretense beyond what Astrophil can envision and a thrift that releases an abundance of feeling.

Astrophil's conclusions represent, in multiple forms, a descent to the actual, a linguistic equivalent to that path of descent I proposed in Chapter 2 to define the life choices of Edward Herbert, Carew, and Suckling. They speak of the frail and fallible human, who exercises his "best wits" in sonnet 19 just as he turns to "inventions fine" in sonnet 1, but who must eventually admit his allegiance to the plain truth of his experience. That experience must abandon the ideal to embrace the actual. In sonnet 5, thirteen lines acknowledge that

> . . . the heavenly part
> Ought to be king, from whose rules who do swerve,
> Rebels to Nature, strive for their owne smart.
>
> (2–4)

True beauty is still virtue. But opposed to that ideal truth is natural experience: "True, and yet true that I must *Stella* love." Sonnet 71 gives a name to experience and endows it with still more power: virtue bends Astrophil's love to good, but the poem closes with desire crying out for its food. Similarly, in sonnet 52, Astrophil wishes to trade Stella's "selfe," her virtuous soul, to Virtue in exchange for her body, abandoning the "heavenly part" in surrender to the claims of earthly desire.

Herbert's Sidneyan echoes may be designed to enforce this contrast: earthly love brings Astrophil down, heavenly love raises Herbert up. In sonnet 62, Astrophil repines against Stella's "Love's authority" that "would not let me, whom she loved, decline / From nobler course, fit for my birth and mind" and in conclusion wittily pleads, "Alas, if this the only mettall be / Of *Love*, new-coind to helpe my beggery, / Deare, love me not, that you may love me more." This turn of wit reappears in Herbert's "Affliction" (I), where he concludes his repining against God's cross-biases, "Ah my deare God! though I am clean forgot, / Let me not love thee, if I love thee not." The echo is subtle and delicate. Astrophil is urging Stella to withdraw her virtuous love if she will not love him in a less noble fashion, an act which would then relinquish her authority over him. Herbert, however, urges God to exercise His authority to protect the poet from offering a false love that cannot endure cross-biases. The parallel wit play points up the crucial difference between Astrophil's demand for a love that declines "From nobler course" to seek its own ends and Herbert's plea for the power to love without insisting that God meet his demands. The conclusions of both poets assert the truths of experience. But Herbert's turn on Sidney's word play transforms Astrophil's limiting recognition that love is grounded in the secular into the desire for a sacred love without limit.[19]

Herbert learns from Sidney to speak in the rhythms of civil conversation, to pare down rhetorical excess, to create the fluidity of a mind musing, meditating, analyzing, exploring its own reactions, to achieve the intensity of emotion that Sidney, like Puttenham, calls *energia*. *Astrophil and Stella*, clearly, can serve later poets as a model either for descent to the actual or for reascent to the ideal. In its linguistic virtuosity, it is a speech model for poets concerned to portray the divided mind torn between the experience of mortal limitation and aspiration for the illimitable. Sidney's innovative power enables poets as apparently diverse as Herbert and the early Cavaliers to apply both courtly conversation and plain-spoken immediacy to such opposite ends.

iii

If Sidney's plain appeals to nature represent the path of descent, the claims of Carew and Suckling that love belongs exclusively to the mortal state constitute an even greater decline.[20] These poets share with Herbert not only the inherited repertoire of verbal strategies, but also a distinctive consciousness deriving from the historical moment which they inhabit together. Recognition of affinities between Herbert and the Cavaliers can show us how much Herbert's figure of God's courtier responds to, perhaps means to redeem, the deliberately tarnished image of the Caroline courtier created by Carew and Suckling.[21]

Carew's courtly conversation is much closer to Sidney's grace and ceremony than Suckling's, and Carew still plays – sometimes seriously – with the traditional image of the courtly lover. But the delicate imbalances of virtue versus desire that plagued Astrophil are now resolved unequivocally in favor of desire. Carew's contrasts empty out value from the ideal and give absolute primacy to the poet's emotional state. His plain speech enormously increases the distance between aspiration and actuality. "A divine Mistris" praises the "divine hands" that formed someone so fair, but concludes, "Shee hath too much divinity for mee, / You Gods teach her some more humanitie." Quite contrary to Petrarchan vows of faithful service, "A prayer to the Wind" closes with a threat that reduces undying – once ennobling – love to a matter-of-fact exchange:

> Up the fire of love in her,
> That alike both flames may shine,
> Or else quite extinguish mine.
> (30–2)

"Ingratefull beauty threatned" not only disequilibrates but uncreates the ideal in its assertion that the lady's divine beauty is solely the poet's making:

> That killing power is none of thine:
> I gave it to thy voyce, and eyes:
> Thy sweets, thy graces, all are mine;
> Thou art my starre, shin'st in my skies;
> (7–10)

and concludes by claiming the new power of the actual:

> Tempt me with such affrights no more,
> Lest what I made, I uncreate;
> Let fooles thy mystique formes adore,
> I'le know thee in thy mortall state:
> Wise Poets that wrap't Truth in tales,
> Knew her themselves, through all her vailes.
> (13–18)

In these poems, immediate feeling takes precedence over all other values. The claims of desire rule that feeling with only an ironic side-glance at what has been lost. Where Sidney's "plain" descents to actuality maintain a tense equilibrium with the effort to live up to the ideal, Carew's endings are triumphant in their assertion of mortality, their vindication of the ego speaking for itself. Suckling carries the process still further, and his language is correspondently plainer. He has even less need than Carew to evoke the idealistic past, which in his poetry exists only to be mocked: "Ere I'le die for love, I'le fairly forgo it," announces "The careless Lover," while "Loves Siege" concludes bluntly: "I hate a fool that starves her Love / Onely to feed her pride" (Clayton, pp. 57, 66).

These poets, like Herbert, have learned from Sidney to "simulate the working mind" in what A. J. Smith calls the "vivid articulation of a dramatic syntax" employed to present a "dialectic of love."[22] Herbert's analysis of his spiritual conflicts offers a no less vividly articulated dialectic of love. The ascent figured by his plain endings counters the acceptance of limits traced by the Cavaliers' descents.[23] Yet these poets exhibit the same minute and responsible attention to the ebbs and flows of emotion that Herbert does in *The Temple,* the same desire to report experience with accuracy, through many of the same linguistic techniques. Herbert undercuts the same fictions of ideality in a worldly setting, implicates himself in those pretensions as do Carew and Suckling, but provides a sacred alternative that the Cavaliers seldom consider in their celebration of this world.

Both Carew and Suckling, however, are acutely aware of the alternative which they reject. In spite of his denigration of Petrarchan idealism, Carew can still praise his king's "strong vertues" in "A New-yeares gift. To the King" in a thoroughly courtly manner. In this sense, too, he is still linked to sixteenth-century tradition. The difference from Wyatt's or Gascoigne's catalogues of courtly abuses lies in Carew's politic obliquity, which masks his diminished conception of courtly virtue. "In answer of an Elegiacall Letter . . . from *Aurelian Townsend . . .*" confesses his inability to write on the death of the king of Sweden because such a heroic subject is entirely inappropriate to the special virtues of the English court. These qualities, we find, in no way resemble those of the traditional courtly ideal. The substance of virtue exists – like the divine beauties of Carew's mistress – only in art: "vertues Carde," which is to guide "Our steerelesse barkes," is directed not by God but by a troop of deities in a masque.[24] Instead of serving the common good, the court sings "Of Revels," and the poem ends with a paean to the power of illusion in a stunning substitution of ideal fictions for the real thing:

> . . . these are subjects proper to our clyme.
> Tourneyes, Masques, Theaters, better become
> Our *Halcyon* dayes; what though the German Drum
> Bellow for freedome and revenge, the noyse

Concernes not us, nor should divert our joyes;
Nor ought the thunder of their Carabins
Drowne the sweet Ayres of our tun'd Violins;
Beleeve me friend, if their prevailing powers
Gaine them a calme securitie like ours,
They'le hang their Armes up on the Olive bough,
And dance, and revell then, as we doe now.

(94–104)

In spite of its protestations, Carew's tone is decidedly elegiac, as are all of his poems to King Charles. If his resolutely secular love lyrics mark a gain, the epistle to Townsend shows that Carew knows very well what has been lost politically. His acknowledgment of religious loss is etched more sharply in the self-revelation of "To my worthy friend Master *Geo. Sands,* on his translation of the Psalmes." His assessment here could stand as a reversed mirror to Herbert's self-portrayal in *The Temple*. The difference between ascending and descending choices has seldom been so clearly imaged as in this work by a "prophane" poet:

I presse not to the Quire, nor dare I greet
The holy place with my unhallowed feet;
My unwasht Muse, polutes not things Divine,
Nor mingles her prophaner notes with thine;

. . . .

Sufficeth her, that she a lay-place gaine,
To trim thy Vestments, or but beare thy traine;
Though nor in tune, nor wing, she reach thy Larke,
Her Lyrick feet may dance before the Arke.

. . . .

Perhaps my restlesse soule, tyr'de with persuit
Of mortall beauty, seeking without fruit
Contentment there, which hath not, when enjoy'd,
Quencht all her thirst, nor satisfi'd, though cloy'd;
Weary of her vaine search below, Above
In the first Faire may find th'immortall Love.
Prompted by thy example, then, no more
In moulds of clay will I my God adore;
But teare those Idols from my heart, and write
What his blest Spirit, not fond Love shall indite. . . .

(1–6; 11–14; 23–32)

It's tempting to read a secondary reference to Herbert's divine poetry in these lines to Sandys.[25] Carew's "unwasht Muse" remains humbly in the church porch that, in *The Temple*, is the place of preparation for entering the church, and clearly the libertine Carew depicts could benefit from the moral lessons of *The Church-porch*. The "restless soule" which seeks a fruitless contentment in mortal beauty, but might be drawn upward to the "first Faire" of immortal love, seems to enact the plight fabled in Herbert's "The Pulley" where peace is the one gift God withholds from man:

> Yet let him keep the rest,
> But keep them with repining restlesnesse:
> Let him be rich and wearie, that at least,
> If goodness leade him not, yet wearinesse
> May tosse him to my breast.
>
> (16–20)

Both Sidney and Herbert, as we've noted, have had much to say about fond Love's inditing and what the blest Spirit may write. Yet we need not assume deliberate allusion in order to recognize how this image of a worldly courtier counterpoises God's courtier in *The Temple*. Carew's humble posture reminds us that Herbert, too, confesses to being "guiltie of dust and sinne," to "quarries of pil'd vanities." The difference lies in Herbert's effort to imitate Christ, to exchange the courtier's flower for His thorns in the moral struggle which Carew only projects as a distant possibility in this poem.[26]

Suckling, even more worldly than Carew in his secular poems, also moves at least tentatively toward the sacred. As L. A. Beaurline discovered, he almost certainly wrote several religious lyrics that show considerable affinity with Herbert's distinctive simplicity of tone and diction. The broken speech rhythms of "Upon *Christ* his birth" are particularly Herbertian:

> Strange news! a Cittie full? will none give way
> To lodge a guest that comes not every day?
> Noe inne, nor taverne void? yet I descry
> One empty place alone, where wee may ly:
> In too much fullnesse is some want: but where?
> Mens empty hearts: let's aske for lodgeing there.
> But if they not admit us, then wee'le say
> Their hearts, as well as inn's, are made of clay.[27]

Beaurline stresses "metaphysical" resemblances between Suckling's "Upon Stephen stoned" and Herbert's poetry,[28] but the links are not limited to Suckling's ingenuity. This brief lyric plays upon the figure of the stony heart, which in *The Temple* is a far more central symbol than Suckling's merely witty conceit; yet we can hear the same undertones:

> Under this heape of stones interred lies
> No holocaust, but stoned sacrifice
> Burnt not by altar-coales, but by the fire
> Of Jewish ire
> Whoes softest words in their hard hearts alone
>   Congeal'd to stone,
> Nor peirceing them recoild in him againe
>   Whoe beeing slaine
> As not forgetfull, whence they once did come,
> Now beeing stones hee found in them a tombe.

The power accorded Stephen's gentleness is much more Herbertian than metaphysical, and the epigrammatic brevity and point of the poem recall similar characteristics in Herbert's Latin verse, at least some of which belong, as do these lyrics of Suckling, to the early 1620s. One, in fact, also took the stoning of Stephen as its subject. Its wit resembles Suckling as much as the gentleness in Suckling's lyric evokes Herbert:

> How Marvelous! Who
> Pounds rock gets fire.
> But Stephen from
> Stones got heaven.[29]

The surprisingly soft tone of Suckling's poem on Stephen and the humble diction of "Upon *Christ* his birth" disclose a quality of mind that is almost unique to Herbert. As with all the similarities outlined here, it should encourage us to rethink our comfortable stereotypes, not only of Suckling, but all "rake-hell Cavaliers" and "pious Metaphysicals."[30] This doubleness of character and personality is simply a more radical version of the complex mingling of worldliness and piety that I wish to demonstrate in Herbert.

Herbert's piety grows out of his worldliness, just as his conception of God's courtier emanates from the secular ideal of the courtier.

His worldliness bestows exemplary power upon his piety. His continuing belief in the virtuous substance of the ideal enables him to recognize its disintegration in his actual world, perhaps even more acutely than Carew or Suckling. Their imbalances are precisely opposite to Herbert's. The actuality of human limitation triumphs in their art as Wyatt or Gascoigne might have predicted, and as Sidney certainly foresaw in his creation of courtly but Christian models of virtue in the revised *Arcadia*.

But the path of descent that leads to the Cavaliers is already begun in Sidney's other major work, *Astrophil and Stella*. The ideal courtier of the sixteenth century stands poised on the threshold of alternative models of courtiership figured by Herbert on the one hand and by the Cavaliers on the other. Herbert's transformation of the worldly courtier into God's courtier is all the more remarkable because it is accomplished by fully confronting the state of worldly actuality and richly employing the stylistic resources of courtly tradition. In sharing both the techniques and the milieu of his Cavalier contemporaries, he nonetheless retains enough faith in tradition to create a new ideal which might purify their poetry and redeem their vision.

Part Two

The Temple

Chapter Four

Shreds of Holiness

> Come away,
> Help our decay.
> Man is out of order hurl'd,
> Parcel'd out to all the world.
> Lord, thy broken consort raise,
> And the musick shall be praise.
> "Dooms-day"

Herbert's apocalyptic vision of man in "Dooms-day" belongs appropriately to the group of poems on the Four Last Things which, with "Love" (III), concludes *The Church,* the central lyric sequence and structural core of *The Temple.* These extraordinarily vivid images of fragmented human bodies hurled piecemeal, in chaotic disorder, over the surface of the earth reflect in the larger perspective of eternity the particular consciousness of disintegration which characterized Herbert's age. This pattern of imagery recurs throughout the lyrics of *The Church,* disordering every aspect of the secular realm and even more powerfully reducing the self to uncontrollable and agonizing divisions. Herbert's individual poems are self-subsistent wholes, yet they incorporate with surprising frequency images of fragmentation, cutting or rending, disintegration and dissolution remarkably resembling the terms of universal dispersion in "Dooms-day." Moreover, some lyrics are constructed out of linguistic fragments, noun clusters or broken phrases, as in "The Quidditie" or "Dotage," in an apparently disordered catalogue of qualities. The structural contrast in "Dooms-day" between the chaotic condition of mortality and the harmonious order to which God's grace might restore these broken fragments can also be understood as a model of the poetic strategy which disorders, and repeatedly attempts to reorder, this collection of 160 separate poems diverse in kind, in subject, and in metrical form.

Herbert's opening lyric in *The Church* invites us to consider this section of *The Temple* as a parcel of parts, a "broken ALTAR . . . / Made of a heart, and cemented with teares." He presents himself as a composition of fragments: God's power cuts the block of stone out of which the altar is made, "Wherefore each part / Of my hard heart / Meets in this frame." Although "The Altar" is primarily concerned to point out the mysterious ways of God which empower even the stony heart of man to praise his Maker, the poem also evokes the paradoxical presence of formlessness as a formal principle within *The Church* and a crucial self-perception for Herbert. The altar that God's servant erects is "broken" rather than whole; its parts are divided and distinguished; that they simply "meet" within the frame depicts a mere juxtaposition rather than a fully-integrated construction.

This perception depends upon a perspectival shift which is itself dispersed among the lyrics of *The Church*. In the heavenly perspective, values customarily associated with the worldly court undergo inversion from the highest to the lowest of earthly positions. Once the heights of worldly power are reduced to the figure of "guilded dust," the attributes of that power can be perceived as fragmentary and disintegrating. The process extends not only to the secular seat of power but also to the chair of ecclesiastical rule and even to the orderly structure of the world, prefiguring the apocalyptic vision of dissolution in "Dooms-day." There, the broken consort of man will be restored to harmony only in the divine perspective of eternity. In earlier lyrics of *The Church*, Herbert strives to recover wholeness by invoking the sacred values of the heavenly perspective as a replacement for the secular values that have initially been fragmented. That wholeness, however, is itself questioned when individual poems are juxtaposed in dissolving sequences or joined as "constellations" across the "leaves" of Herbert's text.

i

The opposed perspectives of earth and heaven are introduced by Christ in the opening stanza of "The Sacrifice," immediately following "The Altar." His address to mankind, echoing the *improperia* for Good Friday and the medieval commonplace once inscribed on many a wayside cross, distinguishes significantly between human and divine vision: "O all ye, who passe by, whose eyes and minde / To worldly things are sharp, but to me blinde. . . ." This juxtaposition suggests that the one mode of vision prevents the other, thereby declaring a need to unlearn the lesser in order to attain the greater.[1]

Later in *The Church*, a canceled couplet of "Charms and Knots" defines the required alteration of vision as an inversion of value:

> The world thinks all things bigg and tall
> Grace turns ye Optick, then they fall.

Herbert's references to worldly kings in *The Church* invert their position in just this way. Their high estate evokes only a mutter of pity in "Church-musick," where it is implicitly contrasted with the power of sacred music to show Herbert "the way to heavens doore":

> Now I in you without a bodie move,
>   Rising and falling with your wings:
> We both together sweetly live and love,
>   Yet say·sometimes, *God help poore Kings.*
>   (5–8)

"Peace" not only lowers kingly power metaphorically to earth but subjects it to fragmentation:

> Then went I to a garden, and did spy
>   A gallant flower,
> The Crown Imperiall: Sure, said I,
>   Peace at the root must dwell.
> But when I digg'd, I saw a worm devoure
>   What show'd so well.
>   (13–18)

The figure of a flower attacked by a natural predator associates the decay of kingly power with the exigencies of mortal existence. "Content" makes a similar connection and carries the process of destruction to its ultimate end in dissolution. Here, the human height of earthly glory is brought down to nothing but a bad smell of decaying flesh:

> The brags of life are but a nine dayes wonder;
>   And after death the fumes that spring
> From private bodies make as big a thunder,
>   As those which rise from a huge King.
>   (21–4)

This negation of secular power and substance also appears in "Praise" (I), where Herbert observes that "Man is all weaknesse; there is no such thing / As Prince or King." As in "Church-musick," he underlines this diminishment by projecting the heights attainable by the spirit: "I go to Church; help me to wings, and I / Will thither flie." In "Content," his figure of the "pliant minde" that can "Let loose to a crown, and yet with pleasure / Take up within a cloisters gates" stresses the ignominy to which even huge kings are reduced by a similar contrast: "This soul doth span the world, and hang content / From either pole unto the centre."

These figures of inversion and fragmentation extend to the values and activities of the court as well as to the ruler of it. Herbert's renaming of conventional courtly "goods" in "Frailtie" inverts their worth and syntactically fragments them into mere insentient particles:

> Lord, in my silence how do I despise
> What upon trust
> Is styled *honour, riches,* or *fair eyes;*
> But is *fair dust!*
> I surname them *guilded clay,*
> *Deare earth, fine grasse* or *hay;*
> In all, I think my foot doth ever tread
> Upon their head.
> (1–8)

The comparison of two "regiments" – the world's and God's – in the following stanza locates the source of these inversions in the substitution of a heavenly for a worldly perspective. Courtly values define the regiment of the world as "fine, / Full of glorie and gay weeds, / Brave language, braver deeds," whereas in the heavenly perspective these fine shows are reduced to nothing more than "Fair dust." Once worldly glories of dress, speech, and action are refigured as earth, grass, or hay for Herbert's feet to tread down still further, these highly-esteemed courtly qualities have descended to the lowest of positions, a process repeated in "Vanitie" (II), where the "flat delights" of the soul "on earth do creep and grow." Here again the courtly references, by metonymy, redefine "earthly delights" by reducing them to attractive but inconsequential parts: "the starres shine not so fair, as eyes; / Nor solid work, as false embroyderies."

"The Quidditie" adds disorder to fragmentation. Courtly values are trivialized by association with fashionable courtly accouterments in an apparently random list of negations:

> My God, a verse is not a crown,
> No point of honour, or gay suit,
> No hawk, or banquet, or renown,
> Nor a good sword, nor yet a lute:
>
> It cannot vault, or dance, or play;
> It never was in *France* or *Spain*;
> Nor can it entertain the day
> With my great stable or demain. . . .
>
> (1–8)

The crown as symbol of regal power, points of honor as standards of aristocratic behavior, renown as the appropriate end of noble aspiration are now contaminated by their intermixture with the stylish Jacobean or Caroline courtier's favorite possessions, while the second stanza associates these values with the most frivolous of courtly activities — vaulting, dancing, playing, aping the French and the Spanish. The figure of worldly verse as nothing but a brittle courtier divided into indifferently related parts thus extends beyond its primary reference. Herbert's telling indictment of the ideals of the court denies them any greater significance than the most superficial courtly activities or possessions.

These configured fragments disclose a courtly world that is crumbling in every aspect of its existence. But the disintegration of power and value spreads far beyond the court, as if the worm devouring the root of the Crown Imperial were infecting everything under its sway. In "Church-rents and schismes," Herbert transfers this image to the ecclesiastical realm, in a truly terrible depiction of dissection and dismemberment:

> Brave rose, (alas!) where art thou? in the chair
> Where thou didst lately so triumph and shine
> A worm doth sit, whose many feet and hair
> Are the more foul, the more thou wert divine.
> This, this hath done it, this did bite the root
> And bottome of the leaves: which when the winde
> Did once perceive, it blew them under foot,

Where rude unhallow'd steps do crush and grinde
    Their beauteous glories. Onely shreds of thee,
    And those all bitten, in thy chair I see.

Why doth my Mother blush? is she the rose,
And shows it so? Indeed Christs precious bloud
Gave you a colour once; which when your foes
Thought to let out, the bleeding did you good,
And made you look much fresher then before.
But when debates and fretting jealousies
Did worm and work within you more and more,
Your colour vaded, and calamities
    Turned your ruddie into pale and bleak:
    Your health and beautie both began to break.

Then did your sev'rall parts unloose and start:
Which when your neighbors saw, like a north-winde
They rushed in, and cast them in the dirt
Where Pagans tread. O Mother deare and kinde,
Where shall I get me eyes enough to weep,
As many eyes as starres? since it is night,
And much of Asia and Europe fast asleep,
And ev'n all Africk; would at least I might
    With these two poore ones lick up all the dew,
    Which falls by night, and poure it out for you!

Just as the roots of secular power are devoured in "Peace," so here the church is torn apart from within. The personification of rents and schisms is grotesque, almost surrealistic: an empty chair occupied only by bitten shreds of the once-whole rose and its predator, a worm possessing "many feet and hair" – the human attribute identifies the agents of division. The immediacy and violence of the process are heightened by savage verbs which act as the principal vehicles of fragmentation: "bite the root / And bottome of the leaves . . . crush and grinde . . . Onely shreds . . . And those all bitten . . . worm and work within you . . . Your health and beauty both began to break. . . . Then did your sev'rall parts unloose and start. . . ."

There is no mitigating balance in this poem. It is pure lament, offering no healing balm other than the author's tears.[2] When only bitten shreds remain, when church roots are torn to pieces, when the several parts of a once organic unity are unloosed, Herbert is envisioning death as the unnatural – yet so inevitably natural – end of divisive and destructive processes within the church just as, by

reducing kings and peasants to decaying flesh, he has leveled all
worldly distinctions to a similar state of dissolution.

"Decay" expands the vision of worldly dissolution:

> I see the world grows old, when as the heat
> Of thy great love, once spread, as in an urn
> Doth closet up it self, and still retreat,
> Cold Sinne still forcing it, till it return,
>   And calling *Justice,* all things burn.
>
>   (16–20)

In "The World," the imagery of natural destruction that we have
seen in "Peace" and "Church-rents and schismes" is repeated in the
figure of Sin "Working and winding slily evermore," but it accumu-
lates still more intensity in the violent verbs of cleaving, tearing, and
razing which follow:

> Then enter'd *Sinne,* and with that Sycomore,
> Whose leaves first sheltred man from drought & dew,
> Working and winding slily evermore,
> The inward walls and sommers cleft and tore:
> But *Grace* shor'd these, and cut that as it grew.
>
> Then *Sinne* combin'd with *Death* in a firm band
> To raze the building to the very floore:
> Which they effected, none could them withstand.
> But *Love* and *Grace* took *Glorie* by the hand,
> And built a braver Palace then before.
>
>   (11–20)

The repetitive pattern of construction and deconstruction here
reaches backward to the beginnings of human time.[3] In two brief
lyrics – "The World" and "Decay" – the vision of disintegration
encompasses the entire span of earthly history. "Peace" and
"Church-rents and schismes," on the other hand, emphasize the
presentness of division and decay; in these poems the forces of
destruction are products of the historical moment.[4] The full scope of
Herbert's perception is difficult to realize because it is itself divided in
form, parceled out among a great many of the lyrics of *The Church*
and functioning as *primary* focus in only a few of these poems. Yet
his images of fragmentation, in spite of their dispersion, form a single
complex of ideas, internal and external, personal and social, woven
throughout the texture of *The Church*.

All of these images follow naturally once the heavenly perspective has been superimposed in the opening lines of "The Sacrifice." Both the necessary consequence of mortality and the immediate tendencies of the secular realm foreshadow disintegration. Yet a heavenly perspective in regard to the world cannot be attained simply by substituting one mode of seeing for another; the personal lyrics of *The Church* must work out the painful result of such an attempt to enlarge vision. If what Herbert sees from this perspective is a world torn apart and disintegrating, if those broken pieces appear to him as dismembered fragments of the courtly life and value system, if huge kings are transformed into decaying corpses in his "mutt'ring thoughts," it is equally evident how agonizingly difficult these visions are to accept. Neither lofty indifference nor cool irony governs these images, but rather regret, disturbance, lament: the tones of a mind divided between heavenly and earthly perspectives, not an easily accomplished dispensation with the one and assumption of the other.

ii

In the third stanza of "Affliction" (IV), we see a court in disarray and a world in chaos. But here the rebellious courtiers and the warring elements stand for the misrule of the passions within the mind that would rule them:

> All my attendants are at strife,
>   Quitting their place
>   Unto my face:
> Nothing performs the task of life:
>   The elements are let loose to fight,
>   And while I live, trie out their right.
>   (13–18)

These images reflect Herbert's earlier call upon God to quell his unruly faculties in "The Temper" (II):

> O fix thy chair of grace, that all my powers
>   May also fix their reverence:
>   For when thou dost depart from hence,
> They grow unruly, and sit in thy bowers.
>   (9–12)

The fourth stanza of "Affliction" (IV) further develops the figure of rebellion at court, again invoking God's assistance in an admission of Herbert's inability to control his passions: "Oh help, my God! let not their plot / Kill them and me. . . ." The abrupt shift from courtly to natural figures in these stanzas signifies his disorderly mental processes. But they also connect chaos in nature with rebellion in the state in a familiar way.[5] In depicting his mind as a court threatened by its unruly attendants, Herbert not only identifies the self with the court but implicates himself in its values. Curiously, division is doubled in "Affliction" (IV) by the presence of two rulers: the self whose attendants are at strife and the greater King to whom Herbert appeals. Thus the internalization of chaos multiplies its power to divide the self, even threatening its own stance as ruler, far beyond the intensity of lamentation we've seen in the allusions to a divided and disintegrating external world considered thus far. The second stanza of "Affliction" (IV) shows the distortions emanating from this fragmented consciousness:

> My thoughts are all a case of knives,
> Wounding my heart
> With scatter'd smart,
> As watring pots give flowers their lives.
> Nothing their furie can controll,
> While they do wound and pink my soul.
> (7–12)

This image of furious cutting and wounding derives from the dismemberment introduced in the poem's opening line, "Broken in pieces all asunder," and transfers to the self the same perception of violent destruction that we have seen in the figure of sin cleaving and tearing apart the brave palace of the world.

"Giddinesse" and "The Familie" expand the consequences of a divided self. The same images define man in general and Herbert in particular, yet the internalizing of these images unlocks their most destructive energies. The opening stanza of "Giddinesse" splits man into a warring multiplicity of identities:

> Oh, what a thing is man! how farre from power,
> From setled peace and rest!
> He is some twentie sev'rall men at least
> Each sev'rall houre.
> (1–4)

In a later stanza, man's mind is figured as a building undergoing violent destruction:

> He builds a house, which quickly down must go,
> As if a whirlwinde blew
> And crusht the building: and it's partly true,
> His minde is so.
>
> (13–16)

In "The Familie," the chaos is enclosed with first-person immediacy within the house of Herbert's own mind. His own unruly passions have created it, and here the responsibility for rule is given over entirely to God:

> What doth this noise of thoughts within my heart,
> As if they had a part?
> What do these loud complaints and puling fears,
> As if there were no rule or eares?
>
> But, Lord, the house and familie are thine,
> Though some of them repine,
> Turn out these wranglers, which defile thy seat. . . .
>
> (1–7)

This invasion of the mind by the divisions of the self, like the courtly insurrection of the faculties in "The Temper" (II) and "Affliction" (IV), suggests not only Herbert's personal sense of division but also the communal multiplicity of poetic "voices" that his extraordinarily various lyrics in fact represent.[6] It is as if the voices of the disintegrating court world, the divided seat of ecclesiastical rule, and all the inhabitants of the brave palace of the world have been incorporated into his mind and cry out their agonies within that house. A certain distancing of affect modifies lament in such poems as "The World" and "Peace," where visions of chaos are set within the framework of allegory. Even "Church-rents and schismes" distances in the extremity of its allegorical fancy and in the formalized hyperbole of Herbert's sorrow: "Where shall I get me eyes enough to weep, / As many eyes as starres?" Only when these voices are internalized, as in "The Temper" (II), "Affliction" (IV), and "The Familie," does the agony consequent upon the vision of a fragmented world multiply beyond the ability of a single consciousness to contain it. That agony becomes a full-throated outcry in the great poems of lamentation, "Deniall," "Complaining," and "Longing," where the fragmentation of consciousness utterly destroys the wholeness of the self.

"Deniall" once more turns the unruly faculties into rebellious courtiers flying in opposite directions, no longer subject to Herbert's control:

> When my devotions could not pierce
>   Thy silent eares;
> Then was my heart broken, as was my verse:
>   My breast was full of fears
>   And disorder:
>
> My bent thoughts, like a brittle bow,
>   Did flie asunder:
> Each took his way; some would to pleasures go,
>   Some to the warres and thunder
>   Of alarms.
>   (1–10)

The possibility of self-rule is abandoned here. The "bent thoughts" split consciousness asunder as the poem enacts a sequence of dissolutions. Two stanzas later, Herbert shifts to a natural image of disintegrated particles that is nearly as surrealistic, though far more moving, than the allegorical conceit of "Church-rents and schismes":

> O that thou shouldst give dust a tongue
>   To crie to thee,
> And then not heare it crying! all day long
>   My heart was in my knee,
>   But no hearing.
>   (16–20)

That a crumb of dust should be endowed with a tongue crying out and that the heart should now be located in the knee reduce the self to the fragmentary condition to which we have seen kings and courtiers reduced. The metonymy here wrenches the human body into a structure of agonized dislocations. In conjunction with the curiously animated fragments of inanimate dust in the stanza's first two lines, the displacement of heart to knee enforces the sense of a body and mind dissolving into disorderly pieces, as if most of its parts no longer serve any function at all in the condition of disharmony to which Herbert is brought by God's refusal to hear his prayers.

This occasion for fragmentation is central in "Deniall" as it is in "Complaining" and "Longing." Yet we cannot attribute these perceptions directly to an attempt to view the world from a heavenly perspective, as it has been possible to do with respect to the images considered earlier. These outcries speak of Herbert's longing for God's presence and repining in His absence, a matter of inner experience rather than external perception. Still the spiritual conflict generates the same figures that detail inversion and disintegration of king and court, church and world. In his misery, Herbert perceives his self-rule threatened by his unruly attendants; as failed ruler of these elements he too is reduced, in God's sight, to "Thy clay that weeps, thy dust that calls." Like "Deniall," "Complaining" dismembers the self:

> Am I all throat or eye,
>   To weep or crie?
> Have I no parts but those of grief?
>   (13–15)

Again, in "Longing," the self is composed of disorderly fragments, subjected to the chaotic instability of its own thoughts:

> With sick and famisht eyes,
> With doubling knees and weary bones,
>   To thee my cries,
>   To thee my grones,
> To thee my sighs, my tears ascend:
>   No end?
>
> My throat, my soul is hoarse;
> My heart is wither'd like a ground
>   Which thou dost curse.
>   My thoughts turn round,
> And make me giddie; Lord, I fall,
>   Yet call.
>   (1–12)

The descent that is regretted, but can be contained when it represents an inverted perspective of the world outside the self, becomes a full outcry of agony only when the self is understood to be equally reduced to the earth and ground into fragments: not poor kings and silly Jacobean courtiers whom Herbert treads under his feet contemptuously as so much gilded dust, but "my cries / . . . my grones / . . . my soul is hoarse; / My heart is wither'd like a ground / Which thou dost curse." Herbert's scornful depiction of man in "Miserie" – other men, mankind in general – as nothing but a "lump of flesh, without a foot or wing / To raise him to a glimpse of blisse" loses its third-person, superior distance in the shocking immediacy of the first-person conclusion, "My God, I mean my self";[7] the "flat delights" that creep and grow upon earth in "Vanitie" (II), like the fair dust of "Frailtie," are now identified with the self and endowed with a voice to cry out against its condition. In "Longing" the dust speaks and the broken parts call out:[8]

> Behold, thy dust doth stirre,
> It moves, it creeps, it aims at thee:
> Wilt thou deferre
> To succour me,
> Thy pile of dust, wherein each crumme
> Says, Come?
>
> . . . .
>
> Lord JESU, heare my heart,
> Which hath been broken now so long,
> That ev'ry part
> Hath got a tongue!
> Thy beggars grow; rid them away
> To day.
> (37–42, 73–8)

The source of Herbert's spiritual conflict, and the basis of his fear that God will not hear his cries, is spelled out in "Frailtie" by the same complex of ideas that signify his attempt to attain a heavenly perspective. He begins with a confident assertion:

> Lord, in my silence how do I despise
> What upon trust
> Is styled *honour, riches,* or *fair eyes;*
> But is *fair dust!*
> (1–4)

But after the neatly-patterned antitheses between God's regiment and the world's in the following stanza, he confesses his own attachment to that fair dust:

That which was dust before, doth quickly rise,
            And prick mine eyes.

O brook not this, lest if what even now
            My foot did tread,
Affront those joyes, wherewith thou didst endow
            And long since wed
    My poore soul, ev'n sick of love:
            It may a Babel prove
Commodious to conquer heav'n and thee
            Planted in me.

                                    (15–24)

The worldly values so easily dismissed from Christ's lofty perspective in "The Sacrifice" are his values, too; the inversion of courtly heights must become his own descent to the state of a crumb of dust. The worldly courtier is Herbert himself.

These internal structures of inversion and fragmentation show the consequence for consciousness of a radical shift in perspective. The images examined in the first section of this chapter described an overwhelming process of disintegration, but never turned that perception back upon the self. They figured Herbert as an observer, looking on his world with new eyes, deploring, even mourning its condition, but enduring the vision in the comforting sense of its externality to the self. And, with few exceptions, the force of disintegration and disorder was contained in a stanza or a phrase, subordinated to other concerns in these poems. Fragmentation within the self, however, focuses Herbert's spiritual conflict in the harsh light of his warring thoughts and impulses. The same vision of a fragmented court world and a disintegrating natural world controls both perceptions. An altered external perception exerts even greater force upon the image of self, breaking up consciousness, crowding the mind with a noise of thoughts, filling Herbert's verse, as well as his heart, with fears and disorder.

These conflicts create enormous pressures toward resolution. The final stanza of "Deniall" projects the possibility of a restored harmony in a microcosmic replication of God's macrocosmic recovery of the broken consort of mankind in "Dooms-day":

        O cheer and tune my heartlesse breast,
            Deferre no time;

That so thy favours granting my request,
> They and my minde may chime,
> > And mend my ryme.
> > (26–30)

The closing line does resolve one source of disorder in the poem: the appeal to God to restore harmony mends the broken rhyme that has closed every stanza except this final one. But it is spoken in the conditional mood; it is only a wish.

"An Offering" also invokes a restoration of order and a resolution of conflict. Herbert addresses his divided mind:

> But all I fear is lest thy heart displease,
> As neither good, nor one: so oft divisions
> Thy lusts have made, and not thy lusts alone;
> Thy passions also have their set partitions.
> These parcell out thy heart: recover these,
> And thou mayst offer many gifts in one.
> (13–18)

This possibility of a recovered wholeness implies the potential value in the painful parceling out of "Deniall," "Complaining," and "Longing." "Many gifts in one" postulates that the restoration of a divided unity may constitute an offering to God even preferable to a unity which never suffers division. The following section examines those poems which contain images of fragmentation within structures that raise what has been brought low and reconstruct values that have been lost in the process of deconstruction. As discrete units, these lyrics do find a way to recover wholeness. But such recoveries, we shall see, are merely momentary attempts to piece together a far less unitary fabric of perception and consciousness. As Herbert recognizes in "Sion," "now thy Architecture meets with sinne; / For all thy frame and fabrick is within." And as "The Sinner" confessed, that fabric is comprised of piled vanities, mere shreds of holiness.

iii

The first stanza of "Dotage" sets forth a disorderly catalogue of worldly pleasures and reduces them to nothing but illusion and deception:

False glozing pleasures, casks of happinesse,
Foolish night-fires, womens and childrens wishes,
Chases in Arras, guilded emptinesse,
Shadows well mounted, dreams in a career,
Embroider'd lyes, nothing between two dishes;
    These are the pleasures here.
     (1–6)

The catalogue of broken phrases imposes no order and establishes no connecting sequence; these empty shadows are merely laid out in disarray for our inspection. It is as if the eye were moving over the surface of a courtly world at random, noting here a tapestry, there some dishes, and intermixing these objects indifferently with words and feelings and fancies. Lies, wishes, and dreams are given the same linguistic weight as what might seem at least materially substantial. "Embroider'd lyes" recall the silly soul's attraction to "false embroideries" rather than "solid work" in "Vanitie" (II), another association of falsity with an elegant surface concealing the lack of substance within. "Chases in Arras" are only figures on a tapestry that might cover a palace wall, while "nothing between two dishes" evokes a palatial banquet where the real lack of food is covered over by the material promise of its presence. The phrase "guilded emptinesse," like the terms "fair dust" and "guilded clay" in "Frailtie," denies that any value is to be found in earthly courts. These associations turn the world into a court, but also identify insubstantial show with the court world.

Although the second stanza catalogues "the sorrows here" in a similar fashion, these syntactic fragments are rather less randomly ordered. The natural references suggest growth rather than the disintegration evoked by Herbert's earlier images of fair dust and gilded clay:

True earnest sorrows, rooted miseries,
Anguish in grain, vexations ripe and blown,
Sure-footed griefs, solid calamities,
Plain demonstrations, evident and cleare,
Fetching their proofs ev'n from the very bone;
    These are the sorrows here.
     (7–12)

The initial contrast between the falsity of pleasures and the truth of sorrows is followed by a miniature sequence tracing a natural cycle from "rooted miseries" to the seed which brings forth life – "Anguish in grain" – to the full flowering of "vexations ripe and blown." The third line, by reference back to the first stanza, contrasts the substanceless with the substantial. "Sure-footed griefs" are paradoxically endowed with more reality than the shadowy evocation of running feet in an imaginary chase embroidered on a tapestry, while the dependable solidity of calamities, in its parallel place in the line, redeems the "guilded emptinesse" of worldly pleasures. The final lines again suggest the idea of sequence by reference to the patterns of logic. The pleasures are empty, delusory, and dream-like; earthly sorrows, no less fragmentary, are nevertheless rooted, "evident and cleare," a matter susceptible of demonstration and proof, as palpable as bone and as solid.

But the final stanza of the poem places both the pleasures and the sorrows of the world in a context that transcends worldly categories altogether and restores the syntactic wholeness that has been absent in all but the refrain lines of the two preceding stanzas:

> But oh the folly of distracted men,
> Who griefs in earnest, joyes in jest pursue:
> Preferring, like brute beasts, a lothsome den
> Before a court, ev'n that above so cleare,
> Where are no sorrows, but delights more true
>   Then miseries are here!
>   (13–18)

Herbert's reductive treatment of the earthly court in the first stanza undergoes a still greater diminution in its implied equation to a "lothsome den" preferred by man over the clear court above. Yet the stanza recovers wholeness by offering a true court to replace the false one whose value has been emptied out at the beginning of the poem. And though "true earnest sorrows" are all the world can offer of either value or substance, these conditions are reversed in the court above, "Where are no sorrows, but delights more true / Then miseries are here!" The movement towards order in the second stanza has initiated the redeeming ascent postulated in the conclusion, which now inverts the destructive reductions of the opening lines.

"Dotage" shows how inversion is a perceptual pattern that can work in two directions. If, when "Grace turns ye Optick," the things that the world thinks "bigg and tall" must undergo a fall, a reversal of this descent is also possible. Furthermore, the fall is a necessary preliminary to the rise, as another couplet of "Charms and Knots" makes clear:

> Who looks on ground with humble eyes,
> Findes himself there, and seeks to rise.
>
> (11–12)

These lines help to explain the structure of "Dotage." Inversion of the worldly perspective brings down to earth and splits into fragments. But that same process, rightly understood, enables what has been brought low to rise and reassembles the fragments into orderly wholes. As "Dotage" shows, this reconstruction is also a transvaluation: in the heavenly context, courtliness once more carries positive implications. Although the earthly court is reduced to a loathsome den of shadows, clarity is still to be found in the court above; when this world's kings are reduced to decaying flesh, there is still a true King who rules over that court. This poem is a useful introduction to the patterns of transvaluation in *The Church,* because it includes so many of the oppositions upon which the process depends: deception and truth, emptiness and substance, shadows and clarity, descent and ascent. These contrasts transform the effects of disorder by enclosing them within an orderly structure that restores the values which have been lost.

The images of destruction considered thus far represent only the first stage in a process whose ultimate end is transvaluation rather than denial of value. The reduction of worldly things that are commonly understood to be "bigg and tall" does bring with it all of the consequences that we have seen, for the self as well as for the court, the church, or the world: fragmentation, disintegration, dissolution. But at the same time there is a source of value beyond the secular which enables the humbled soul to rise. The fragmentation that disintegrates also restores; the same images that have traced an arc of descent, transvalued, also describe the curve of ascent.

"Paradise" recovers the dispersed fragments of the self through a reversal of perspective which reveals that rending is, in fact, a process of healing:

> I blesse thee, Lord, because I　　　GROW
> Among thy trees, which in a　　　ROW
> To thee both fruit and order　　　OW.

What open force, or hidden   CHARM
Can blast my fruit, or bring me   HARM
While the inclosure is thine   ARM?

Inclose me still for fear I   START.
Be to me rather sharp and   TART,
Then let me want thy hand &   ART.

When thou dost greater judgements   SPARE,
And with thy knife but prune and   PARE,
Ev'n fruitfull trees more fruitfull ARE.

Such sharpnes shows the sweetest   FREND:
Such cuttings rather heal then   REND:
And such beginnings touch their   END.

The extent of such a reversal can best be measured by comparison
with similar images in "Affliction" (IV), where, as we have seen, the
knives that wound his heart and pink his soul are Herbert's thoughts.
One line of the second stanza suggests that these wounds possess
some value, but it is engulfed in the linguistic extremity of the
remaining five lines:

My thoughts are all a case of knives,
            Wounding my heart,
            With scatter'd smart,
As watring pots give flowers their lives.
        Nothing their furie can controll,
        While they do wound and pink my soul.
                        (7–12)

That the "scatter'd smart" of Herbert's thoughts might be as saving a
grace to his heart as water to flowers could represent an attempt to
"naturalize" his affliction, as figuring the self as growing tree indeed
succeeds in doing in "Paradise." But the clash of sense between the
image of flowers and watering pots versus thoughts as dueling opponents leaves little room for the fully comprehended healing that is
worked out in the latter poem.

The final stanza of "Affliction" (IV) also adumbrates the more
thoroughgoing reversals of "Paradise." With God's help, Herbert
perceives that his rebellious passions might become forces of
reconstruction rather than deconstruction:

> Then shall those powers, which work for grief,
>   Enter thy pay,
>   And day by day
> Labour thy praise, and my relief;
>   With care and courage building me,
>   Till I reach heav'n, and much more, thee.
>   (25–30)

Although Herbert has recognized in the first stanza of this poem that he is "A wonder tortur'd in the space / Betwixt this world and that of grace," his conclusion, like that of "Deniall," is put as a wish, in the future tense, while "Paradise" is present, declarative, even imperative: "Inclose me still . . . / Be to me rather sharp and T A R T. . . ." Here, the same figures that we have seen repeatedly producing pain and disturbance are now transformed by an enabling discovery. It is God's knife, not alone the knives of Herbert's thought, that is doing the rending: the knife prunes to make him more fruitful, its sharpness is sweet, this cutting is a healing.

Herbert's perception of himself as a growing tree, both fruitful and one of an orderly row, represents still another perspectival shift. The tree is as natural an image as the crumb of dust in the lamentations, still close to the lowest level of creation and certainly below the presumed place of man in the hierarchy, but now the image is one of reaching upward rather than falling, growth rather than disintegration. These reversals, moreover, are given form in the orderly structure of the whole. The neat paring-away of each three-line stanza cuts away the rhyme word in a diminishment which in fact represents the means of increase: the pruning makes more fruitful. As the last line says, "such beginnings touch their E N D." The poem's opening claim to order and fruitfulness "touches" its end in the final stanza's explanation of the process of sharp cutting that has produced that condition.[9]

"The Quidditie" recovers wholeness through both structure and style. Rather than assembling its fragments within an orderly frame or reversing their signification, it inverts the pattern of descent in the first ten lines by the ascent claimed in the last two:

> My God, a verse is not a crown,
> No point of honour, or gay suit,
> No hawk, or banquet, or renown,
> Nor a good sword, nor yet a lute:

It cannot vault, or dance, or play;
It never was in *France* or *Spain;*
Nor can it entertain the day
With my great stable or demain:

It is no office, art, or news,
Nor the Exchange, or busie Hall;
But it is that which while I use
I am with thee, and *most take all.*

This concluding ascent is weighted all the more because of the
enormous extent of fragmentation compressed into the preceding
lines. Disordered though they are, these linguistic parts constitute an
entire court world, from the symbol of its ruler and the values of its
inhabitants to their businesses, recreations, arts, and fashions. The
geography of the poem encompasses the boundaries of the courtier's
world from the continental destinations favored by young gentlemen
completing their education to the London scene of their daily life in
the world to the great houses in which their society is centered when
they are not in attendance at court.

The poem seems to say that verse is not courtly poetry. But in fact
it says that verse is neither the world of the court, nor the life of the
courtier, nor even his values. All these parts are rejected in favor of
the quiddity; the verse that unites Herbert with God replaces the
entire court world with a higher source of value and allegiance.[10]
"The Quidditie," in distinction to those poems discussed up to this
point, adopts a stylistic strategy to work its transvaluation. The claim
for sacred verse could not be higher, both in its effect on him and in
its absolute value over and above all the parts of court verse and the
court world: "*most take all.*" And yet it is a slang term for the
winning hand in a card game which asserts that absolute value:[11] low
language, pithy and compressed, with none of the high associations
evoked — and reduced — by the courtly fragments in the poem's
preceding ten lines. A phrase in the low style inverts expectation just
as the couplet of "Charms and Knots" does in pointing out the need
for the humble soul to find itself by looking on the ground. This
stylistic inversion all the more magnifies the difference between the
sacred and substantial versus the secular and inconsequential.

"The Quidditie" exemplifies those lyrics which recover wholeness not simply by reordering fragmented images but by incorporating within their structure the rise that must follow descent. This
pattern appears also in Herbert's other poems on poetry, where the

revaluation of style is his explicit subject. The oppositions of "Jordan" (I) can best be understood by glancing back to "The Temper" (II), immediately preceding:

> The grosser world stands to thy word and art;
>   But thy diviner world of grace
>   Thou suddenly dost raise and race,
> And ev'ry day a new Creatour art.
>
> O fix thy chair of grace, that all my powers
>   May also fix their reverence:
>   For when thou dost depart from hence,
> They grow unruly, and sit in thy bowers.
>
> Scatter, or binde them all to bend to thee:
>   Though elements change, and heaven move,
>   Let not thy higher Court remove,
> But keep a standing Majestie in me.
>
>   (5–16)

Here, as in "Dotage," the "grosser world" is contrasted to "thy diviner world of grace." God in this poem is every inch a king, whose "chair of grace" is situated in a "higher Court" which, Herbert realizes, might restore order and stability to his unruly faculties. These allusions to the higher court and its divine ruler enable us to place the plain assertion of Herbert's allegiance to "*My God, My King*" in "Jordan" (I):

> Who sayes that fictions onely and false hair
> Become a verse? Is there in truth no beautie?
> Is all good structure in a winding stair?
> May no lines passe, except they do their dutie
>   Not to a true, but painted chair?
>
> Is it no verse, except enchanted groves
> And sudden arbours shadow course-spunne lines?
> Must purling streams refresh a lovers loves?
> Must all be vail'd, while he that reades, divines,
>   Catching the sense at two removes?
>
> Shepherds are honest people; let them sing:
> Riddle who list, for me, and pull for Prime:
> I envie no mans nightingale or spring;
> Nor let them punish me with losse of rime,
>   Who plainly say, *My God, My King*.

Most critics of this poem have pointed out the Platonic reference of the "painted chair" of line 5,[12] but their analyses don't really account for the action controlling the metaphor: "May no lines passe, except they do their dutie / Not to a true, but painted chair?" In the light of the conclusion, the image of a courtier kneeling to his king ought to be read more literally than is customarily done. The painted chair to which allegiance is owed by shepherd-poets is the throne of the earthly ruler, the other king shadowed in this poem. That Herbert describes the chair as painted is puzzling unless we accept Anthony Low's reading of the poem as a rejection of fictionality in the masque,[13] though the fragmentary allusions to poetic fictions, nightingales, and spring seem far more specifically coded to pastoral and allegory – favorite modes of poets at the courts of James and Charles as they had been with the Elizabethans.[14] But within the poem's immediate context, to call an earthly throne a painted chair is to use the Platonic image of distance from the true idea of a chair in a fashion directly parallel to the contrast in "The Temper" (II) between the grosser world and the divine world, where there is a higher court and a ruler to whose true "chair of grace" Herbert offers his allegiance.[15]

Here, to an even greater degree than in "The Quidditie," Herbert shifts styles after the manner of Sidney to designate the difference between two orders of language. The first is richly and appropriately decorative, spun out over thirteen lines that, in their grace and smoothness of movement, any Cavalier might have written. But this order is reduced to elegant trivia by the bare statement compressed into four words in the concluding line. And the "course-spunne" denomination – my God "who is" my King – supplants the shadowy presence of a secular king in his painted chair receiving the duty of poets who have nothing more to offer than "fictions onely." It is the plainness and brevity of the statement which give it such power to outweigh the elaborate imagery of the preceding lines.[16] Yet in supplanting fictions and shadows, Herbert is still courtly. He directs his verse to the true King of whom all others are copies, at two removes from reality as they appear in their courtiers' poetry. As his artful deployment of their language makes clear, he offers his verse to this King as a plain-spoken but true courtier who might have chosen the other forms of verse.

The same pattern of descent followed by ascent occurs in "Jordan" (II), although here the rather facile rejection of poetic fictions accomplished in "Jordan" (I) becomes far more problematic when Herbert applies it to his own religious verse:

> When first my lines of heav'nly joyes made mention,
> Such was their lustre, they did so excell,
> That I sought out quaint words, and trim invention;
> My thoughts began to burnish, sprout, and swell,
> Curling with metaphors a plain intention,
> Decking the sense, as if it were to sell.
>
> Thousands of notions in my brain did runne,
> Off'ring their service, if I were not sped:
> I often blotted what I had begunne;
> This was not quick enough, and that was dead.
> Nothing could seem too rich to clothe the sunne,
> Much lesse those joyes which trample on his head.
>
> As flames do work and winde, when they ascend,
> So did I weave my self into the sense.
> But while I bustled, I might heare a friend
> Whisper, *How wide is all this long pretence!*
> *There is in love a sweetnesse readie penn'd:*
> *Copie out onely that, and save expense.*

Just as the fragmenting considered thus far has extended to Herbert's own consciousness as well as to the exterior world, so the two Jordan poems reject fashionable poetic styles in both contexts. The language of the court is inverted and fragmented in these poems: arbors, streams, nightingales, and springs are nothing but veiled fictions, shadows ominously anticipatory of "Dotage," in Jordan (I), while in "Jordan" (II), all of Herbert's quaint words, inventions, metaphors, and notions offer an "ascent" that is no more than a busy show, a luster that raises him up in self-esteem – but not to his God.

In "Jordan" (II), Herbert implicates himself in the same process of decorative excess that he has condemned in courtly pastoral: "My thoughts began to burnish, sprout, and swell, / Curling with metaphors a plain intention." But the scornful comment that follows, "Decking the sense as if it were to sell," makes his efforts even more suspect than the veiled fictions of the pastoralists, while the whisper of a "friend" points out a still worse deception, a bustling self-concern that falsifies the self: "*How wide is all this long pretence!*" Here, too, a plain and simple mode of utterance outweighs the elaborations confessed (and evidenced) in the preceding fourteen lines. To copy "sweetnesse readie penn'd" in fact releases the poet from his obsessive self-concern: it is there for him without effort.[17] As in "Jordan" (I), this plainness recovers wholeness out of the fragments of stylistic excess and poetic pride that have been devalued initially; the deliberate echo of Sidney's comparable endings in *Astrophil and Stella* ("And love doth hold my hand, and makes me write") lays claim to a transformed language, a new but still courtly poetic.

"The Forerunners" returns to the same issue, though here the process of rejecting one poetic mode and adopting another is even less simple than the advice of "Jordan" (II) to copy out sweetness already penned. Herbert's exposition shows how one poem's momentary recovery is challenged by a later poem's re-engagement with the problem:

> The harbingers are come. See, see their mark;
> White is their colour, and behold my head.
> But must they have my brain? must they dispark
> Those sparkling notions, which therein were bred?
>   Must dulnesse turn me to a clod?
> Yet they have left me, *Thou art still my God.*
>
> Good men ye be, to leave me my best room,
> Ev'n all my heart, and what is lodged there:
> I passe not, I, what of the rest become,
> So *Thou art still my God,* be out of fear.
>   He will be pleased with that dittie;
> And if I please him, I write fine and wittie.
>
> Farewell sweet phrases, lovely metaphors.
> But will ye leave me thus? when ye before
> Of stews and brothels onely knew the doores,
> Then did I wash you with my tears, and more,
>   Brought you to Church well drest and clad:
> My God must have my best, ev'n all I had.
>
> Lovely enchanting language, sugar-cane,
> Hony of roses, whither wilt thou flie?
> Hath some fond lover tic'd thee to thy bane?
> And wilt thou leave the Church, and love a stie?
>   Fie, thou wilt soil thy broider'd coat,
> And hurt thy self, and him that sings the note.

Let foolish lovers, if they will love dung,
With canvas, not with arras, clothe their shame:
Let follie speak in her own native tongue.
True beautie dwells on high: ours is a flame
            But borrow'd thence to light us thither.
Beautie and beauteous words should go together.

Yet if you go, I passe not; take your way:
For, *Thou art still my God,* is all that ye
Perhaps with more embellishment can say.
Go birds of spring: let winter have his fee;
            Let a bleak palenesse chalk the doore,
So all within be livelier then before.

Here Herbert weaves God into the sense and structure of the poem
and attempts to weave himself out of it. The plain statement "*Thou
art still my God*" outweighs all his sweet phrases and lovely enchanting metaphors and sparkling notions. The language that he rejects is
again associated with the secular court: "Let foolish lovers, if they
will love dung, / With canvas, not with arras, clothe their shame."
This recollection of the "lothsome den" and "Chases in Arras" of
"Dotage" suggests that the ornaments of courtly poetry conceal its
mortal taint. On the other hand, the language pleasing to God will be
"fine and wittie" even though it allows only plain words to offer his
allegiance to this higher King. Wholeness is restored by Herbert's
recognition that the flame borrowed from beauty's dwelling on high,
whatever "bleak paleness" it might seem to possess from the earthly
perspective, is still sufficiently beautiful to offer praise to God and
thus signify a spiritual "liveliness within." Yet "The Forerunners"
admits, as "Jordan" (II) does not, the real pain entailed by relinquishing "sweet phrases" and "lovely metaphors." His rewriting of "Jordan" (II) is radical and revealing.[18]

   "The Posie" transvalues by presenting, in two contexts, the same
courtly conceit of an inscription upon a ring or book or picture. It
follows the injunction of "Jordan" (II) to copy out sweetness ready
penned, borrowing the "True beautie" of scripture:

                Let wits contest,
      And with their words and posies windows fill:
                Lesse then the least
      Of all thy mercies, is my posie still.

> This on my ring,
> This by my picture, in my book I write:
> Whether I sing,
> Or say, or dictate, this is my delight.
>
> Invention rest,
> Comparisons go play, wit use thy will:
> *Lesse then the least*
> *Of all Gods mercies,* is my posie still.

Here, the posies dear to worldly courtiers are trivialized in the compressed and scornful aside – "Invention rest, / Comparisons go play, wit use thy will" – while a plain recognition replaces all these elegant efforts by joining the humble soul's descent with its means of rising – "*Lesse then the least of all Gods mercies.*" Here, as in "The Forerunners," the poet's pride must give over even its invention; "thy will" here must be God's will, not Herbert's. "The Posie" does transvalue, since Herbert appropriates the courtly conceit and adopts the courtly image for himself, but the low and simple transference of courtly wit to the scriptural source relieves Herbert's need to "invent" as it reinstates the value of courtly inscribing.

This pattern, incorporating an inversion of secular values as a necessary preliminary to their displacement by sacred values, can be recognized most clearly in the poems on poetry. It is found in other lyrics as well, sometimes combining images of fragmentation and inversion as in "Dotage." In "Divinitie," the elaborate complexities of theological speculation are outweighed by the actual simplicity of divine Wisdom:

> As men, for fear the starres should sleep and nod,
>   And trip at night, have spheres suppli'd;
> As if a starre were duller then a clod,
>   Which knows his way without a guide:
>
> Just so the other heav'n they also serve,
>   Divinities transcendent skie:
> Which with the edge of wit they cut and carve.
>   Reason triumphs, and faith lies by.
>
> Could not that Wisdome, which first broacht the wine,
>   Have thicken'd it with definitions?
> And jagg'd his seamlesse coat, had that been fine,
>   With curious questions and divisions?

But all the doctrine, which he taught and gave,
    Was cleare as heav'n, from whence it came.
At least those beams of truth, which onely save,
    Surpasse in brightnesse any flame.

Love God, and love your neighbour. Watch and pray.
    Do as you would be done unto.
O dark instructions; ev'n as dark as day!
    Who can these Gordian knots undo?

                          (1–20)

The destructive fragmentation of excess wit in the pursuit of heavenly wisdom, consisting of nothing more than definitions, questions, and divisions, is set over against the redeeming wholeness of three plain sentences, the doctrine "clear as heav'n" which Herbert copies out from the scriptures. The sarcastic aside on these "dark instructions" and "Gordian knots" reminds us of the dark worldly perspective to which Christ had called attention in the opening lines of "The Sacrifice": "*O all ye who passe by,* whose eyes and minde / To worldly things are sharp, but to me blinde." Herbert displays the ability of his own worldly wit to "cut and carve" in his account of these errors, but he abandons metaphysical excess in the poem's closing lines: "Faith needs no staffe of flesh, but stoutly can / To heav'n alone both go, and leade." It is this language which truly serves "Divinities transcendent skie," and moves towards it in the homely closing image that demonstrates the mode of rising available only to a humble soul.

The poems discussed in this section recover wholeness either by assigning new values to the process of fragmentation, or by incorporating within their structure an ascent to the realm of sacred values after the secular realm has been emptied of any substantial worth. All of them reflect the central perceptual shift resulting from an inversion of the worldly perspective required by the attempt to achieve a heavenly perspective. To speak in these terms is to claim the influence of such a shift upon the structure and even the style of the lyrics in *The Church*. A great many other poems share the structure outlined here, establish similar contrasts between court and Court, and differentiate the language appropriate to these two realms.[19] Still another consequence of the transition from a worldly to a heavenly perspective demands a greater shift than either the perceptual or the experiential: the altered conditions of serving a ruler so different from earthly kings. The contrast between worldly and heavenly perspectives in the opening stanza of "The Sacrifice" is followed by two stanzas in which Christ declares the paradoxes of worldly and heavenly power:

> The Princes of my people make a head
> Against their Maker: they do wish me dead,
> Who cannot wish, except I give them bread:
> > Was ever grief like mine?
>
> Without me each one, who doth now me brave,
> Had to this day been an Egyptian slave.
> They use that power against me, which I gave:
> > Was ever grief like mine?
> > > (5–12)

Christ's own behavior inverts the image of kingly power in another way. He allows these debased rulers to "buffet him, and box him as they list" even though He "grasps the earth and heaven with his fist"; He points out that Herod's soldiers "deride me, they abuse me all: / Yet for twelve heav'nly legions I could call"; and the inversion of height and lowliness is nowhere so sharply figured as in the lines on His mockers:

> They bow their knees to me, and cry, *Hail king:*
> What ever scoffes & scornfulnesse can bring,
> I am the floore, the sink, where they it fling.
> > (173–5)

Just as the opening three stanzas contrasted Christ's extraordinary acceptance of lowliness with the genuinely base behavior of earthly princes, so this stanza's assertion that a willing descent models divinity is followed by an equally remarkable denial of secular power. Christ's attributes are transferred, in a terrible prophetic irony, to the kings of this world:

> Yet since mans scepters are as frail as reeds,
> And thorny all their crowns, bloudie their weeds;
> I, who am Truth, turn into truth their deeds. . . .
> > (177–9)

Christ's example thus inverts the pattern of power as the earthly perspective sees it:

> A king my title is, prefixt on high;
> Yet by my subjects am condemn'd to die
> A servile death in servile companie. . . .
>   (233–5)

These inversions control the anxious questioning of "The Thanksgiving," which follows "The Sacrifice." Herbert presents himself as a courtier who would emulate his King, yet the model set by Christ offers only incongruities from the worldly viewpoint:

> Oh King of grief! (a title strange, yet true,
>   To thee of all kings onely due)
> O King of wounds! how shall I grieve for thee,
>   Who in all grief preventest me?
> Shall I weep bloud? why, thou hast wept such store
>   That all thy body was one doore.
> Shall I be scourged, flouted, boxed, sold?
>   'Tis but to tell the tale is told.
>   .   .   .   .
> Shall I then sing, skipping thy dolefull storie,
>   And side with thy triumphant glorie?
> Shall thy strokes be my stroking? thorns, my flower?
>   Thy rod, my posie? crosse, my bower?
> But how then shall I imitate thee, and
>   Copie thy fair, though bloudie hand?
>   (1–8, 11–16)

The opening lines distinguish Christ's kingly role from that of any earthly prince, while Herbert's proposed transpositions from flower to thorn, posy to rod, and bower to cross attest the inadequacy of the worldly courtier's equipment to aid him in emulating such an exemplar. Herbert continues to suggest means of imitation more suited to service at an earthly court and even, perhaps, constituted by such service: "If thou dost give me honour, men shall see, / The honour doth belong to thee." Like any true courtier of his time, he evokes Ovid in a witty attempt to parallel sacred and secular texts: "Nay, I will read thy book, and never move / Till I have found therein thy love, / Thy art of love, which I'le turn back on thee: / O my deare

Saviour, Victorie!" But these incongruous substitutions and worldly offerings dissolve into an admission of defeat in the face of the crucifixion: "Then for thy passion − I will do for that − / Alas, my God, I know not what."

The inverted view of earthly kings in "The Sacrifice" empties their position of any substantial worth and initiates the process of fragmentation that I have been tracing in later lyrics of *The Church*. "The Thanksgiving" not only distinguishes Christ from these mortal models but also, in reiterating the principle of emulation fundamental to the courtly ideal, underlines the incapacity of the courtier's role once service to the King no longer provides either a pattern or an object worthy of imitation. By presenting the *imitatio Christi* in courtly terms, and by depicting himself as a courtier, Herbert exposes the failing power of the secular ideal even as he evokes the spirituality it once contained.

The descent that we have seen in Herbert is far more sweeping in its implications and absolute in its rejection of the secular ideal than either Sidney or any Cavalier − at least before the Civil Wars − ever conceived. Although earlier poets and historians had begun to foresee its disintegration, Herbert's treatment of the court in *The Church* confronts that disintegration fully and details all of its consequences. His resolution is brilliant within individual lyrics that simultaneously acknowledge all of the pressures upon the ideal that were mounting as he wrote, and yet still visualize its transvaluation to the higher realm which in fact had always been the ultimate goal of the courtier and the originary source of courtly value.

But the problem of exemplifying God's courtier, serving the heavenly King, demands the exercise of virtues that the worldly courtier of "The Thanksgiving" has clearly not yet learned to attain or even to articulate. As Herbert confesses in "The Sinner," he finds in himself "quarries of pil'd vanities" but only "shreds of holiness." The transformation of this worldly courtier into God's courtier takes more than a single poem to resolve, as the weightiness of piled vanities in contrast to his slight shreds of holiness might imply. The fine integration of individual lyrics in *The Church* is fragmented once more when Herbert confronts this disproportion between the ideal to which he aspires and the actual condition of his soul that still stands in his way. What one poem resolves, the next discovers to be still a problem. Recovery all too often leads only to new disclosures. The conclusion of "The Temper" (I) and the opening of "The Temper" (II) are paradigmatic:

> Whether I flie with angels, fall with dust,
>   Thy hands made both, and I am there:
> Thy power and love, my love and trust
>   Make one place ev'ry where.
>   "The Temper" (I)

> It cannot be. Where is that mightie joy,
> Which just now took up all my heart?
>   "The Temper" (II)

Herbert attempts recovery of these divisions in the larger structure of *The Church*. They constitute a configuration of lyrics[20] tracking the course of Herbert's conflicts in respect to the service that God requires of him. Actualizing the ideal, the making of God's courtier, is the subject of the following chapter.

Chapter 5

The Circumference of Earth

Lord, how I am all ague, when I seek
  What I have treasur'd in my memorie!
  Since, if my soul make even with the week
Each seventh note by right is due to thee.
I finde there quarries of pil'd vanities,
  But shreds of holinesse, that dare not venture
  To shew their face, since crosse to thy decrees:
There the circumference earth is, heav'n the centre.
In so much dregs the quintessence is small:
  The spirit and good extract of my heart
  Comes to about the many hundred part.
Yet Lord restore thine image, heare my call;
  And though my hard heart scarce to thee can grone,
  Remember that thou once didst write in stone.
                                        "The Sinner"

"The Sinner" states the problem which Herbert cannot resolve within the scope of any single lyric in *The Church*. These scant shreds of holiness are insufficient to weave the "frame and fabrick" of a Temple within[1] that might be fit for Christ to inhabit. Nor can they restore God's image and thus transform the worldly courtier who, in "The Thanksgiving," cannot conceive of a way to imitate his Lord, into the dedicated priest of God who celebrates his assumption of office in "Aaron." The broken parts of Herbert's "hard heart" in "The Altar," his courtly self-portrait in "The Thanksgiving," and the soul overwhelmed by its weight of piled vanities in "The Sinner" all direct our attention to the "I" whose struggle toward holiness is recorded in the first-person lyrics of *The Church*.

This person is Herbert himself. His poetic voice and presence in *The Church* not only encourage but, I believe, require us to read the personal lyrics in the light of Herbert's biography. To the seventeenth-century reader of *The Temple*, the life unquestionably informed and even justified the art. Just as John Hacket introduced his memoir of Bishop Williams by stressing the value of presenting a "real Cyrus," a model of virtue drawn from life, so Nicholas Ferrar's prefatory description of Herbert as "a pattern or more for the age he lived in" links *The Temple*'s benefit to the reader with the exemplary design modeled by Herbert's life choices. Ferrar claims, in fact, that some knowledge of the life is necessary if we are to understand the poetry:

> Onely for the clearing of some passages, we have thought it not unfit to make the common Reader privie to some few particularities of the condition and disposition of the Person;
>   Being nobly born, and as eminently endued with gifts of the minde, and having by industrie and happy education perfected them to that great height of excellencie, whereof his fellowship of Trinitie Colledge in Cambridge, and his Oratorship in the Universitie, together with that knowledge which the Kings Court had taken of him, could make relation farre above ordinarie. Quitting both his deserts and all the opportunities that he had for worldly preferment, he betook himself to the Sanctuarie and Temple of God, choosing rather to serve at Gods Altar, then to seek the honour of State-employments. As for those inward enforcements to this course (for outward there was none) which many of these ensuing verses bear witness of, they detract not from the freedome, but adde to the honour of this resolution in him. As God had enabled him, so he accounted him meet not only to be called, but to be compelled to this service: Wherein his faithfull discharge was such, as may make him justly a companion to the primitive Saints, and a pattern or more for the age he lived in.[2]

Ferrar's contrast between Herbert's worldly "deserts" and "opportunities," and the "freedome" and "honour" of the choice which he ultimately made, rightly implies that his rejection of "State-employments" in favor of service at God's altar is central to our reading of *The Temple*. Thus we need to examine the role of vocation in the personal lyrics of *The Church* in order to recognize the nature of those inward enforcements leading to Herbert's choice of a calling. Of course the spiritual progress traced in this section of *The Temple* figures any Christian's struggle toward God,[3] but as Ferrar's preface makes perfectly clear, the power of the pattern to *represent* for others arises out of the particularities of this individual life.

The sinner configured in *The Church* is a very worldly courtier whose anxiety to discover God's purpose for him is deeply contaminated by his wish to gain honor for himself in serving God. His repining at God's refusal to hear his prayers and his impatience under the burden of afflictions reflect not only the attachments to this world which enmesh every Christian seeker, but also those particular entanglements deriving from Herbert's own worldly position and its expectations of great place. Since the progress of vocational choice in *The Church* reflects Herbert's life in the world outside the poem, it cannot be considered solely an artifice created by and for the poetic fiction: the actual life exterior to the work is re-presented within it by deliberate design.

God's courtier configures Herbert's ultimate service at Bemerton together with the hopes for great place in the world with which he began, according to Ferrar. The biographical space between Herbert's acceptance of the Oratorship at Cambridge in 1619 and his assumption of the priesthood at Bemerton in 1630 is a space within *The Church* framed by "Affliction" (I) and "Aaron."[4] Inside that space, the choice of a calling recurs over and over at nodal points as the worldly courtier tries to imagine himself serving God in one way or another, awaits a call from God that does not come, attempts without success to emulate Christ. Circumscribed by earth, he can neither reach his center in God nor discover a means to miraculously transform his world-bound self into the "quintessence" which might animate Christ within his heart. Herbert's images in "The Sinner" show why the linearity of "sequence" fails to account for the process detailed in poems concerned with his search for a calling. "Circumference" and "center," like the configurations and constellations of "The H. Scriptures. II," *outline* relationships between parts of the divided self or between poems or parts of poems, and those relationships change continually as we move through the sequence in a merely linear way:[5] each reappearance of an image or an emotion sets new relationships in play, may mark an advance or a retreat. In the search for vocation, it is retreat – the binding of the impatient soul within its circumference of earth – which carries the emotional weight of quarries of piled vanities and the temporal burden of delay that Herbert bears with such ill grace in so many poems. The outcome of his search for a calling depends upon figures of transformation, rather than progress: animating the Christ within the old man full of "defects and darkness" in "Aaron," in "The Elixir" the marvelous extraction of the quintessence "The Sinner" only longs to discover. These processes are not sequential, but configurative, in still another sense: the old courtier is not left behind but incorporated within the new figure, once Godly center and earthly circumference are set into right relationship – a reciprocity – by Herbert's own perception that his life, even the contingent and the chaotic, is capable of generating an intelligible pattern.

Although I shall be moving through a sequence that seems to have a defined beginning and end, I use such terminology only to suggest its inadequacy to a "progress of choices," which outlines a very different design. My aim in studying the "vocation sequence" is to disclose how its power as pattern is generated by its circular, encompassing, configurating movements rather than by the more rigid ordering imposed by ideas of linearity, progress, inevitable advance. If the space between "Affliction" (I) and "Aaron" is filled with moments of insight about the choice of vocation – nodal points reaching out to other lyrics to cluster or constellate acts of recognition[6] – the entire sequence may be perceived as a binding together of circumference and center in reciprocity, as an animation of the soul's divine center which nevertheless does not exclude the earthly circumference that not only binds us to our mortality, but bonds us with one another in our shared and fallible humanity.

i

Herbert, however, initially confronts his search for a calling as if it could be a sequence of inevitable advances. The concept of vocation as both a progress of choices and the revelation of an unfolding purpose reflects orthodox thought on the matter in Herbert's time. Each person's particular calling was understood to be ordained by God, but at the same time it was one's own responsibility to make the proper choice. As William Perkins puts it:

> Men of years make choice of fit callings for themselves when they try, judge, and examine themselves to what things they are apt and fit and to what things they are not. And every man must examine himself of two things: first, touching his affections; secondly, touching his gifts. For his affections, he must search what mind he hath to any calling, and in what calling he desireth

most of all to glorify God. For his gifts, he must examine for and to what calling they are fittest. Having thus tried both his affections and gifts, finding also the calling to which they tend with one consent, he may say that is his calling, because he liketh it best and is every way the fittest to it. . . .[7]

Perkins' emphasis upon "gifts and affections" reflects the humanists' concern with the right education of future leaders of the state, and indeed he goes on to urge that parents and schoolmasters must consider these same matters in attempting to determine what God might have fitted their charges to do. The secular writers of courtesy books make the same point: it is man's obligation to discover his proper place in God's order through a process of self-examination.[8]

As Perkins says later in the *Treatise of the Vocations,* "we must consider the main end of our lives, and that is to serve God in the serving of men in the works of our callings" (p. 457). This point becomes a key element in humanist doctrine and, consequently, dominant in a humanist education such as Herbert received. The expectations established initially by his birth into a great family would have been reinforced by his own training; both would lead him to value the active life of service to the common good. *The Country Parson* confirms his orthodoxy with respect to the doctrine promulgated in courtesy books like Aegremont Ratcliffe's and in moral treatises like William Perkins'. In "The Parson's Surveys," Herbert argues that since the "great and national sin of this Land [is] Idlenesse," the parson must warn his parishioners against the vice:

> And because Idleness is twofold, the one in having no calling, the other in walking carelessly in our calling, he first represents to every body the necessity of a vocation. The reason of this assertion is taken from the nature of man, wherein God hath placed two great Instruments, Reason in the soul, and a hand in the Body, as ingagements of working: So that even in Paradise man had a calling, and how much more out of Paradise, when the evils which he is now subject unto, may be prevented, or diverted by reasonable imployment. Besides, every gift or ability is a talent to be accounted for, and to be improved to our Masters Advantage. Yet it is also a debt to our Countrey to have a Calling, and it concerns the Commonwealth, that none should be idle, but all busied. (p. 274)

The parson's reply to the scornful objection of a "Gallant" to useful work reflects the obligation of choice and the necessity for self-examination:

> Now because the onely opposer to this Doctrine is the Gallant, who is witty enough to abuse both others, and himself, and who is ready to ask, if he shall mend shoos, or what he shall do? Therfore the Parson unmoved, sheweth, that *ingenuous and fit* implyment is never wanting to those that seek it. But if it should be, the Assertion stands thus: All are either to have a Calling, or prepare for it: He that hath or can have yet no imployment, if he truly, and seriously prepare for it, he is safe and within bounds. Wherefore all are either presently to enter into a Calling, if they be fit for it, and it for them; or else to examine with care, and advice, what they are fittest for, and to prepare for that with all diligence.   (p. 275)

The doctrine of callings provides two crucial points to be taken into account in studying Herbert's vocation poems: first, although one's particular calling, finally arrived at, reflects God's unfolding purpose, the determination of it remains uncertain – yet that determination is one's own responsibility; second, the goal of this self-examination should be an active life of service to one's fellow man. Herbert's progress of choices casts light on the evident dilemma that the theory of callings must often have presented, especially to the well-born and well-educated in Herbert's time. William Perkins points out how the double source of a true calling may lead to an erroneous choice:

> Now that every man must certainly know himself to be called of God to this or that calling, he must have two things: gifts for the calling from God and allowance from men. For the first, whom God calleth, to them he giveth competent and convenient gifts, or knowledge, understanding, dexterity to this or that, and such-like; and thereby makes them able for the performance of the duties of their callings. Contrariwise, they that enter into any calling being utterly unable to perform the duties thereof, were never called of God. For the second, men are to be set apart to their particular callings by the appointment of men whom God hath left on earth as his instruments for the ordering and disposing of vocations. . . . And he that would truly say that God hath

placed him in any particular calling must also have the outward
calling of men. And here it is to be remembered that trial of gifts
and free election without partiality should be in the designment
of all, specially of public callings. . . .[9]

Herbert's own inclination toward the priesthood would need to be
tested by two essential considerations: above all, his own sense of
unworthiness for the office, but also the need for an "outward
calling" by his fellow men as God's "instruments for the ordaining
and disposing of vocations."[10]

A study of the vocation poems in the light of Herbert's biography
has only two firm reference points, those stressed in Nicholas Ferrar's preface to *The Temple:* assumption of the office of Public
Orator at Cambridge in 1619 and entrance into sacred orders at
Bemerton in 1630 – or, put in another way, the subject matter of the
first vocation poem in *The Church,* "Affliction" (I), and the last,
"Aaron." These offices point in very different directions, as Herbert's
predecessor in the Oratorship, Francis Nethersole, had warned when
Herbert was actively courting the post. Uncertainty as to God's
wishes, dominant in all the vocation poems up to "The Priesthood,"
might seem less opaque in light of the general principle that other
men are God's instruments in disposing of vocations, while Herbert's
anxiety concerning his academic employment in "Affliction" (I)
seems far more understandable in view of Perkins' comments on the
academic calling:

> Here is a special rule for all young students in the universities.
> Such as are brought up in the schools of the prophets desire to
> know what particular calling is best for them, because they have
> liberty to be either schoolmasters, physicians, or lawyers, or
> ministers of the word of God. Saint Paul, according to this
> general rule, showeth that a choice must be made of the best
> calling. And in the first place, if gifts will serve a choice must be
> made of the calling of a prophet or teacher, and that above all
> other. Academical callings must have the first place. (p. 460)

Herbert's early inclination toward the "academical calling" is
suggested by his M.A. degree and his reference to "setting foot into
Divinity, to lay the platform of my future life" in the 1617 request
that his stepfather provide him with money for books. Even his delay

in formally relinquishing the Oratorship after he had ceased to be active in the post may seem less surprising in light of Perkins' claim for the priority of academic service. Since every calling is sent by God, but not necessarily heralded by explicit and unambiguous signs, Herbert would indeed have been wise to consider any alternative form of service — even that of the cure of souls — with extreme caution. Our hindsight predisposes us to believe that from the first Herbert was dedicated to becoming an ordained priest and leads to elaborate speculations that might account for his seemingly interminable delays in taking up that office.[11] But the configuration of Herbert's search for a calling spells out a far more lengthy process of determining God's will in the matter than our wish to pinpoint a "moment of decision" or to laud his early resolve might allow. Uncertainty is built into this progress of choices; no perfect assurance follows the resolved identifications of "Aaron"; no fixed constellation finally defines the self-portrait.

ii

"The Thanksgiving," immediately following the two opening poems in *The Church*, "The Altar" and "The Sacrifice," introduces the problem of serving the heavenly King and establishes an initial portrait of God's would-be courtier. But "Affliction" (I) is the first lyric to set the problem in an extended biographical context and to stress that desire for usefulness and anxiety over delay which will become leitmotifs for all the vocation poems:

> When first thou didst entice to thee my heart,
>   I thought the service brave:
> So many joyes I writ down for my part,
>   Besides what I might have
> Out of my stock of naturall delights,
> Augmented with thy gracious benefits.
> .   .   .   .
> Whereas my birth and spirit rather took
>   The way that takes the town;
> Thou didst betray me to a lingring book
>   And wrap me in a gown.
> I was entangled in the world of strife,
> Before I had the power to change my life.

Yet, for I threatened oft the siege to raise,
> Not simpring all mine age,
Thou often didst with Academick praise
> Melt and dissolve my rage.
I took thy sweetned pill, till I came where
I could not go away, nor persevere.
> (1–6, 37–48)

Although Herbert's intention of serving God is apparent from the opening stanza, the means of that service is at issue throughout the poem. As the vocational treatises make clear, *all* callings render service to God if properly chosen and virtuously undertaken. In arguing that his "birth and spirit rather took / The way that takes the town," Herbert evokes the worldly courtier of "The Thanksgiving" and implicates himself in expectations of great place. This desire conflicts with the academic life which entangles him so that he "could not go away, nor persevere" and, even more surprisingly, represents a "world of strife."[12]

His scorn for the place – "a lingring book," "not simpering all mine age" – reveals his unwillingness to accept this as God's calling for him even as his accusation, "Thou didst betray me," admits that indeed this post might be the service God requires. The force of God's "sweetned pill" of praise in countering his sense of betrayal becomes more comprehensible when we remember William Perkins' remarks about the primacy of an academic calling. If God should so call him, Herbert has no right to decline. Yet his birth and spirit still invite him toward the active life of the governor in the humanist pattern of service to the state – great place after the model of an Andrewes or a Williams, perhaps, and still a noble service.

These explicit biographical references begin to clarify the ambiguities of the poem's opening stanzas, which unequivocally declare his commitment to God's service but also suggest a worldly setting for it. The lines "both heav'n and earth / Payd me my wages in a world of mirth" (11–12) recall Herbert's hope that an academic position such as the Oratorship "hath no such earthiness in it, but it may very well be joined with Heaven," and we also notice that here "naturall delights" are not opposed to God's "gracious benefits" but, on the contrary, augmented by them.[13] "There was no moneth but

May" further evokes the courtier who would of course assume that God's "furniture" and "houshold-stuffe" are expressly provided for his delight. In admitting that his "thoughts reserved no place for grief or fear" and that his "sudden soul caught at the place," Herbert recognizes his imprudence and impatience. Yet by blaming God for his mistaken optimism, he essentially denies his own responsibility in the matter: "Thus argu'd into hopes . . . thou gav'st me milk and sweetnesses."

The poem details the conflicting attitudes and desires that circumscribe Herbert's progress of choices and ultimately account for the afflictions and delays portrayed here with such a painful mixture of resentment on the one hand and effort to comprehend on the other. That "pil'd vanities" outweigh the "shreds of holinesse" is evident not only in his ready assumption that the goods of this world are natural perquisites of God's favor, but also in the curious syntactic parallelism of the dulling of his wit – "My mirth and edge was lost" – with what might seem far more serious causes for complaint: "Sicknesses cleave my bones . . . Sorrow was all my soul . . . my friends die."[14]

The two final stanzas establish the terms of Herbert's dilemma: "Now I am here, what thou wilt do with me / None of my books will show." The afflictions sent by God take him from his "wayes" – even the academic path in which he is so unwillingly entangled; still worse, they reduce him to a state of uncertainty and inutility. If he were a tree, he would be a worthy addition to God's "glorious houshold-stuffe," serviceable at least to other creatures; as it is, nothing is open to him except endurance of God's cross-biases. The abrupt shifts of the closing stanza model his struggle to accept and the countervailing impatience of a "sudden soul" which is as yet closer to a falcon than a tree, unacquainted with meekness and unable to realize fully that the endurance of affliction might be the exact service which God at this point requires of him:

> Yet, though thou troublest me, I must be meek;
> > In weaknesse must be stout.
> Well, I will change the service, and go seek
> > Some other master out.
> > > (61–4)

This threat is not to be taken very seriously, but the poem's concluding lines show how doubtfully Herbert regards his ability to attain the requisite humility and fortitude:

> Ah my deare God! though I am clean forgot,
> Let me not love thee, if I love thee not.
>
> (65–6)

The rebellion implied by Herbert's threat to "change the service" is substantially qualified by his wish to love God wholly even to the point of accepting His cross-biases without repining, but he conveys no assurance that he will be able to fulfill this condition.[15]

"Employment" (I) still repines. Requesting God to "extend me to some good, / Before I were by frosts extremitie / Nipt in the bud," Herbert again assumes that God's gracious benefits might augment his natural delights:

> For as thou dost impart thy grace,
> The greater shall our glorie be.
> The measure of our joyes is in this place,
> The stuffe with thee.
>
> (9–12)

The prideful assertiveness of Herbert's desire to serve God in "Affliction" (I) is heard here too, though the final stanzas sound the note of the humble soul more strongly than did the longing to be at least as useful as a tree in the earlier poem:

> Let me not languish then, and spend
> A life as barren to thy praise,
> As is the dust, to which that life doth tend,
> But with delaies.
>
> All things are busie; only I
> Neither bring hony with the bees,
> Nor flowres to make that, nor the husbandrie
> To water these.
>
> I am no link of thy great chain,
> But all my companie is a weed.
> Lord place me in thy consort; give one strain
> To my poore reed.
>
> (13–24)

Herbert places himself on the lowest level of creation in the first lines of the poem, effecting the same inversions of high place that we have noticed in Chapter 4.[16] Here, however, the means of rising is only projected as possibility. His state is one of disconnection – he is "no link," and of disharmony – he belongs to the barren company of weeds, rather than to the fruitful and well-tuned consort of creation, while his anxiety over delay is heightened by the fear that his entire life will be useless. The overt reference to great place and the courtly self-image of "Affliction" (I) are now somewhat muted: "garland" and "glory" are associated with heaven rather than earth, but since earth still might "measure" Herbert's joys, it is not entirely repudiated.

This further descent was anticipated in "Faith," two poems after "Affliction" (I), and there linked to the pattern set by Christ:

> If I go lower in the book,
> What can be lower then the common manger?
> Faith puts me there with him, who sweetly took
>   Our flesh and frailtie, death and danger.
>
> If blisse had lien in art or strength,
> None but the wise or strong had gained it:
> Where now by Faith all arms are of a length;
>   One size doth all conditions fit.
>
> A peasant may beleeve as much
> As a great Clerk, and reach the highest stature.
> Thus dost thou make proud knowledge bend & crouch,
>   While grace fills up uneven nature.
>
>   (21–32)

The value of being a "great Clerk" is here humbled even beyond the scorn that Herbert heaped on God's sweetened pill of academic praise in "Affliction" (I), and grace in this poem no longer serves simply to augment a rich store of natural delights. But this impersonal praise of lowliness does not lead Herbert to assume the position himself. The closing stanza of "Faith" presents the figure of dust as only "that which we all must come to." In "Employment" (I), however, it has become "that state, both barren and seemingly endless, which I myself experience." "Faith" depicts a certain jaunty unconcern very different from the longing to rise above the barren state in which he languishes in the latter poem:

What though my bodie runne to dust?
Faith cleaves unto it, counting evr'y grain
With an exact and most particular trust,
Reserving all for flesh again.

(41–4)

One other lyric between "Affliction" (I) and "Employment" (I) casts light on the language of inversion that marks Herbert's impatience for a useful place in God's consort. "The Temper" (I) first asks God, "Wilt thou meet arms with man, that thou dost stretch / A crumme of dust from heav'n to hell?" Then Herbert acknowledges that his state of disharmony signifies a process of necessary rectification:

Yet take thy way; for sure thy way is best:
    Stretch or contract me, thy poore debter:
This is but tuning of my breast,
    To make the musick better.

Whether I flie with angels, fall with dust,
    Thy hands made both, and I am there:
Thy power and love, my love and trust
    Make one place ev'ry where.

(21–8)

The attempt to accept God's tempering is, as we have seen, undone at once by the sudden descent to despair announced in the opening lines of "The Temper" (II) immediately following: "It cannot be. Where is that mightie joy, / Which just now took up all my heart?" And two poems later, we arrive at the impatient repining over delay in "Employment" (I).

This pattern of interconnections suggests how the vocation poems function as nodal points for the poems surrounding them, enabling us to "read" their configuration by cutting back and forth as we might read the design of constellations in the sky from star-point to star-point. Reading from one poem to another enables us to track backslidings and advances in the uneven course of Herbert's search for a calling. But each poem also reaches out to surrounding poems to contextualize images of Herbert's spiritual state at any given moment of the sequence. When one poem cancels the resolution of another, as the opening of "The Temper" (II) radically undoes the serene assurance in the final lines of "The Temper" (I), we are given no means of "placing" such emotional shifts in any direct biographical sense: yet the juxtaposition unites the "I" of both poems by disjoining Herbert's emotional states.[17]

The vocation poems create context: the anxiety over delay stretches Herbert's alternating emotions over the time that uses up an entire life, while his wish to be serviceable to God projects a pattern for that life which in the doctrine of callings is not only desirable but necessary. Still the vocation poems are only points, nodes of meaning in a network or configuration, requiring the more detailed articulation of Herbert's condition in the poems surrounding them for a full interpretation.[18] In this sense, their meaning is partial and fragmentary, depending finally not only on the constellation of which each is a part, but also on the entire sequence – "All the constellations in the storie."[19]

At no point does the sequence trace a smooth advance in insight or a steadily unfolding comprehension of Herbert's means of service to God. "Praise" (I) again contrasts the state of inutility with the serviceable function of the lowest of God's creatures and laments the continuation of delay.[20] Like "Employment" (I), this poem qualifies the apparent assent to a lowly state in "Faith":

> To write a verse or two is all the praise,
> > That I can raise:
> > Mend my estate in any wayes,
> > Thou shalt have more.
>
> I go to Church; help me to wings, and I
> > Will thither flie;
> > Or, if I mount unto the skie,
> > I will do more.
>
> Man is all weaknesse; there is no such thing
> > As Prince or King:
> > His arm is short; yet with a sling
> > He may do more.
>
> An herb destill'd, and drunk, may dwell next doore,
> > On the same floore,
> > To a brave soul: exalt the poore,
> > They can do more.

O raise me then! Poore bees, that work all day,
        Sting my delay,
    Who have a work, as well as they,
        And much, much more.

Here, the request to "Mend my estate" and the appeal "O raise me then" sound much more like the courtier who considers God's service "brave" in the early stanzas of "Affliction" (I) than the humbled "great Clerk" of "Faith" who realizes that if he goes "lower in the book" his model is Christ in the common manger. Though it is true that "there is no such thing / As Prince or King," God's help can not only "exalt the poore" but raise Herbert; and if his estate is mended, God will benefit – "Thou shalt have more." The pious denial of secular power has given way to an aspiration with a distinct taint of worldliness. Herbert's offer of benefits to God recalls his courtly propositions in "The Thanksgiving":

    If thou dost give me wealth, I will restore
    All back unto thee by the poore.
    If thou dost give me honour, men shall see,
    The honour doth belong to thee.
                                (19–22)

"Content," however, moves in a direction quite contrary to the active aspiration of the earlier vocation poems:

    Peace mutt'ring thoughts, and do not grudge to keep
        Within the walls of your own breast:
    who cannot on his own bed sweetly sleep,
        Can on anothers hardly rest.

    Gad not abroad at ev'ry quest and call
        Of an untrained hope or passion.
    To court each place or fortune that doth fall,
        Is wantonnesse in contemplation.
            .   .   .   .
    Give me the pliant minde, whose gentle measure
        Complies and suits with all estates;
    Which can let loose to a crown, and yet with pleasure
        Take up within a cloisters gates.

> This soul doth span the world, and hang content
> From either pole unto the centre:
> Where in each room of the well-furnisht tent
> He lies warm, and without adventure.
>   (1–8, 13–20)

The opening lines again depict a worldly courtier, but here the aspiration for great place is treated with reductive scorn in the image of a seeker for preferment gadding about indiscriminately looking for any "place or fortune" that might come to hand. Such efforts are not only ignorant – "untrained" – but even worse, intemperate, "wanton" in contemplation if not in act.

Contrasted with this figure of excessive and undirected ambition is the "gentle measure" of the "pliant minde," which is self-sufficient, like fire in flints, but also capable of suiting with "all estates," no more tempted by the crown than by the cloister.[21] This reference to Charles V, the most famous Renaissance example of the contemplative choice and a favorite subject of the Ferrar family's formal "conversations" at Little Gidding, links "Content" to the exemplars as well as to the vocational choices of Herbert's own circle of acquaintance.

The biographical context cannot explain, but may cast some light on a poem whose concerns seem, on any reading, to point in a rather different direction from the clearly defined path of divinity that will be declared in "The Priesthood" and adopted in "Aaron." The "mutt'ring thoughts" that Herbert rejects in "Content" concern worldly "place or fortune," both in his reductive image of the courtier seeking preferment in the second stanza and in his relinquishment of the desire for fame – "Onely thy Chronicle is lost" – in stanzas seven and eight. The "nourisht fame" that results from noble deeds worthy to be chronicled by others was considered, in both courtesy books and vocational treatises, a suitable aspiration for the nobly born: great deeds serve the common good and provide an exemplary model for others. Here, however, Herbert attacks the desire for fame from both worldly and heavenly perspectives. In the light of eternity, the huge king is leveled with the peasant to no more than decaying flesh, while in the light of earthly history, the power of others' pens and tongues to gnaw a reputation to pieces can convert fame into infamy – an argument hardly foreign to Edward Herbert or to Ben Jonson in their later days.

The conclusion of "Content" implies a life of contemplative retirement in the service of personal growth, much closer to Sidney's argument for "thorough self-examination" as the highest form of activity in his defensive letter to Languet, or to the comfortable simplicity of country life celebrated by Caroline poets,[22] than the way of humble service to a small village of farmers that Herbert finally chose at Bemerton. Yet this poem's great place and courtly ambitions are reversed once more in the tone of active aspiration heard in the opening stanzas of "Employment" (II):

> He that is weary, let him sit.
> My soul would stirre
> And trade in courtesies and wit,
> Quitting the furre
> To cold complexions needing it.
>
> Man is no starre, but a quick coal
> Of mortall fire:
> Who blows it not, nor doth controll
> A faint desire,
> Lets his own ashes choke his soul.
> . . . .
> Oh that I were an Orenge-tree,
> That busie plant!
> Then should I ever laden be,
> And never want
> Some fruit for him that dressed me.
>
> But we are still too young or old;
> The Man is gone,
> Before we do our wares unfold:
> So we freeze on,
> Untill the grave increase our cold.
> (1–10, 21–30)

"Trad[ing] in courtesies and wit," rather than being scornfully viewed as gadding about in an effort to realize wanton desires for any place or fortune that might turn up, now signifies the assumption of one's rightful station in God's hierarchy. The element of "mortal fire" in aspiring man simply reflects God's will, which "Ordain'd the highest to be best": Herbert's desire to put his courtesies and wit to use is perceived as a right and proper service to God. In wishing that he might "never want / Some fruit for him that dressed me," he once more claims that the best means to honor God would be God's bestowal of honor upon him – the same ambition that has flickered in and out of these poems since "The Thanksgiving."

The poem is a curious mixture of humbleness and hauteur. Herbert still recognizes that he is less useful than the lowest level of creation, yet he longs to raise himself above that level. The conclusion engulfs his longing in the fear of being reduced to a nearly inanimate state: "freez[ing] on," unblessed by a purpose, lower than the vegetative level of created life. The break-up of verse in "Deniall," immediately following, disintegrates Herbert's easy assumption that he belongs in man's superior place at the top of creation, only a little lower than the angels:

> O that thou shouldst give dust a tongue
> To crie to thee,
> And then not heare it crying!
>
> (16–18)

Lowliness, here, is not welcomed as it was in "Faith," but rather resisted with all the pride of one who would cast off the role that God has assigned him.

These poems prepare us for the halting course of Herbert's progress of choices in the long midsection of *The Church*. The courtier aspiring to great place in order to render back to God the honor that he hopes God will bestow upon him, the great clerk who would reject the sweetened pill of academic praise in favor of a descent to the exalted lowliness of Christ in the common manger, the seeker after self-knowledge and self-sufficiency remote from the strife, indignity, and ephemerality of worldly position: all are potential models of Herbert's service to God, projections of possibility weighed and considered in the manner recommended by the vocational treatises, including Herbert's own brief essay on the subject in *The Country Parson*. Aspiration for great place need not, of course, have signified a rejection of divinity in favor of strictly secular "employment"; Herbert's worldly exemplars were far more likely to have been men like Lancelot Andrewes, Bishop of Winchester and member of the Privy Council, John Williams, Bishop of Lincoln and Keeper of the Great Seal, or John Donne, Dean of St. Paul's and preacher of sermons to his King.[23]

The alternatives implied in the early vocation poems of *The Church* weigh position in the world – an active life attended with honor – against a rejection of the world, in "Content," which might entail either the cloistered life that a community like Little Gidding represented to its members as well as to its visitors,[24] or the retired life in pursuit of self-knowledge free from the "press of men" that grew more attractive in the period as the world of strife increased its pressures.[25] The uncertainty figured by these alternating choices and conflicting attitudes partially accounts for the long span of poems preceding the first explicit reference to Herbert's ultimate choice of a calling in "The Priesthood." But that uncertainty rests also upon the condition that one's calling depends on God's will as well as man's inclination. The following section examines the process of retreat and advance through which Herbert apprehends the painfully slow unfolding of God's purpose for him.

iii

The vocation poems speak over and over of delay as Herbert obsessively re-examines his longing for service and his inability to discover its precise and proper form. These obsessive repetitions transform his early recognition that God requires him to be patient in adversity, humble in lowliness, constant even in idleness into an exercising of these virtues rather than a mere acknowledgment of their value. Each new attack on the problem of service sets it within a fresh configuration of images and imagined responses, thus constituting an advance of sorts.

But the lack of advance is more striking, and ultimately far more important in this long recital of the complications that stand in Herbert's way. The sense of duration that dominates his reaction to his condition within this portion of *The Church*, like the minuteness of his gains, attests the cost of his effort to comprehend the service required of him. What seems to have been learned in one poem is a problem still to be mastered ten leaves off, as the resolute rejection of the world in "Content," but renewal of worldly aspiration in "Employment" (II), would suggest.

"The Pearl" represents a genuine advance. Herbert's elaborate rejections of Learning, Honor, and Pleasure now put in first-person particularity what he has already claimed in the third-person

asseveration of "Vanitie" (II): these worldly pursuits neither lead
him to God nor represent the knowledge that God requires him to
gain. These "ways," so well-known, so long possessed ("I . . . have
them in my hand"), configure an academic, a courtier, a pleasure-
lover. The second stanza is especially telling in its echoes of earlier poems:

> I know the wayes of Honour, what maintains
> The quick returns of courtesie and wit:
> In vies of favours whether partie gains,
> When glorie swells the heart, and moldeth it
> To all expressions both of hand and eye,
> Which on the world a true-love-knot may tie,
> And bear the bundle, wheresoe're it goes:
> How many drammes of spirit there must be
> To sell my life unto my friends or foes:
> > Yet I love thee.
> > > (11–20)

The echo of "Employment" (II), where Herbert's soul "would
stirre, / And trade in courtesies and wit," marks a shift in his attitude
toward the worldly gifts which, earlier, he would devote to God's
service. Here he discovers their complicity in mortal desires for glory;
they are only so many "drammes of spirit" useful not in the service of
God but in servitude to corrupt worldly ends – "To sell my life unto
my friends or foes." The self-disgust here anticipates the insight in
"Jordan" (II) that all Herbert's "curling metaphors" are but "Decking the sense, as if it were to sell." Each stanza's nine lines entirely
encompass Herbert's world, bundling it into a "true-love-knot" of
entanglement. Yet that world of possessive attachment is poised
against the four-word refrain that gives the weight to Herbert's love
of God.

The final stanza explains the alteration in perspective that has led
to these judgments:

> I know all these, and have them in my hand:
> Therefore not sealed, but with open eyes
> I flie to thee, and fully understand
> Both the main sale, and the commodities;
> And at what rate and price I have thy love;
> With all the circumstances that may move:

> Yet through these labyrinths, not my groveling wit,
> But thy silk twist let down from heav'n to me,
> Did both conduct and teach me, how by it
>   To climbe to thee.
>
>   (31–40)

Where in "Affliction" (I), these labyrinthine temptations had been perceived as God's maze entangling him in the world of strife, here Herbert finally assigns the labyrinths, like his "groveling wit," to the world: the movement of ascent required of him – the rate and price of God's love – depends upon a reciprocal descent of God's silk twist by which he might escape his self-made maze.[26]

"Affliction" (IV), placing him in the ambiguous space "Betwixt this world and that of grace," confirms that the knot of earthly entanglements in which his thoughts enmesh him are of his own making, not God's:

> Broken in pieces all asunder,
>   Lord, hunt me not,
>   A thing forgot,
> Once a poore creature, now a wonder,
>   A wonder tortur'd in the space
>   Betwixt this world and that of grace.
>
> . . . .
>
> Oh help, my God! let not their plot
>   Kill them and me,
>   And also thee,
> Who art my life: dissolve the knot,
>   As the sunne scatters by his light
>   All the rebellions of the night.
>
> Then shall those powers, which work for grief,
>   Enter thy pay,
>   And day by day
> Labour thy praise, and my relief;
>   With care and courage building me,
>   Till I reach heav'n, and much more, thee.
>
>   (1–6, 19–30)

The means of ascent out of this world and into the world of grace is now perceived with a certain clarity as an ordered, ceremonious, but above all *continual* process.

The ascent envisioned in "The Pearl" and "Affliction" (IV) not only rejects the worldly implications of "courtesies and wit" but also marks a substantial advance in his understanding. God, reciprocating Herbert's desire, reaches down to him. Although his own unassisted efforts are insufficient to the task, he begins to see that he need not remain entrapped by the circumference of earth that has enclosed him since "The Sinner." "Rising" is no longer linked to Herbert's desire for great place in the world that he might render honor back to God. In this new light, he begins to perceive God's cross-biases as an aid to ascent rather than a "hurling down" that condemns him to the limits of mortality.

"Submission" shows the gain that has been made but retreats once more to Herbert's earlier desire for great place:

> But that thou are my wisdome, Lord,
>   And both mine eyes are thine,
> My minde would be extreamly stirr'd
>   For missing my designe.
>
> Were it not better to bestow
>   Some place and power on me?
> Then should thy praises with me grow,
>   And share in my degree.
>
> But when I thus dispute and grieve,
>   I do resume my sight,
> And pilfring what I once did give,
>   Disseize thee of thy right.
>
> How know I, if thou shouldst me raise,
>   That I should then raise thee?
> Perhaps great places and thy praise
>   Do not so well agree.
>
> Wherefore unto my gift I stand;
>   I will no more advise:
> Onely do thou lend me a hand,
>   Since thou hast both mine eyes.

"Place and power" still represent appropriate means of rendering service to God, though he now at least conditionally – "Perhaps" – acknowledges that great place might be antithetical to his desire that his calling praise God. In promising "I will no more advise," we might think that Herbert has not only relinquished his longing for great place but also given over the decision wholly to God. But the movement of submission is no more than momentary, as the following poem, "Justice" (I), admits.[27] The structure weighs God's perplexing ways against Herbert's own, first repining, "Lord, thou didst make me, yet thou woundest me," only to confess:

> But when I mark my life and praise,
>   Thy justice me most fitly payes:
> For, *I do praise thee, yet I praise thee not:*
> *My prayers mean thee, yet my prayers stray:*
> *I would do well, yet sinne the hand hath got:*
> *My soul doth love thee, yet it loves delay.*
>   I cannot skill of these my wayes.
>
> (6–12)

Both "Submission" and "Justice" (I) develop the double perspective introduced in "The Pearl," embracing God's purpose as well as Herbert's inclination. They continue the attempt to understand his afflictions and delays as a process of construction rather than destruction, "building him with care." "Justice" (I) is followed by "Charms and Knots" where, as we have noted, the couplet "Who looks on ground with humble eyes, / Findes himself there, and seeks to rise" points out the right relation between humility and aspiration. "Affliction" (V) then attempts to see the problem first raised in "Affliction" (I) in "this new light":[28]

> At first we liv'd in pleasure;
> Thine own delights thou didst to us impart:
> When we grew wanton, thou didst use displeasure
> To make us thine. . . .
>
> (7–10)

The figure of affliction which follows dissociates Herbert from the "knot of man" in "Home" whose soul is "pinion'd with mortalitie, / . . . an intangled, hamper'd thing":

> Affliction then is ours;
> We are the trees, whom shaking fastens more,
> While blustring windes destroy the wanton bowres,
> And ruffle all their curious knots and store.
>
> (19–22)

To welcome affliction in this manner is to relinquish the courtly desire for "place and power." "Wanton bowres" and "curious knots" *are* destroyed by affliction and, implicitly, ought to be; Herbert would be the tree fastened all the more stably by endurance of shaking afflictions. Here he accepts the humbling descent which, in "Faith," could link him with the lowliness of Christ but, in "Employment" (I), plunged him into the barren company of weeds and dust, denying the possibility of useful service to God entirely.

"Miserie" then dramatizes Herbert's attempt to welcome affliction as a necessary corrective to his worldliness in an extraordinary shift from third-person denunciation to first-person confession. Herbert commences by addressing God and presuming to share His judgment of man: "Lord, let the Angels praise thy name / Man is a foolish thing, a foolish thing." The aspiration to serve God is demolished utterly in the reduction of man to the base state suitable to his preferred pleasures:

> Man cannot serve thee; let him go,
> And serve the swine: there, there is his delight:
> He doth not like this vertue, no;
> Give him his dirt to wallow in all night. . . .
>
> (43–6)

He shifts to direct accusatory address — "Ah wretch! what verse / Can thy strange ways rehearse?" — and in the final stanzas neatly balances the "Glorie and grace" of man's first creation against the extent of his fall into sin. "Now he is / A lump of flesh, without a foot or wing / To raise him to a glimpse of blisse." But the superior stance from which Herbert makes this eloquent indictment dissolves absolutely in the plain admission of the final line:

> My God, I mean my self.

"Miserie" represents a nodal point for the poems surrounding it in the same way as "The Pearl" and "Submission." By introducing the possibility that Herbert's labyrinths are of his own devising and that God might reach His silk twist down to assist Herbert to rise, "The Pearl" enabled him in the following poems to entertain the possibility that God might in fact be building him, rather than hurling him down and tearing him to pieces. By disjoining his longing for great place from his desire to serve God, "Submission" led to a re-examination of perspective in the following poems, as Herbert weighed his inclinations against his intimations of God's purpose. "Miserie" betrays the prideful self who so easily indicts mankind in general; it is this particular self, not "all those others," who is unfit to serve God.[29] The confession marks a turn in Herbert's handling of affliction and leads to successive attempts to bring himself into harmony with God's wishes for him, as in his request in "Obedience," "Let me not think an action mine own way, / But as thy love shall sway, / Resigning up the rudder to thy skill." "Prayer" (II) shows that the relinquishment of worldliness is still a halting process. Here, as in "Submission," Herbert contemplates it conditionally:

> I value prayer so,
> That were I to leave all but one,
> Wealth, fame, endowments, vertues, all should go. . . .
> (20–2)

This curious list betrays Herbert's stubborn attachment to worldly values in their implied equation with "vertues." The positive drive for "destroying that which ty'd thy purse," sin, is contaminated by the worldly aspirations so hesitantly offered up in exchange for prayer.

"The Quip" once more configures Herbert's academic great place and the gallant courtier in an attempt less conditional than that of "Prayer" (II) to turn his choices over to God, with its confident refrain, "*But thou shalt answer, Lord, for me.*" The allegorical fancifulness of the poem mingles oddly with the autobiographical image of Wit and Conversation:

> Then came quick Wit and Conversation,
> And he would needs a comfort be,
> And, to be short, make an Oration.
> *But thou shalt answer, Lord, for me.*
> (17–20)

But such a deliberate identification suggests that Beauty, Money, and brave Glory "puffing by / In silks that whistled" – now so decisively placed outside the self – may also have been temptations for Herbert, however much we would like to believe that he was always too holy for such worldly matters to be a trouble to him.

These assured rejections might definitively separate Herbert's now humbled soul from the gadding courtier of "Content" who trades in courtesies and wit in "Employment" (II). The distancing of his image as Orator, far more controlled than the "noise of thoughts" in "The Familie" or the rebellious faculties of "Affliction" (IV), would tend to confirm his increasing freedom from worldly entanglements. But "Vanitie" (II), immediately thereafter, shows him still enmeshed in the "flat delights" of earth:

> Poore silly soul, whose hope and head lies low;
> Whose flat delights on earth do creep and grow;
> To whom the starres shine not so fair, as eyes;
> Nor solid work, as false embroyderies;
> Heark and beware, lest what you now do measure
> And write for sweet, prove a most sowre displeasure.
>
> (1–6)

"Dialogue" and "Dulnesse" confirm the state of contradiction. In "Dialogue," Herbert seems to take responsibility for the apparent lack of "gains" from God: "I disclaim the whole designe: / Sinne disclaims and I resigne." But "Dulnesse" once more longs for courtesy and wit, echoing the bitter repining at their loss – "a blunted knife / Was of more use then I" – of "Affliction" (I):

> Why do I languish thus, drooping and dull,
>   As if I were all earth?
> O give me quicknesse, that I may with mirth
>   Praise thee brim-full!
>
> (1–4)

Herbert wishes once again here for at least as much quickness and mirth as the "wanton lover" can muster to praise his "fairest fair," yet the circumference of earth still surrounds him:

> But I am lost in flesh, whose sugred lyes
>   Still mock me, and grow bold:
> Sure thou didst put a minde there, if I could
>   Finde where it lies.
>
> (21–4)

The conclusion of "Dulnesse," however, states a moderated desire far more appropriate to the humble soul lost in flesh and unable to discover, let alone make use of, the mind that God has given him than the easy assurance in "The Quip" that Beauty, Money, Glory, and Wit-and-Conversation can all be answered by God in Herbert's place:

> Lord, cleare thy gift, that with a constant wit
> I may but look towards thee:
> *Look* onely; for to *love* thee, who can be,
> What angel fit?
>
> (25–8)

This humble aspiration accords with Herbert's confession that he is unfit to serve God in "Miserie" and his admission in "Dialogue" that he is so "full of staines" that his soul is not "worth the having." "Sinnes Round," modeling in its repetitive form the stasis in which Herbert has imprisoned himself, completes the recognition that it is Herbert, rather than God, who creates the delay – "Words suffice not where are lewd intentions." The silk twist let down by God that Herbert might climb in "The Pearl," like God's careful building of Herbert till he might reach heaven in "Affliction" (IV), is undone by the entirely opposite construction of the worldly self: "my sinnes ascend three stories high, / As Babel grew. . . ."

To confess responsibility is also to discover insufficiency because, as "Giddinesse" puts it, man needs God's hand in the building:[30]

> Lord, mend or rather make us: one creation
> Will not suffice our turn:
> Except thou make us dayly, we shall spurn
> Our own salvation.
>
> (25–8)

In "Sinnes Round" Herbert is isolated from God, "lost in flesh" where his "offences course it in a ring" just as his emblematic poem returns to its beginning, "Sorrie I am, my God, sorrie I am." He can only build the towering structure of sins that the poems we have been considering represent. But in their obsessive repetition of the same complaints, they begin to redefine the meaning of delay – the subject of Herbert's repinings ever since "Affliction" (I) and the signifier that he is still lost in the worldly perspective.

"Time," immediately following "Sinnes Round," traces the same process of self-delusion and discovery that we have seen in "Miserie." In all assurance, Herbert points out to Time that, since Christ's coming, he is no longer an executioner, but rather an usher "to convey our souls / Beyond the utmost starres and poles." As the impatience to be done with earthly trials bursts out in "Home," so it does in "Time":

> And this is that makes life so long,
> While it detains us from our God.
> Ev'n pleasures here increase the wrong,
> And length of dayes lengthen the rod.
>   Who wants the place, where God doth dwell,
>   Partakes already half of hell.
>
> Of what strange length must that needs be,
> Which ev'n eternitie excludes!
>   (19–26)

But Time undermines Herbert's pretensions:

> Thus farre Time heard me patiently:
> Then chafing said, This man deludes:
>   What do I here before his doore?
>   He doth not crave lesse time, but more.
>   (27–30)

"The Bunch of Grapes" confirms Time's insight by admitting that delay has, thus far, constituted no progress at all:

> Joy, I did lock thee up: but some bad man
>   Hath let thee out again:
> And now, me thinks, I am where I began
>   Sev'n yeares ago: one vogue and vein,
>   One aire of thoughts usurps my brain.
> I did towards Canaan draw; but now I am
> Brought back to the Red sea, the sea of shame.
>   (1–7)

Although the scriptural story of the Jews spans each Christian's journey, "pennes and sets us down," Herbert's own pathway circles upon itself rather than crossing over to Canaan:

> But where's the cluster? where's the taste
> Of mine inheritance? Lord, if I must borrow,
> Let me as well take up their joy, as sorrow.
>
> (19–21)

There is no need to puzzle out the exact years to which this poem might refer in order to comprehend the function of such a pointed time signature in the very middle of the *Church* sequence. Herbert is measuring the intensity of delay by giving it an exact span: seven years of repetitive building of a tower of sins, seven years of impatience to take up joy as well as sorrow, seven years that comprise an imprisoning circle as absolute as that traced linguistically in "Sinnes Round."

As "Time" has implied, however, from the heavenly perspective delay means time enough – to remake Herbert, to restore God's image, to transform the worldly courtier into a fit servant of God. The final stanza of "The Bunch of Grapes" suggests that the means of remaking derives from the acceptance of affliction in time, after the model set by Christ:

> But can he want the grape, who hath the wine?
>   I have their fruit and more.
> Blessed by God, who prosper'd *Noahs* vine.
>   And made it bring forth grapes good store.
>   But much more him I must adore,
> Who of the Laws sowre juice sweet wine did make,
> Ev'n God himself being pressed for my sake.
>
> (22–8)

This recognition circles back to the problem of imitating a model so different from worldly kings that Herbert had posed, but been unable to resolve, in "The Thanksgiving": "But how then shall I imitate thee, and / Copie thy fair, though bloudie hand?" If the seven years measure Herbert's lack of progress up to this point in *The Church*, the poems following "The Bunch of Grapes" in some sense represent a new beginning. The following section traces the progress growing out of Herbert's attempt to take up Christ's sorrow rather than the joy that he would have reserved to himself, if only he could have gained it, throughout the seven years' worth of poems now dismissed as "Sinnes Round."

iv

Herbert's fruitless attempts to resist the imperatives of affliction now give way to a converse effort to accept affliction after the model of Christ. St. Ambrose, whose vocational shift from secular to sacred service might well have made him an exemplar for Herbert, suggests how difficult that "true fortitude" required of "Christ's warrior" may be to achieve: "Or does that call to fortitude seem to thee but a poor one: 'Tribulation worketh patience, and patience, experience, and experience, hope'? . . . Entangle not thyself in the affairs of this life, for thou art fighting for God."[31] St. Ambrose argues that there is "a blessedness even in pains and griefs" (p. 45); it is this blessedness to which Herbert, still entangled in the affairs of this life, can only assent as a proposition until he finally extracts the essential blessing out of the experienced pains and griefs of the poems following "The Bunch of Grapes."

His tribulations up to this point have clearly not yet led to the development of patience, nor have his efforts to avoid tribulation produced any fruit other than increased anguish. But in "Love unknown," following directly after "The Bunch of Grapes," he sees that, from God's perspective, the afflictions of his "foul," "hard," and "dull" heart belong to that process of "mending and making" that he had, in "Giddinesse," begun to envision: *All did but strive to mend, what you had marr'd.*

As St. Ambrose advises, Herbert has been attempting to disentangle himself from the world, though we have seen how doubtful his gains in that respect have been. His recognition in "Mans medley" that "Mans joy and pleasure / Rather hereafter, then in present, is" recalls, but now frees him from, his earlier worldly attachment in "Employment" (I), where he could still say that "The measure of our joyes is in this place." The "throbbing conscience spurred by remorse" that quits the earth to besiege God in "The Storm" also leaves behind earthly attachments: "Glorie and honour are set by, till it / An answer get." Here, as in "Love unknown," affliction is perceived to be beneficial, and we can assume that among the poets who have misunderstood its value is Herbert himself: "Poets have wrong'd poore storms: such dayes are best, / They purge the aire without, within the breast." And "Paradise," whose transposition of cutting into healing we have already noticed, follows appropriately in this cluster of lyrics that work out Herbert's acceptance of the state of affliction.

Just as the initial rejection of earthly "goods" in "The Pearl" depended upon Herbert's realization that God's reciprocal action of reaching down His silk twist might help him climb toward the world of grace, and just as, in "The Bunch of Grapes," the contemplation of "Ev'n God himself being pressed for my sake" enabled him to accept the value of affliction in the following poems, so the image of a kingly God grieved for His humble servant in "Ephes. 4. 30." inspires the effort to emulate his Lord:

> And art thou grieved, sweet and sacred Dove,
>> When I am sowre,
>> And crosse thy love?
> Grieved for me? the God of strength and power
>> Griev'd for a worm, which when I tread,
>> I passe away and leave it dead?
>> (1–6)

The effort is put in language as elegant as any love poet's, yet Herbert reserves something to himself, sets a limit upon his capacity for grief:

> O take thy lute, and tune it to a strain,
>> Which may with thee
>> All day complain.
> There can be no discord but in ceasing be.
>> Marbles can weep; and surely strings
>> More bowels have, then such hard things.
>
> Lord, I adjudge my self to tears and grief,
>> Ev'n endlesse tears
>> Without relief.
> If a cleare spring for me no time forbears,
>> But runnes, although I be not drie;
>> I am no Crystall, what shall I?
>
> Yet if I wail not still, since still to wail
>> Nature denies;
>> And flesh would fail,
> If my deserts were masters of mine eyes:
>> Lord, pardon, for thy Sonne makes good
>> My want of tears with store of bloud.
>> (19–36)

He is unwilling to allow his deserts to master his eyes completely; if "Nature denies," he is still identifying himself with the state of nature, rather than ascending out of it toward the world of grace. But the measuring of his ability to accept affliction against that of Christ maintains the connection between him and that higher world which he had recognized in "The Pearl"; as he will put it in "The Glimpse," "a slender thread a gentle guest will tie."

In "The Size," a similar comparison with Christ enables him finally to disentangle himself from the earlier aspiration to great place:

> Content thee, greedie heart.
> Modest and moderate joyes to those, that have
> Title to more hereafter when they part,
> > Are passing brave.
> Let th' upper springs into the low
> Descend and fall, and thou dost flow.
>
> What though some have a fraught
> Of cloves and nutmegs, and in cinamon sail;
> If thou hast wherewithall to spice a draught,
> > When griefs prevail;
> And for the future time art heir
> To th' Isle of spices, is 't not fair?
>
> To be in both worlds full
> Is more then God was, who was hungrie here.
> Wouldst thou his laws of fasting disanull?
> > Enact good cheer?
> Lay out thy joy, yet hope to save it?
> Wouldst thou both eat thy cake, and have it?
>
> Great joyes are all at once;
> But little do reserve themselves for more:
> Those have their hopes; these what they have renounce,
> > And live on score:
> Those are at home; these journey still,
> And meet the rest on Sions hill.
>
> Thy Saviour sentenc'd joy,
> And in the flesh condemn'd it as unfit,
> At least in lump: for such doth oft destroy;
> > Whereas a bit
> Doth tice us on to hopes of more,
> And for the present health restore.

> A Christians state and case
> Is not a corpulent, but a thinne and spare,
> Yet active strength: whose long and bonie face
>   Content and care
>   Do seem to equally divide,
>   Like a pretender, not a bride.
>
>   Wherefore sit down, good heart;
> Grasp not at much, for fear thou losest all.
> If comforts fell according to desert,
>   They would great frosts and snows destroy:
>   For we should count, Since the last joy.
>
>   Then close again the seam,
> Which thou hast open'd: do not spread thy robe
> In hope of great things. Call to minde thy dream,
>   An earthly globe,
>   On whose meridian was engraven,
>   *These seas are tears, and heav'n the haven.*

Herbert has not, since "The Thanksgiving," directly associated his hope of "great things" with his desire to imitate Christ. The orderly measuring out of "modest and moderate joyes" against the "Title to more hereafter," the weighing of his wish to be "in both worlds full" against Christ's willingness to be "hungrie here," and the contrast between a journey that ends on Sion's hill and one which, in its greed for "Great joyes . . . all at once" must find its only home on earth – all define Herbert's ends by placing them in the perspective of Christ's practice rather than man's.

Even the tone of this address to the self, with its encouraging "sit down, good heart," is markedly different from the scorn and impatience we have heard earlier. There is a certain gentle humor in Herbert's image of the thin and spare Christian in whose long and bony face content and care are equally divided.[32] This implied self-portrait balances the opposites that have driven him up to this point with an equanimity which "equals" a genuine acceptance of care instead of a merely pious self-exhortation. The finality with which he enjoins himself to "close again the seam, / Which thou hast open'd" suggests that he is looking back over the span of years in which he has aspired to great things. The new self-image, so distant from "The Sinner" or "The Thanksgiving," allows a perspective that now links him sufficiently to the world of grace to enable him to reduce not only his own past desires, but the whole world, merely to a globe in a dream.

"The Size" functions as a nodal point in the decisive shift in attitude marked in all the poems that, since "The Bunch of Grapes," have welcomed affliction and begun to compare Herbert's spiritual state with the exemplary model of Christ. It returns to the same issue raised in the poems preceding "The Bunch of Grapes" — his impatience at delay and his urging that God should raise him so that Herbert might serve Him in a fashion suitable to his estate. But here the return signals a departure from the obsessive repetitions of the earlier poems. His serene acceptance of care as well as content denotes a sober realism concerning the earthly condition which identifies "The Size" as a point of genuine advance, for the first time suggesting that he has learned to consider his griefs "nothing beyond what is natural" to his mortal condition.[33]

Once Herbert has reached this point of understanding, he is able to promise God, in "Artillerie," that "I will do or suffer what I ought." He does continue to suffer, for he is not done with either complaining or aspiring upward to heaven. But the emphasis is now on giving himself to God rather than imposing his will upon Him: although his tears and prayers "wooe, / And work up to thee," even if "thou shunnest, I am thine." "The Discharge" gives over all anxiety about his future into God's hands in a further undoing of the knot of earthly entanglements which reverses the querulous anxiety of his early complaint, in "Affliction" (I), that "What thou wouldst do with me / None of my books will show":

> Hast thou not made thy counts, and summ'd up all?
> Did not thy heart
> Give up the whole, and with the whole depart?
> Let what will fall:
> That which is past who can recall?
>
> Thy life is Gods, thy time to come is gone,
> And is his right.
> . . . . .
> Either grief will not come: or if it must,
> Do not forecast.
> And while it cometh, it is almost past,
> Away distrust:
> My God hath promis'd; he is just.
>   (6–12, 51–5)

These poems exercise fortitude – not as a magical point after which Herbert's attitudes are suddenly reversed entirely, but as a process which must be worked out again and again, one of endurance and duration of affliction rather than its instant conversion into joy. Herbert's delay has become God's time – "his right." Grief, no less than joy, may be one of those "present things requir'd of thee."

Yet as Ambrose points out, "What so difficult as . . . to despise what one has decided to be worthless, as of no good?" Even the seam closed with such finality in "The Size" is opened once more in "The Collar":

> Shall I still be in suit?
> Have I no harvest but a thorn
> To let me bloud . . .
>
> . . . .
>
> Is the yeare onely lost to me?
> Have I no bayes to crown it?
> No flowers, no garlands gay? all blasted?
> All wasted?
> (6–8, 13–16)

The relationship of "The Collar" to "The Size" confirms the uneven and sometimes crab-like nature of Herbert's progress. But it also suggests the inadequacy of a term like "sequence" to account for the way the vocation poems function in the structure of *The Church*. "The Collar" yields one meaning in its position a few leaves after "The Size" and a few leaves before "The Priesthood." If, as is usually assumed, its title refers to the clerical collar, it points toward the explicit choice of divinity asserted in "The Priesthood," recounting a determined effort to pull away from that path.[34] Herbert's inclinations toward worldly bays and garlands are poised against the "inward enforcements" implied by God's call to his "child" in the concluding lines, and "The Collar" refers also to the "caller" whom Herbert at first resists.

If, however, we read the vocation poems as configuration rather than sequence, the most useful referent for "The Collar" is neither "The Size" nor "The Priesthood" but rather "The Thanksgiving," many leaves away indeed at the beginning of the *Church* sequence. "The Collar" recapitulates Herbert's courtly self-depiction in the earlier poem, again contrasting Christ's attributes with the worldly perquisites of the courtier. Whereas in "The Thanksgiving" Herbert

is conscious primarily of their incongruity, in "The Collar" the loss
of flowers and gay garlands and the possession of "no harvest but a
thorn" are bitterly resisted. He is now able to realize the full impact
of their loss and to face his regret with a far sturdier honesty than he
could even conceive in the earlier poem.

The conclusions of the two poems also measure out a progress
that we could not recognize simply by reading "The Collar" in
sequence and noting its backsliding to a problem which had seemed
solved in "The Size." Herbert's ambitious catalogue of offerings to
match Christ in "The Thanksgiving" concludes with a baffled admission that the task is impossible: "Then for thy passion – I will do for
that – / Alas, my God, I know not what." "The Collar," however,
closes in a movement of dependence, thus achieving the reciprocity
that had been unimaginable in the earlier poem: the "doing" here
rests in and responds to God, even though, and in fact precisely
because, Herbert is unequal to the task.[35]

In "The Priesthood," on the other hand, there is no hint of any
calling from God at all. But here, for the first time, Herbert is able to
assemble the images that have defined his separation from God into a
pattern capacious enough to comprehend both his actual position –
the barren and useless state of a crumb of dust – and his aspiration to
serve. At the same time he accepts the necessity to wait upon God's
use of him rather than himself setting the terms of service and
determining the time of its inception:

> Blest Order, which in power dost so excell,
> That with th' one hand thou liftest to the sky,
> And with the other throwest down to hell
> In thy just censures; fain would I draw nigh,
> Fain put thee on, exchanging my lay-sword
> > For that of th' holy Word.
>
> But thou art fire, sacred and hallow'd fire;
> And I but earth and clay: should I presume
> To wear thy habit, the severe attire
> My slender compositions might consume.
> I am both foul and brittle; much unfit
> > To deal in holy Writ.
>
> . . . .
>
> Wherefore I dare not, I, put forth my hand
> To hold the Ark, although it seem to shake

Through th' old sinnes and new doctrines of our land.
Onely, since God doth often vessels make
Of lowly matter for high uses meet,
                    I throw me at his feet.

There will I lie, untill my Maker seek
For some mean stuffe whereon to show his skill:
Then is my time. The distance of the meek
Doth flatter power. Lest good come short of ill
In praising might, the poore do by submission
                    What pride by opposition.
                                        (1–12, 31–42)

The poem is a brilliant recovery of wholeness and a true progress, even though it marks no gain from God. Herbert now explicitly chooses to exchange his courtier's lay-sword for "that of th' holy Word," though he has been sufficiently humbled to recognize that, without God's "enforcements," he "dare not" put forth his hand to hold the Ark. He confesses to the same condition so scornfully dismissed as useless in "Employment" (I) and (II) and in the lamentations: as "but earth and clay, . . . both foul and brittle," he is indeed unfit to "deal in holy Writ."

But here, the persistent self-image as inanimate earth and clay, of less use than any of the creatures, becomes a vivifying metaphor of a serviceable vessel wrought by the transformative power of God as artist. Like the enabling image of God as architect in "The Church-floore," "whose art / Could build so strong in a weak heart," the scriptural figure of God the potter, molder of men, allows Herbert at least to conceive that even his "wretched earth" might be given not only renewed life, but a substantial form: that of a holy preacher "fitted by the fire and trade" of the most skillful artist of all.

The insight derives from Herbert's recognition that all men share the "fellowship of dust": not only he himself, but "those great ones, be they ne're so great," also "Come from the earth, from whence those vessels come." This realization reduces the highest earthly estates no less than his image of the huge king's decaying flesh in "Content," but now he focuses on the "high uses" for which the "lowly matter" of mortality is suited, rather than the disintegration to which it must naturally come. Yet even here, though Herbert willingly gives up his lay-sword, the language of submission in the final stanza is still the language of the courtier: "The distance of the meek / Doth flatter power." What Herbert might, in another pattern of choices, have said of James or Charles is spoken of God by his entirely courtly servant, determined now to enter the service but able to await his master's will.[36]

The sequence of poems separating "The Priesthood" from "Aaron" spells out the rate and price of the submission to which Herbert has acceded. The pattern of alternating joy and grief is still not complete. In "The Search," following "The Priesthood," his images of being wracked and stretched over infinite distances recall the "wonder tortur'd in the space / Betwixt this world and that of grace" that Herbert had felt himself to be in "Affliction" (IV), long before this point in *The Church:*

> My knees pierce th' earth, mine eies the skie;
>   And yet the sphere
> And centre both to me denie
>   That thou art there.
>   .   .   .   .   .
> Thy will such a strange distance is,
>   As that to it
> East and West touch, the poles do kisse,
>   And parallels meet.
>   .   .   .   .   .
> When thou dost turn, and wilt be neare;
>   What edge so keen,
> What point so piercing can appeare
>   To come between?
>
> For as thy absence doth excell
>   All distance known:
> So doth thy nearenesse bear the bell,
>   Making two one.
>   (5–8, 41–4, 53–60)

Just as Herbert's repeated rewriting attacked the problem of delay until, in enduring the experience of delay, he achieved the patience required of him, and just as his descents to the lowest stages of creation attacked the problem of inutility until, by experiencing the self as a crumb of dust, he conceived a use for that wretched earth, so here the oscillations between confidence and despair attack the separation between his will and God's, the distance between the world of nature and that of grace, by experiencing the tortures of those infinite disparities until finally the gap is closed by a principle of reciprocity so beyond man's powers that it can only be initiated by God, "Making two one."

Though the initiative is God's, the rise to the world of grace does demand a reciprocal movement from Herbert, a harmonizing of wills that he finally masters in "The Crosse":

> To have my aim, and yet to be
> Further from it then when I bent my bow;
> To make my hopes my torture, and the fee
>   Of all my woes another wo,
> Is in the midst of delicates to need,
> And ev'n in Paradise to be a weed.
>
>   Ah my deare Father, ease my smart!
> These contrarieties crush me: these crosse actions
> Doe winde a rope about, and cut my heart:
>   And yet since these thy contradictions
> Are properly a crosse felt by thy Sonne,
> With but foure words, my words, *Thy will be done.*
>   (25–36)

Until the final three lines, Herbert recapitulates all the themes and images which have dominated the vocation poems: the extent of his desire to serve God, the endless duration of delay, lament at his uselessness, demands to be released from affliction. His wish that "all my wealth and familie might combine / To set thy honour up" recalls his promise in "Praise" (I): "Mend my estate in any wayes, / Thou shalt have more." God is still cross-biasing him, "Taking me up to throw me down," as He was doing in "Affliction" (I); and he is no less one of the company of useless weeds here than he was in "Employment" (I). This time, however, he closes with no conditions that imprison him still in the world of nature. Instead, following his exemplary model from the world of grace, Herbert restores the contradictions to harmony – properly – by accepting his own cross as Christ accepted His, in the same four words: *"Thy will be done."*

This act of identification leads directly to the transforming insight of "The Flower." Here, as in "The Crosse," the themes that have dominated Herbert's struggle since the beginning are brought together in fruitful interchange. His barren self-perception as a weed in the midst of Paradise gives place to a complementary, but now transvalued, image of the flower recovering greenness. The wracking spaces "bringing down to hell / And up to heaven in an houre" are now redefined in the perspective of eternity: "We say amisse, / This or that is: / Thy word is all, if we could spell."[37]

As in "The Crosse," Herbert also recapitulates the contrary longings that have held him in the state of nature and withheld him from the world of grace: "O that I once past changing were, / Fast in thy Paradise, where no flower can wither!" Still enmeshed in the state of mortality, for the first time he is able to accept it as a succession of killings and quickenings, and to welcome the declines as necessary forerunners of the returns:

> And now in age I bud again,
> After so many deaths I live and write;
>   I once more smell the dew and rain,
> And relish versing: O my onely light,
>   It cannot be
>   That I am he
>   On whom thy tempests fell all night.
>
> These are thy wonders, Lord of love,
> To make us see we are but flowers that glide:
>   Which when we once can finde and prove,
> Thou hast a garden for us, where to bide.
>   Who would be more,
>   Swelling through store,
>   Forfeit their Paradise by their pride.
>   (36–49)

These poems do not lead at once to the fully experienced transformation of the profane priest Herbert, "Defects and darknesse in my breast," into the new-dressed holiness given life by Christ within, "Perfect and light in my deare breast," that we will see in "Aaron." Herbert remains in the mortal condition of "flowers that glide," though he has "found and proven" not only the wonders of God's power to renew the shriveled heart, but also his own capacity to experience his alternations between confidence and despair without repining.

Probatio has indeed worked hope at last. "Bitter-sweet," one of the shortest and plainest poems in *The Church*, touches the condition of mortality that Herbert has so intensely resisted with the grace of a "plain simplicity of mind."[38] Here we realize that Herbert can now say, with St. Ambrose, that there is "a blessedness even in pains and grief":

Ah my deare angrie Lord,
Since thou dost love, yet strike;
Cast down, yet help afford;
Sure I will do the like.

I will complain, yet praise;
I will bewail, approve:
And all my sowre-sweet dayes
I will lament, and love.

This recognition enables Herbert to become the holy priest of God celebrated in "Aaron." The poem unites the reciprocity between divine and human first understood in "The Crosse" with the acceptance of mortal limitation first achieved in "The Flower":

Holinesse on the head,
Light and perfections on the breast,
Harmonious bells below, raising the dead
To leade them unto life and rest:
Thus are true Aarons drest.

Profanenesse in my head,
Defects and darknesse in my breast,
A noise of passions ringing me for dead
Unto a place where is no rest:
Poore priest thus am I drest.

Onely another head
I have, another heart and breast,
Another musick, making live not dead,
Without whom I could have no rest:
In him I am well drest.

Christ is my onely head,
My alone onely heart and breast,
My onely musick, striking me ev'n dead;
That to the old man I may rest,
And be in him new drest.

> So holy in my head,
> Perfect and light in my deare breast,
> My doctrine tun'd by Christ, (who is not dead,
> But lives in me while I do rest)
> Come people; Aaron's drest.

Herbert begins, as he does in "The Priesthood," by contrasting the excellence of this "Blest Order" with his own insufficiencies, though here the symmetry of the lines exactly parallels every point of perfection with his imperfections. The entire figure is shaped as a blazon: profaneness, defects, darkness, and noise of passions are in every respect opposed to what is required of "true Aarons." These qualities encompass the self-perceptions we have seen throughout the *Church* lyrics: the piled vanities that overwhelm his scant shreds of holiness, the "noise of thoughts" that invades his heart in "The Familie" and, since the passions ring him "Unto a place where is no rest," the same reduction to dust that until "The Priesthood" defined his useless state. This echo intensifies his contrast with the capacity of true Aarons not merely to rise themselves, but to accomplish the raising of others. Where Herbert would emulate Christ but has been too entangled in mortality to do so, true Aarons serve Him by "imitating" – carrying out on earth – His primary office of leading the dead "unto life and rest."

The turn of the third stanza, with equal symmetry, fills up Herbert's "uneven nature" with the grace of Christ's presence within, converting the noise of passions into well-tuned music and reversing the direction of decay in the essential vivifying act, "making live not dead." The fourth stanza extends even beyond Herbert's recognition that he has "another head / . . . another heart and breast" to declare identity, the complete co-inherence of Christ with Herbert that fits this "poore priest" to become a true Aaron. The shift from "another" to "My alone onely" marks the moment of transformation that, striking "ev'n dead" the "old man" of defects and darkness, clothes Herbert in Christ's holiness. But this interior transformation, as the image of being "new drest" in Christ suggests, leads outward to Herbert's identification with the true Aarons in the final stanza.

Each defect, in its order, is now filled: it is "my head / . . . my deare breast / My doctrine" which are holy, perfect, and light, harmoniously tuned by Christ's presence within. The orderly sequence works a still greater wonder. Herbert is not only himself revivified, and in consequence now enabled to take up his service in an earthly emulation of Christ's office, but in perfect reciprocity he too brings Christ to life: the vivified soul, by providing a fit habitation for its Master, returns life to Him. The circularity is as complete as "Sinnes Round," but unlike the sad cycle there traced, the harmonious ordering of "Aaron" patterns a series of risings that finally spread still further beyond the self and the company of true priests to reach out to all humankind in the invitation of the closing line: "Come people; Aaron's drest."

The order of transformation in "Aaron" recapitulates the order of the vocation sequence, which began with Herbert's recognition of Christ's perfections, turned to the bitter realization of his own defects and darkness, and in the poems following "The Bunch of Grapes" traced a slowly growing movement toward the exemplary model without whom he "could have no rest," leading finally to the harmonizing of Herbert's will with that of God in "The Crosse" which prepares him for the choice of a calling declared in "The Priesthood" and his investiture as God's servant in "Aaron." In the retrospective view provided by "Aaron," we see that this progress does indeed possess the pure and simple inevitability of God's unfolding purpose for Herbert. Yet the presence of the "old man" still within the poem reminds us also of how painful a process it has been for one so composed of piled vanities to stitch together his shreds of holiness into the dress of the true priest which he has been called to assume.

The paean of praise to Herbert's Master in "The Odour," immediately following, celebrates the reciprocity which has enabled him for the service:

> For when *My Master,* which alone is sweet,
>   And ev'n in my unworthinesse pleasing,
>   Shall call and meet,
>   *My Servant,* as thee not displeasing,
> That call is but the breathing of the sweet.
>
> This breathing would with gains by sweetning me
>   (As sweet things traffick when they meet)
>   Return to thee.
>   And so this new commerce and sweet
> Should all my life employ and busie me.
>   (21–30)

This is the language of God's courtier, cleansed of the incongruities and disproportions between servant and master that Herbert had stressed in "The Thanksgiving." But we notice that Herbert is pleasing to his master "ev'n in" his unworthiness. As "Love" (III) also points out, grace does not depend upon an absolute worth which man, marred and mortal, cannot expect to attain.[39] The final stanza of "The Odour" defines the reciprocity which Herbert has been striving toward since "The Pearl" and "The Bunch of Grapes." Now we watch the reascension of his service to God after God's "sweetning" descends to him, in another pattern of circularity signifying a cycle of fulfillment, as in "The Flower" and "Aaron," rather than the sterile and repetitive cumulation of "Sinnes Round."

The process of transformation traced in this chapter concludes most appropriately with "The Elixir," which now articulates the means of restoring God's image:

> Teach me, my God and King,
> In all things thee to see,
> And what I do in any thing,
> To do it as for thee:
> . . . .
> This is the famous stone
> That turneth all to gold:
> For that which God doth touch and own
> Cannot for lesse be told.
>   (1–4, 21–4)

Here the "spirit and good extract of my heart," which in "The Sinner" was a minute quintessence overwhelmed in its circumference of earth, is transformed by the alchemical tincture that "turneth all to gold." The restoration of God's image that has taken virtually all the lyrics of *The Church* to complete is condensed into a single essence:

> Not rudely, as a beast
> To runne into an action;
> But still to make thee prepossest,
> And give it his perfection.
>   (5–8)

What is essential is that every action should have God in it, be taken "for thy sake." The fluid alchemical imagery and the move-

ment generated by this stress upon action transforms the static picture in "The Sinner" of Herbert's hard heart frozen in its quarries of
piled vanities. "The Sinner" presented a tableau and envisioned the
simple replacement of the one portrait by another – God's image – if
God would only, once more, "write in stone." Nothing seemed to be
required of Herbert. But in "The Elixir" restoration is a process by
no means completed by the transformation celebrated in "Aaron"
which enables him to do God's work. It is a continuous and ongoing
effort, not simply "In all things thee to see" but "What I do in any
thing, / To do it as for thee." This definition justifies the long duration of affliction and explains the wavering pattern of repetition,
retreat, and advance that marks the personal lyrics of *The Church*.
These poems witness to Herbert's fulfillment of the requirement
stressed by Ambrose – the exercise of virtue rather than the desire for
it alone, or even its possession:

> A servant with this clause
> Makes drudgerie divine:
> Who sweeps a room, as for thy laws,
> Makes that and th' action fine.
>   (17–20)

Herbert's homely image of the servant whose drudgery is, by
"this clause," made divine links action pleasing to God with a
descent to lowliness rather than an ascent to great place. While in
"The Thanksgiving" Herbert envisioned his service to God as a
restoration of wealth or honor that he comfortably assumed God
might bestow on him, in "The Elixir" he chooses an image of the
humblest form of service to show forth the means of perfection. It is,
of course, a far more accurate figure for his role as country parson in
a small farming community – a humble way – than the images of
bravery and glory that marked Herbert's earlier promises of what he
would do for God, now rightly ordering the humble soul's ascent
toward heaven by assigning him, with Christ, a lowly position on
earth in service at the court of the poor and simple.

The resolution of Herbert's search for a calling in this way
structures the *Church* sequence by endowing its personal lyrics with
a shape drawn from life. This configuration incorporates the disorder
and lack of progress which man in his fallen condition must endure
with fortitude even as he strives toward the perfection that, in "The

Elixir," is understood to be a continuous "mending and making." It is the inclusion of God in every act that transforms it into fine service, but Herbert's emphasis upon continuous and repeated action — "what I do in any thing . . . still to make thee prepossest" — stresses this perfection as the work of a whole life and, indeed, a perfecting rather than a process that once understood, can be completed once and for all.

"Giddinesse" points out that we need God to "mend . . . [or] make us dayly," and it is this continual action which the personal lyrics of *The Church* bring into being by their very form. Since the shape of the transformed self is never merely a static image of the new man, its articulation must extend over time, in a multiplicity of retreats and advances which detail the labyrinthine entanglements with the world in which the old man is enmeshed. Within the scope of a single poem, Herbert can perceive that what seems to natural man a descent leading only to disintegration is, in the heavenly perspective, his only means of ascent to God. But telling the story of the transformation of the self, spelling its elements, requires a configuration of many structures, a group of interwoven patterns constituting both the knot of complications and the means of its unraveling.

By juxtaposition, Herbert can show the competing pulls of earth and heaven, the "contrarieties" that reveal the insufficiency of any single moment of insight to work a permanent alteration in the pattern of a life. The irregular and wavering sequence of the vocation poems, on the other hand, introduces the element of time and relates the problem of delay to Herbert's indecisive shifts between the expectations of the world and his aspiration toward heaven. Constellations of meaning formed by groups of poems establish still wider interrelationships that move fluidly either backward or forward throughout the sequence to measure progress by how far Herbert has come, or its lack by how far he still has to go. Only when all these patterns are read together does the pattern of life choice come clear; only then is it possible to realize the harmony of God's unfolding purpose for Herbert with Herbert's progress of choices.

Yet Nicholas Ferrar's description of Herbert as a pattern for his age points out that the transformation into a true priest which resolves Herbert's search for a calling is in no sense an end in itself. It is simply a means to enable Herbert, in his turn, to serve others as

Christ has served man. Even the account of the self remade in "Aaron" concludes with an expansive outward address – "Come people; Aaron's drest" – that invites all, however "mean," to partake in the process of transformation.

This movement outward to the world returns the poem from the realm of Herbert's art to the setting of his life, uniting the action of the poet within *The Church* with the service which, he hopes in "The Odour," "should all my life employ and busie me." The central action traced by the personal lyrics of *The Church* is neither reconstruction nor, finally, resolution: the transformed self is subject to continual mending and making. The larger structure of *The Temple* as a whole refigures Herbert's world and in turn refigures the role of God's courtier within that world. We too often read *The Temple* as if it were only the poems of *The Church*. Such readings deny the configuration of Herbert's Temple that, he hoped in his Dedication, would "make a gain" for his readers.

Chapter 6

All the Frame and Fabric Is Within

Lord, with what glorie wast thou serv'd of old,
When Solomons temple stood and flourished!
 Where most things were of purest gold;
 The wood was all embellished
With flowers and carvings, mysticall and rare:
All s. w'd the builders, crav'd the seeers care.

Yet all this glorie, all this pomp and state
Did not affect thee much, was not thy aim;
 Something there was, that sow'd debate:
 Wherefore thou quitt'st thy ancient claim:
And now thy Architecture meets with sinne;
For all thy frame and fabrick is within.

There thou art struggling with a peevish heart,
Which sometimes crosseth thee, thou sometimes it:
 The fight is hard on either part.
 Great God doth fight, he doth submit.
All Solomons sea of brasse and world of stone
Is not so deare to thee as one good grone.

And truly brasse and stones are heavie things,
Tombes for the dead, not temples fit for thee:
 But grones are quick, and full of wings,
 And all their motions upward be;
And ever as they mount, like larks they sing;
The note is sad, yet musick for a King.

           "Sion"

"Sion" rejects the value of material structures and challenges our definition of Herbert's Temple. If "now thy Architecture meets with sinne," if "all thy frame and fabrick is within," how are we to interpret the curious three-part form of *The Temple*?[1] The only

Temple figured in "Sion," displacing Solomon's elaborate building of old, is the human heart. It is built of groans winging upward, sad music aspiring toward and pleasing to the one true King.[2] These lines recognizably depict the experience of *The Church,* but that interior and spiritual structure is apparently framed by *The Church-porch* and *The Church Militant.* *The Church-porch* is usually read as preparation for entrance into *The Church,* but this interpretation does not quite account for the way Herbert draws the world of contemporary English society into its precincts. The closing frame, *The Church Militant,* traces a history of the Church on earth continually not only meeting with sin but being overrun by it. More important, Herbert clearly figures England "now," as he writes, subjected to the overtakings of sin. The last voice we hear in *The Temple* speaks a refrain which can only affirm its trust that God's providential design will work itself out at the end of time.

This structure unmakes, turns back within, denies closure, configures a world that *must* be unmade, will never until time ends be wholly mended. It can be created *only* out of groans, struggles, crosses. The building that is never completed, a work of continual mending and making, takes place in the human heart, neither within the institution of the church in England nor even the body of Christianity on earth. In human history, *The Temple* exacts an acceptance of disintegration; the promise of integration is finally prophecy, not fulfillment.

Herbert converts structure into figure in "Sion" and also unframes the external world. Yet it is that exterior which predominates in both "framing" poems of *The Temple.* This chapter will consider how *The Church-porch* and *The Church Militant* work as insufficient frames, inadequate structures for the work of building God's courtier is required to do. Yet I hope also to show how they do frame the world in which God's courtier attempts to make himself into a Temple. Within *The Church,* we shall see how these worldly frames, interiorized and restructured, play their part in piecing the fabric of that Temple. Worldliness is still figured within Herbert's courtly self-representation, providing a thoroughly realistic "frame" — a circumference of earth — for the heart always in process of reconstruction, only on the way to transformation.

i

The Church-porch grounds the courtly speaker of *The Temple* in a particular society. Even as it offers preparation for entrance into *The Church,* however, the conditions of that society and the sensible, often traditional advice dispensed within the poem disclose a fabric rent by schism, contradiction, falsity. The world of the Porch cannot provide a substantial frame, or an adequate preparation, for courtiers who would serve their heavenly king. "Superliminaire," the verses marking the threshold between Porch and Church, figures both the possibility of preparation and recognition of its inefficacy:

> Thou, whom the former precepts have
> Sprinkled and taught, how to behave
> Thy self in church; approach, and taste
> The churches mysticall repast.
>
> Avoid, Profanenesse; come not here:
> Nothing but holy, pure, and cleare,
> Or that which groneth to be so,
> May at his perill further go.

If the first stanza's claim that "the former precepts have / Sprinkled and taught" affirms the *Porch* as preparation, the second stanza revises that claim substantially. The moral instructions of the *Porch,* we now see, only seem to offer purification. Far more dubiously, the qualifying line "Or that which groneth to be so" suggests only a possibility, a need, a desire. It is the struggle traced in "Sion," rather than an assured state, "holy, pure, and cleare," which accurately describes the agonistic consciousness within *The Church* and reveals the inadequacies of the *Porch*'s moral instruction.

These instructions initially promise to guide a very courtly young man through the hazards of a worldly society, to provide him with a structure of virtuous practice to build upon as he approaches the spiritual realm of *The Church.* The image of a world emptied of value when "worth and service fail" dominates the superficial facades of courtliness depicted in *The Church-porch.* The poem denies "surfaces" but seems — like the courtesy books it resembles so closely — to affirm the virtues of *habitus,* to confirm the value of striving toward the good:

Slight those who say amidst their sickly healths,
Thou liv'st by rule. What doth not so, but man?
Houses are built by rule, and common-wealths.
Entice the trusty sunne, if that thou can,
    From his Ecliptick line: becken the skie.
    Who lives by rule then, keeps good companie.

Who keeps no guard upon himself, is slack,
And rots to nothing at the next great thaw.
Man is a shop of rules, a well truss'd pack,
Whose every parcell under-writes a law.
    Lose not thy self, nor give thy humours way:
    God gave them to thee under lock and key.
                            (stanzas 23, 24)

Here Herbert stresses man's ability to acquire virtue: he is assumed to possess the capacity to maintain control of himself, even to maintain his self-identity – very unlike the courtly figure within *The Church* so beset with inner wranglers, so fiercely resisting the losses of self that will finally be exacted of him. That the precepts of the Porch are to be practiced by a future governor or courtier is clear from the Verser's opening address to a "sweet youth," whose "early hopes inhance / Thy rate and price, and mark thee for a treasure" straight through to the urbane reminder of proper deportment at divine service in stanza 68: "Kneeling ne're spoil'd silk stocking: quit thy state. / All equall are within the churches gate."[3] The Verser, to be sure, addresses "you" – England's youth – but we can recognize that young man too as an externalized projection of the *Church*'s courtly speaker.

Herbert attributes to the decline of the aristocracy the necessity for "rules" in order to develop a "mast'ring minde":

O England! full of sinne, but most of sloth;
Spit out thy flegme, and fill thy brest with glorie:
Thy Gentrie bleats, as if thy native cloth
Transfus'd a sheepishnesse into thy storie:
    Not that they all are so; but that the most
    Are gone to grasse, and in the pasture lost.
                            (stanza 16[4])

As the next stanza points out, "This losse springs chiefly from our education." This echo of Elyot places the poem squarely in the tradition of courtesy books designed to make up that deficiency and

evokes the values of the courtly ideal as the standard against which
its present decline is to be measured.

The poem's courtly references contrast the substance of true
worth and the mere appearance of it, just as we have seen the
disintegration of the ideal lamented in other seventeenth-century
sources:

> Spend not on hopes. They that by pleading clothes
> Do fortunes seek, when worth and service fail,
> Would have their tale beleeved for their oathes,
> And are like empty vessels under sail.
>   Old courtiers know this; therefore set out so,
>   As all the day thou mayst hold out to go.
>   (stanza 31)

Here interior virtue is still perceived as a proper – and possible –
aspiration. Herbert's advice to England's parents recommends quality of mind over quantity of matter:

> The way to make thy sonne rich is to fill
> His minde with rest, before his trunk with riches:
> For wealth without contentment climbes a hill
> To feel those tempests, which fly over ditches.
>   But if thy sonne can make ten pound his measure,
>   Then all thou addest may be call'd his treasure.
>   (stanza 19)

Stanza 32 urges the interior and spiritual virtue of discretion in
preference to the merely external and material show of fine lace:

> In clothes, cheap handsomnesse doth bear the bell.
> Wisdome's a trimmer thing then shop e're gave.
> Say not then, This with that lace will do well;
> But, This with my discretion will be brave.
>   Much curiousnesse is a perpetuall wooing,
>   Nothing with labour, folly long a-doing.

"Pleading clothes" are thus rejected in favor of the superior form of
ornament provided by wisdom and brave discretion, while in stanza
38, the "thinne webbe" of "poysonous fancies" is weighed and
found wanting in comparison to the honor of great soldiers, "com-
pos'd / Of thicker stuffe, which would endure a shake."[5]

These precepts for right action define Herbert's intended audience as courtly but transform the ideal of courtly relationship to the
ruler. In stanza 21, Herbert appeals to the courtier's concern with the
earthly king's opinion of him, but invokes instead the heavenly King
to whom earthly rulers and their servants alike are accountable:

> Doe all things like a man, not sneakingly:
> Think the king sees thee still; for his King does.
> Simpring is but a lay-hypocrisie:
> Give it a corner, and the clue undoes.
>   Who fears to do ill, sets himself to task:
>   Who fears to do well, sure should wear a mask.

In these stanzas interior virtue is contrasted with the falsity that not
only deceives, but corrupts an entire society. Speech as well as action
must stem from a harmony of exterior and interior, since words
measure the truth of "worth and service" no less than deeds:

> Lie not; but let thy heart be true to God,
> Thy mouth to it, thy actions to them both:
>   .   .   .   .
> Dare to be true. Nothing can need a ly:
> A fault, which needs it most, grows two thereby.
>
> (stanza 13)

This ideal of courtly conversation, like the standard of the courtier's
behavior, is compromised by contemporary preoccupation with hol-
low rhetoric rather than a more solid value. Again a showy exterior
weighs light compared to interior substance:[6]

> In conversation boldnesse now bears sway.
> But know, that nothing can so foolish be,
> As empty boldnesse: therefore first assay
> To stuffe thy minde with solid braverie;
>   Then march on gallant: get substantiall worth.
>   Boldnesse guilds finely, and will set it forth.
>
> (stanza 35)

This distinction between an elegant and elaborate surface
appearance of courtliness and the interior emptiness of substance is
familiar to us also in Jacobean drama and in the contemporary
indictments of courtly corruption cited in Chapter 2. Herbert chal-

lenges worldly aspiration to turn inward, redirects the striving toward virtue to the king of heaven. In denying exterior "surfaces," he is rejecting worldly values. Yet, by evoking the modes of acquiring virtue typical in the courtesy books, as well as by adopting their tropes for measuring inner substance against outward appearance, Herbert links the courtly values which he sees degenerating into nothing but surface "bravery" with the Christian progress toward holiness which will be his subject within *The Church*. Insofar as these values accumulate in the Porch as possibility, they do prepare for the mending and making within *The Church*. They initially configure the courtier as the aspiring "I" whose sense of self must be transformed, whose allegiances must be redirected, whose *inner* surface must be restitched into substance.

Like Wyatt and Gascoigne, Herbert figures the loss of courtly virtue in terms of linguistic duplicity. Stanzas condemning such vices of speech as swearing and lying reflect the particular temptations of youth[7] but also emphasize once more the double aspect of external behavior as both words and deeds, each of which ought to reflect the principle that Herbert will state in "Constancie": "His words and works and fashion too / All of a piece, and all are cleare and straight." Herbert's summary to these opening stanzas suggests that the control of youthful passions is only a preliminary step:

> The cheapest sinnes most dearely punisht are;
> Because to shun them also is so cheap:
> For we have wit to mark them, and to spare.
> (stanza 12, 67–9)

Stanza 15 addresses the young man as an independent adult whose worth is to be tested by his virtuous performance of whatever office he attains:

> Art thou a Magistrate? then be severe:
> If studious, copie fair, what time hath blurr'd;
> Redeem truth from his jawes: if souldier,
> Chase brave employments with a naked sword
>   Throughout the world. Fool not: for all may have,
>   If they dare try, a glorious life, or grave.

This stanza, like those following Herbert's apostrophe to England (stanzas 16–19), emphasizes the standard of interior virtue which ought to control behavior – "When thou dost purpose ought within thy power, / Be sure to do it, though it be but small" – but stanza 25 stresses the internal state still further in its reminder that the sweet youth ought not to be dependent upon the social world:

> By all means use sometimes to be alone.
> Salute thy self: see what thy soul doth wear.
> Dare to look in thy chest, for 'tis thine own:
> And tumble up and down what thou find'st there.
>   Who cannot rest till hee good-fellows finde,
>   He breaks up house, turns out of doores his minde.

Yet just as, within *The Church*, the stress upon self-knowledge in "Content" is significantly qualified by the precepts of service to one's neighbor as well as oneself in "Constancie," so in *The Church-porch* the world of society is not to be rejected entirely, but rather becomes another testing ground in which virtue, or the lack of it, can be demonstrated. The standard against which progress is to be measured is that of the four cardinal virtues; Herbert's examples, as well as his definitions, are traditional.

Temperance, as the mean between extremes of defect and excess, is applied to a wide variety of activities in stanzas 26 to 45, providing a vividly detailed, if miniaturized, picture of the courtly world.[8] Money, clothing, gambling, dueling, wit and conversation, and behavior to the great are all evaluated according to their proper use. "A sad wise valour is the brave complexion, / That leads the van, and swallows up the cities," while "respective boldness" toward those of great place renders what is due to them "and yet doth take / Nothing from thine." In distinguishing between the place of honor and the possibly less-than-honorable person who holds it, Herbert once more adopts the figure of outward adornment to contrast substance and show, though here it is the substance of the office, rather than its holder, which deserves respect:

> When baseness is exalted, do not bate
> The place its honour, for the persons sake.
> The shrine is that which thou dost venerate,
> And not the beast, that bears it on his back.
>   I care not though the cloth of state should be
>   Not of rich arras, but mean tapestrie.
>
>   (stanza 45)

Concern with the proper mode of courtly service shifts gradually toward an emphasis upon obligations to others in stanzas 46 to 64, exemplifying the cardinal virtue of justice as it was traditionally understood. This group of precepts again covers a range of activities from domestic and private obligations to the art of civil conversation to a culminating statement of the ultimate aim of the courtly life. Courtesy is once more given an ideal value and the court is credited with the power to inculcate it:

> In thy discourse, if thou desire to please,
> All such is courteous, usefull, new, or wittie.
> Usefulnesse comes by labour, wit by ease;
> Courtesie grows in court; news in the citie.
> > Get a good stock of these, then draw the card
> > That suits him best, of whom thy speech is heard.
> > > > > (stanza 49)

As stanza 52 shows, the basis for this emphasis upon courtly conversation is the power of love to bind together the social world:[9]

> Be calm in arguing: for fiercenesse makes
> Errour a fault, and truth discourtesie.
> Why should I feel another mans mistakes
> More then his sicknesses or povertie?
> > In love I should: but anger is not love,
> > Nor wisdome neither: therefore gently move.

Here Herbert anticipates the courteous exchanges between Christ and his soul, "guiltie of dust and sinne," in "Love" (III), where the principle of "gently moving," and the loving acceptance of limitation, are exemplified by Christ and followed by Herbert – a first-person transformation into sacred terms, and into the dramatic mode of experience, for which this second-person exhortation seems to be preparing the way.

Richard Strier reads in this stanza a Stoic prudence – "'Wisdome,' not love, is the guiding ideal" ("George Herbert and the World," p. 231) – and points out that these lines "accept quite casually a world in which men do not take to heart the sickness or poverty of others." I agree that the "prudential ethics" of the *Porch* are, from the revised perspectives of *The Church*, revealed as insufficient, tainted with an irreducible worldliness. If we read *The*

Church-porch as a poem in need of rewriting within *The Church,* as the speaker of the *Porch* refigures and interiorizes his world, we begin to recognize the calculated betrayals of opportunism that even a would-be courtier of God reveals in the external virtues of *habitus* extolled in the *Porch.* But when Strier argues that "Self-interest is the only motive to which [*The Church-porch*] appeals" (p. 228), I think he overstates the way in which this explicit fashioning of courtesy-book precepts establishes the limitations which *will* require revising in the "virtues" poems within *The Church.* The sweet youth of the *Porch* is being advised to strive for virtue even in his most worldly relations; the worldliness of the Verser is, I'd argue, deliberately latent in the *Porch,* since the interiorizing process of self-discovery cannot take place in this world of surfaces. I think Strier is absolutely correct, however, in commenting, "It is difficult not to conclude that the quality of Herbert's otherworldliness and anti-worldliness later has a good deal to do with the quality of his worldliness – and of his religion – here" (p. 232).

Stanza 55 enlarges the insight of stanza 52 beyond speech to action, prefiguring the concern with "use" which will be so central to Herbert in the lyrics of *The Church* concerning his own vocation:

> Be useful where thou livest, that they may
> Both want and wish thy pleasing presence still.
> Kindnesse, good parts, great places are the way
> To compasse this. Finde out mens wants and will,
>   And meet them there. All worldly joyes go lesse
>   To the one joy of doing kindnesses.

In the Porch, great place is still a worthy object of aspiration. But stanza 56 adumbrates the pattern of humility and aspiration that, in *The Church,* will be finally transvalued through its redirection toward the court and king of heaven – though it does not yet acknowledge that the humble way may entail a loss of self:

> Pitch thy behaviour low, thy projects high;
> So shalt thou humble and magnanimous be:
> Sink not in spirit: who aimeth at the sky,
> Shoots higher much then he that means a tree.
>   A grain of glorie mixt with humblenesse
>   Cures both a fever and lethargicknesse.[10]
>   (stanza 56)

Beyond the narrow confines of the courtly class, persons of low estate are equally to be valued: "Scorn no mans love, though of a mean degree; / Love is a present for a mightie king"; furthermore, "Man is Gods image; but a poore man is / Christs stamp to boot." These assurances are easily prescriptive – and, of course, linguistically "exterior": they project an absorption of humble values into the worldly model of courtiership that the speaker of *The Church* will discover to be impossible.

In spite of its didactic confidence and stanzaic uniformity, in one respect *The Church-porch* resembles *The Church* and anticipates a crucial aspect of its structure. There is an element of randomness, a lack of precise neatness to its sequences, just as *The Church* incorporates the disorderly processes of a mind continually moving over its world and its experience in an attempt to create a unity out of its "partitions" and "divisions."[11] A sense of order, however, is also built into the structure of *The Church-porch* from the first task of youth, controlling the passions, through the right tempering of worldly office and activity, to a just "rendering to every man his due" throughout the whole frame of a courtly world even to its farthest spatial and social limits, finally concluding with a still more expansive movement beyond the quotidian into the realm of the spiritual. As Herbert notes, to attend church is to "Restore to God his due in tithe and time": Sundays are to be observed because "God then deals blessings: If a king did so, / Who would not haste, nay give, to see the show?"[12] The entrance into church, again paralleling the moral significance of earthly and heavenly kings, serves as the initial step in ascending to a higher level, for "God is more there, then thou: for thou art there / Onely by his permission. Then beware, / And make thyself all reverence and fear."

Whereas the previous stanzas have detailed the counsels of worldly prudence, these set forth precepts of behavior designed to prepare the soul to receive heavenly wisdom, the higher application of the same virtue,[13] though they remain on the worldly level in their primary concern with outward behavior rather than the state of the soul: "Look to thy actions well: / For churches are either our heav'n or hell." The concluding stanzas, however, emphasize a harmonizing need for attention to the state of the soul as well as the body:

> Summe up at night, what thou hast done by day;
> And in the morning, what thou hast to do.

Dresse and undresse thy soul: mark the decay
And growth of it: if with thy watch, that too
   Be down, then winde up both; since we shall be
   Most surely judg'd, make thy accounts agree.
                         (stanza 76)

The metaphor of external ornament is now given an entirely spiritual signification, reflecting but also intensifying the concern with internal substance which we have noticed in earlier stanzas. Herbert denies the worth of all worldly pleasures, yet can still assign a worldly term – "acquit thee bravely" – to the effort to live in the world according to the standard of moral virtue:

In brief, acquit thee bravely; play the man.
Look not on pleasures as they come, but go.
Deferre not the least vertue: lifes poore span
Make not an ell, by trifling in thy wo.
   If thou do ill; the joy fades, not the pains:
   If well; the pain doth fade, the joy remains.
                         (stanza 77)

Within *The Church*, the process of purification will radically disjoin the values of the courtly world and those necessary to the soul who would follow Christ. Transformation of courtly virtues to the king and court of heaven exacts inversions and perspectival shifts as the limitations of human will and grace are experienced by the "I" who now speaks directly. *The Church-porch* offers a dream of order, to which courtly aspiration is sufficient. *The Church* rewrites the texts of the *Porch* from within, un-making its certainties in order to recover an actuality of continuous mending.

ii

The transition from an exterior *Church-porch* to the interior of *The Church* represents far more than a movement in space dependent upon the architectural figure implied by these two titles. The mode of address changes from second-person concern with the sweet youth whom Herbert wishes to "rhyme to good" in the *Porch* to first-person intimacy and immediacy, predominant in the *Church*. As Joseph Summers has pointed out (*George Herbert*, p. 104), the sweet youth is just such a young man as Herbert himself, yet he is also distinguished from the poet who, in the *Porch*, adopts the role of a Verser making his poem into a "bait of pleasure" but in the *Church*, offers his poems to God as the "parts" of his hard heart which meet within the frame. In *The Church*, the "I" discovers how much his own poetry provides him with "baits of pleasure" which fail to "rhyme him to good."

The Church traces its speaker's aspiration to spiritual progress: worldly behavior, like his choice of a calling in the world, is measured against this single standard. Yet the exterior world is still present in all of its aspects and in many of its characteristics, though now it is presented through the medium of Herbert's controlling consciousness and in relation to his own attempt to comprehend God's design, thereby transcending the limitations of a merely worldly perspective. The uniform didactic stanzas of the Porch give place in the Church to a dazzling multiplicity of genres and kinds which, in their reflection of contemporary literary modes and their rich variety of reference to contemporary life, internalize the world that has been so vividly depicted in *The Church-porch*. That internalizing fragments the world into disorderly parts. The hope of a purifying, transforming wholeness that *The Church-porch* seems to anticipate gives way to interior struggles that are scarcely imagined by the confident Verser.

A telling phrase of J. Hutchison in 1873 can help define the structural complexity of *The Temple*:

> Herbert's strong point was spiritual anatomy.
> His probing and exposure of the deceits and
> vanities of the human heart, and his setting
> forth of the dangers of the world to spiritu-
> ality of mind, is at once quaint and incisive.[14]

Hutchison does not associate Herbert's "spiritual anatomy" with Burton's *Anatomy of Melancholy*, nor does he relate his brief observation to the generic problem of *The Temple* as a whole. His term, however, is valuable in just this connection. *The Church* is not, like Burton's anatomy, an encyclopedic assemblage of human knowledge disposing its diverse materials in elaboration of a single state at once psychological, physical, and spiritual. Its multiple lyric forms and kinds are disposed about a far less unified center: the construction of a broken altar "Made of a heart, and cemented with teares: / Whose parts are as thy hand did frame" which Herbert announces as his theme in the opening poem of this section of *The Temple*. These parts are surrounded by the wide social perspective of *The Church-porch* and the vast span of time of *The Church Militant*, both portrayals of an exterior failure of virtue. Within the *Church* is a continually-constructed Temple, the human heart. God's courtier animates the entire work and holds it together within one frame, from the confident Verser of the *Porch* who would rhyme his world to good to the chastened speaker of *The Church Militant*'s hopeful prophecy; but that courtly figure has discovered the delusions of recovery and the illusions of wholeness.

Louis Martz considers the multiplicity of kinds to represent Herbert's desire that everything in his world should unite to praise God, but they serve another purpose as well: to trace the disintegration and decay of all merely earthly values. Transference of value to the heavenly realm entails rejecting not only the claims of earth but also the self who aspires to worldly glory. In *The Church-porch*, Herbert contrasts the empty show of courtly virtue with the interior moral substance required of one who aims toward the good, and defines that substance by reference to the cardinal virtues which man must endeavor to acquire. Within *The Church*, these virtues are remeasured: certain courtly qualities are now shown to have been so contaminated by their deterioration into mere surface attributes that they no longer represent any meaningful relation to interior virtue.

Worldly honor, given positive significance in the *Porch* – "Pitch thy behaviour low, thy projects high" – is reduced to one of the disorderly collection of meaningless fragments in "The Quidditie," while its virtuous substance is now assigned only to God, depicted as a thoroughly courtly king in "Affliction" (III):

> My heart did heave, and there came forth, O *God!*
> By that I knew that thou wast in the grief,
> To guide and govern it to my relief,
>   Making a scepter of the rod:
>   Hadst thou not had thy part,
> Sure the unruly sigh had broke my heart.
>
> . . . .
>
> Thy life on earth was grief, and thou art still
> Constant unto it, making it to be

A point of honour, now to grieve in me,
And in thy members suffer ill.
They who lament one crosse,
Thou dying dayly, praise thee to thy losse.

                          (1–6, 13–18)

Although the earthly king appears only as a disembodied crown in
the list of disvalued parts in "The Quidditie," the scepter as well as
the honor proper to a king regain value in being assigned to God
in "Affliction" (III). This recovery of the "worth and service"
whose loss Herbert lamented in *The Church-porch* depends upon
the process of transvaluation exemplified by "Dotage," discussed
in Chapter 4.

"Affliction" (III) belongs to a constellation of poems, including
"Content," "The Quidditie," "Humilitie," "Frailtie," and "Constancie," which reconstitute the courtly ideal, affirmed in *The
Church-porch* in spite of its actual decline, by retaining its traditional
virtues as the standard of value but raising that which has become
mere exterior show in the courtly world to a higher level where it
once more possesses true worth. This restructuring makes up the
virtues' insufficiencies by adding the distinctive values of Christianity
and by establishing Christ as the model to be emulated.

"Humilitie" is the most interesting – and also the most difficult –
example of the process, since this allegory retains the traditional four
cardinals except for a single significant substitution:

I saw the Vertues sitting hand in hand
In sev'rall ranks upon an azure throne,
Where all the beasts and fowl by their command
Presented tokens of submission.
Humilitie, who sat the lowest there
                          To execute their call,
When by the beasts the presents tendred were,
                          Gave them about to all.

The angrie Lion did present his paw,
Which by consent was giv'n to Mansuetude.
The fearfull Hare her eares, which by their law
Humilitie did reach to Fortitude.
The jealous Turkie brought his corall-chain;
                          That went to Temperance.
On Justice was bestow'd the Foxes brain,
                          Kill'd in the way by chance.

At length the Crow bringing the Peacocks plume
(For he would not) as they beheld the grace
Of that brave gift, each one began to fume,
And challenge it, as proper to his place,
Till they fell out: which when the beasts espied,
                              They leapt upon the throne;
And if the Fox had liv'd to rule their side,
                              They had depos'd each one.

Humilitie, who held the plume, at this,
Did weep so fast, that the tears trickling down
Spoil'd all the train: then saying, *Here it is*
For which ye wrangle, made them turn their frown
Against the beasts: so joyntly bandying,
                              They drive them soon away:
And then amerc'd them, double gifts to bring
                              At the next Session-day.

Like Herbert's attribution of honor to Christ's grief in "Affliction" (III), the substitution of Mansuetude for Prudence introduces distinctively Christian overtones into the well-known list and suggests the insufficiency of an ideal which does not stress the imperatives of the New Testament.[15] Hutchinson's interpretation of the "beasts" as the passions[16] is certainly plausible, though they may more precisely refer to the vices opposite to each virtue. The lion's gift to Mansuetude signifies the submission of wrath to mercy, while the fearful hare's gift of its ears is appropriately presented to Fortitude, the cardinal virtue denoting courage; the immoderate vice of jealousy is properly given up to Temperance, and the gift of the fox's brain, perhaps evoking Machiavellian practices of craft and deceit, belongs rightly to Justice.

The central role of Humilitie as both servant of the virtues, who sits "the lowest there / To execute their call," and the sole force capable of restoring their sovereignty, emphasizes still further the limitations of acquired virtue and the need of this essential Christian principle if they are to be either harmonious or efficacious. The fable once more points out the falsity and corruptive power of the merely external, since it is the "grace / Of that brave gift," the peacock's plume, by tradition signifying worldly attachment,[17] that tempts the Virtues into such wrangling that the vices, or passions, leap upon the throne to usurp the seat of rule.

As the final stanza makes clear, neither Fortitude, Temperance, Justice, nor even Mansuetude is capable of resisting worldly temptation or of regaining its rightful position of rule without the action of Humilitie, who willingly gives up to them that for which they wrangle. Humilitie alone chooses to serve and give rather than to fight over what is "proper to his place," and in this sense represents a higher value that, after the pattern of Christ making a "point of honour" of His grief in "Affliction" (III), relinquishes the world rather than seizing upon it.

As Hutchinson points out, "Humilitie" appears to be a redaction of Sidney's eclogue, "As I my little flocke on *Ister* banke," in the *Arcadia*. Herbert's introduction of Humilitie's healing action, however, redresses Sidney's account of man's inability, "swelling in tyranny," to rule wisely. Man's excessive pride and arrogance indict him as unworthy to hold the office allotted to him by Jove, since it is, Philisides observes, a "rage . . . beyond thy neede."

In Herbert's version of the fable, Sidney's vision of the inherent corruption of man, rendering him incompetent to rule the created world, is transformed into an internal drama of passions and virtues whose outcome is a restoration of harmony, suggesting the possibility of man's harmonious tempering. But this process depends upon the Christian relinquishment of place and position signified by the action of Humilitie: graces that man can at least aspire toward although, as Herbert's own halting progress toward grace in the more personal lyrics of *The Church* attests, they must await infusion, since they cannot be possessed simply by willing or even endeavoring to acquire them.[18] By recording the limits of the will, the poem rewrites the prideful aspirations of *The Church-porch*.

"Constancie" contrasts and implicitly revises the contemplative quietism postulated in "Content," where Herbert concludes, "He that by seeking hath himself once found, / Hath ever found a happie fortune." Here he raises to "godliness" the standard of moral virtue that had been introduced in *The Church-porch* but not there developed beyond its worldly applications:

> Who is the honest man?
> He that doth still and strongly good pursue,
> To God, his neighbour, and himself most true:
> Whom neither force nor fawning can
> Unpinne, or wrench from giving all their due.
>
> Whose honestie is not
> So loose or easie, that a ruffling winde

Can blow away, or glittering look it blinde:
    Who rides his sure and even trot,
While the world now rides by, now lags behinde.

. . . .

            Whom nothing can procure,
When the wide world runnes bias from his will,
To writhe his limbes, and share, not mend the ill.
    This is the Mark-man, safe and sure,
Who still is right, and prayes to be so still.
                                    (1–10, 31–5)

Like the soul in "Content," and unlike the sweet youth of *The Church-porch* who is presumed to be easily tempted by his worldly companions, the constant man does not try to keep pace with the world. This constancy represents a far more active virtue than that celebrated in "Content," since it is to be measured by the principles of justice and prudence and it is one of the traditional parts of fortitude. These courtly and classical virtues are now rewritten, amended by substituting the needs of others for the aspirations of the self. The good of one's neighbor, "giving all their due" and paying "What place or person calls for," is to be pursued as well as one's own good, a standard that reflects the counsels of justice. "When great trials come," the constant man neither "seeks, nor shunnes them; but doth calmly stay / Till he the thing and the example weigh." These precepts of both fortitude and patience are more than merely stoic, since they define the acceptance of continual "crosses" depicted by God's courtier in "The Crosse" and anticipate the constructive groans that, in "Sion," help build the Temple within.[19]

Unlike the brave shows masking an interior emptiness exposed in *The Church-porch*, the constant man is so composed of moral virtue that exterior and interior are joined in one continuous fabric: "His words and works and fashion too / All of a piece, and all are cleare and straight." This goodness operates in dark or light alike, nor can the tortuous twistings of worldliness cause him to "writhe his limbes, and share, not mend the ill." It is the confidence of the poem that must – in its turn – be rewritten in later lyrics of *The Church*, not the perception.

Although "Constancie" owes as much to classical as to Christian values, its initial definition of the honest man as "He that doth still and strongly good pursue, / To God, his neighbor, and himself most true" depends on what, in "Divinitie," Herbert will ironically term the "dark instructions" of Christ: "*Love God, and love your neighbour. Watch and pray. / Do as ye would be done unto.*" The principle of service to others is affirmed in classical descriptions of justice, but here Herbert chooses to open his poem by repeating the scriptural injunction, thus raising this "character" of moral virtue to the level of godliness which takes divine rather than human words for a guide.

Just as, in "Humilitie," it is the Christian virtue which restores the (revised) cardinals to their rightful position of rule, so the stoic steadiness and social responsibility of "Constancie" lead to Herbert's recognition in "Affliction" (III) that the ultimate and perfect exemplar of these virtues is Christ, whose "life on earth was grief," who is "still / Constant unto it, making it to be / A point of honour, now to grieve in me." In each of these poems, the Christian application radically re-defines, and thereby amends, the courtly quality. Just as the active braveries associated with classical fortitude are, in "Frailtie," subordinated to the "sad events" of God's regimen, so the lesson of suffering in "Affliction" (III) sanctifies the struggle to achieve patience in adversity – the second part of fortitude – by association with Christ's noble role as the suffering servant of man, while the "Mark-man, safe and sure, / Who still is right, and prayes to be so still" in "Constancie" not only models himself upon Christ's exemplary constancy in grief but also follows Christ's clear instructions to serve God and his neighbor as well as himself.

Herbert's position here begins to shadow forth the life of service as a country parson, directed to God through the cure of souls, on which he ultimately embarked and thus accords with the struggle to acquire virtue in the more personal lyrics discussed in Chapters 4 and 5. The poem is important for its affirmation of a virtue as moral as it is religious, as courtly as it is holy. Here Herbert's conception of the proper mode of serving God overcomes the limits of the moral virtues by configuring Christ as their exemplar, just as his definition of the country parson couples the classical virtues with gravity and holiness in order to construct a complete pattern of service which the cardinals alone cannot achieve. In this sense, "Affliction" (III) revises the classicism of "Constancie" rather than qualifying it.

"Constancie" also reconciles the disparity between exterior and interior identified in *The Church-porch.* The poems within *The Church* stress the need for infused virtue if exterior behavior is to

regain the virtuous substance which, Herbert has pointed out, is lost
in present-day England. This internalizing is also, of course, a "raising," since the virtues of *habitus* commended in the Porch, alone, are
insufficient preparation for the higher infusion of God's grace which,
in the Church, Herbert finds necessary if he is to become a Temple fit
for Christ to inhabit. The virtues are restored to their proper place in
the exemplary Christian life by being "raised to godliness" – thus
recovering the Christian values which in fact had always been at the
heart of the courtly ideal.

In "The Size," however, concerned also with a cardinal virtue –
temperance – but occurring later in *The Church* than the constellation of virtues poems we have just considered, Herbert depicts the
enormous and consequential difference between a nobility that is
simply of the world and a divine nobility which totally rejects all
standards of earthly achievement:

> Content thee, greedie heart,
> Modest and moderate joyes to those, that have
> Title to more hereafter when they part,
> Are passing brave.
> Let th' upper springs into the low
> Descend and fall, and thou dost flow.
>
> . . . .
>
> To be in both worlds full
> Is more then God was, who was hungrie here.
> Wouldst thou his laws of fasting disanull?
> Enact good cheer?
> Lay out thy joy, yet hope to save it?
> Wouldst thou both eat thy cake, and have it?
>
> . . . .
>
> Then close again the seam,
> Which thou hast open'd: do not spread thy robe
> In hope of great things. Call to minde thy dream,
> An earthly globe,
> On whose meridian was engraven,
> *These seas are tears, and heav'n the haven.*
>   (1–6, 13–18, 42–7)

The "great things" of the exterior world, and even that world
itself, are now reduced to an imaginative projection, a globe in a
dream, and furthermore decisively detached from the exemplar who

was "hungrie here." The proverbial homeliness of "Wouldst thou both eat thy cake, and have it?" underlines the plainness of this apprehension of value in contrast to the fine show of brave deeds and eloquent language, while the heart flows in smooth serenity assisted by a willing acceptance of descent: "Let th' upper springs into the low / Descend and fall. . . ."

"The Size" also redefines the virtue of temperance in terms which paradoxically raise it above its usual applications by defining it as a lowering of worldly expectation. In *The Church-porch,* Herbert urged the sweet youth to "Pitch thy behaviour low, thy projects high," and by recommending "great places" as well as kindness and "good parts" as a means to usefulness in the preceding stanza, he acknowledged the value of such positions and allowed for virtue within them. But in "The Size," neither great things nor great joys are to be expected or, even more important, desired from this world. "Modest and moderate joyes" define a humble way and reject aspiration for great place absolutely. "The Size" transvalues temperance, which in the context of divine nobility takes on a form very different from its original associations with moral nobility. Herbert's definition of temperance in "The Size" allows for no continuity between moral and divine virtues when they are worked out in the individual life. They trace a path that leads to Bemerton, not to the court; they require God's courtier to serve the humble rather than the great.

All these poems figure the same courtly virtues that have shaped an ideal of conduct throughout the sixteenth century. They particularly resemble George Meriton's concept of divine nobility, and reflect La Primaudaye's emphasis upon the Christian end of the courtier's aspirations, in their insistence that virtue modeled after the example of Christ requires a rejection of worldly glory, an acceptance of affliction rather than the desire to rise above the condition.

In this respect the "virtues" poems in *The Church* recover the ideal in the only way possible, given the disintegration of worldly values that we have noted in Chapter 4, by raising them to a higher level after an initial humbling of the soul who would "pitch its projects high." Aspiration, too, is transvalued rather than rejected. In *The Country Parson,* it is presented in a similar figure of speech. Herbert defines the work as

> the Form and Character of a true Pastour, that I may have a Mark to aim at: which also I will set as high as I can, since hee

shoots higher that threatens the Moon, then hee that aims at a
Tree.   (p. 224)

These poems not only transform the courtly ideal by restoring Christian elements that had always been inherent within it, but also help to
transform Herbert's individual life choices into a pattern for his age.
Within *The Church*, the primary emphasis is upon his own experience, yet he enlarges the application and the significance of that
experience when such impersonal lyrics as "Humilitie" accomplish
the same transvaluation that we find in an explicitly personal poem
like "The Size," or when a third-person "character" lyric like "Constancie" is juxtaposed to the first-person "Affliction" (III) and con-
tributes substantially to its meaning.

    These patterns of significance reflect Herbert's dual insight in
"The H. Scriptures. II" that his life "makes good" and "comments
on" the secrets which, in scriptural verses, "make up some Christians
destinie." In just this way, whether we consider the evidence of the
poems or the response of his seventeenth-century readers, the first-
and third-person lyrics of *The Church* create an interconnected web
of meaning in which Herbert's life comments on the destiny of other
Christians by refiguring the traditional virtues and values which he
shares with his age. The work of virtue is accomplished in the
first-person poems that detail Herbert's inner experience, but the
way of virtue expands beyond the limits of the self in the third-person
lyrics which attempt to rhyme his whole age to good. In this effort,
both the self and the courtly society must abandon their worldly
identity. Herbert's loss of self in a humble way is not only confirmed
in lyrics of *The Church*, but implicitly recommended as a pattern for
others to follow.

iii

    As Nicholas Ferrar's preface to *The Temple* points out, it is the
exemplary model of its author's life, not alone the persuasive power
of his poetry, the truth of his vision, or the value of his precepts,
which commends the work to its readers. This design harmonizes the
life of its author with that of Christ, whose "sweet art," we are
reminded in "Easter," might "bear a part / And make up our defects." It is Herbert's attempt to emulate the pattern set by Christ –

or, as he says in "Lent," at least to "go part of that religious way" –
which enables him to pattern for his readers the way in which Christ
might also make up their defects, not simply his own.

The defective action of Herbert's will is therefore specific to his
own relationship with God, yet also represents the defects his readers
must struggle against. His recognition in "Providence" that, within
the plan of creation, "All things have their will, yet none but thine,"
stands as a precept applicable to Herbert or to any Christian, but we
have also seen in Chapter 5 how Herbert's worldly willfulness separates him from God and from the service which God has designed
him to fulfill. "The Search" points out that in Herbert's experience,
God's will

> such a strange distance is,
> As that to it
> East and West touch, the poles do kisse,
> And parallels meet.
>   (41–4)

The harmony with God enjoyed by "all things" in the third-person
assurance of "Providence" contrasts painfully with Herbert's distance from Him in "The Search":

> My knees pierce th' earth, mine eies the skie;
> And yet the sphere
> And centre both to me denie
> That thou art there.
>
> Yet can I mark how herbs below
> Grow green and gay,
> As if to meet thee they did know,
> While I decay.
>
> Yet can I mark how starres above
> Simper and shine,
> As having keyes unto thy love,
> While poore I pine.
>   (5–16)

This difference between the well-tuned consort of creation and
the infinite distance from God experienced by the searching soul is
bridged only by an interiorizing process which enables Herbert to

bring his own will into consonance with that of God just as, in "The Size," we have seen the world interiorized, transformed into nothing more than an emblem for Herbert's rejection of its delusory attractions. This pattern helps to explain the place of such visions of order as "Man" and "Providence" in the structure of lyrics that compose *The Church.* They are necessary elements in the building of a frame and fabric within the individual heart, because they represent moments of correct perception, achievements of a perspective large enough to recognize the workings of God's designs even in a universe that, as "The World" points out, is continually razed by man's propensity to sin. These perceptions are lessons to man, serviceable finally to teach the seeking soul its right relationship to its maker, but in themselves such perceptions do not possess sufficient power to transform the soul.

That power depends upon the action of man's will, which Herbert defines in "The Elixir" as the deliberate effort to do "any thing . . . as if for thee," and on the reciprocal movement of God's will toward man which accomplishes what all of man's striving cannot. As the final stanza of "The Search" puts it:

> For as thy absence doth excell
> > All distance known:
> So doth thy nearnesse bear the bell,
> > Making two one.
> > > (57–60)

Herbert has used the metaphor of physical space throughout "The Search" to signify man's infinite spiritual distance from God. His resolution of the distance in these lines consequently reveals the miraculous nature of such divine intervention. The action of God's will is a work of grace that supersedes the laws of creation, enabling man to become not simply one of the creatures, but "more," as "Providence" points out.

In "Mans medley," it is clear that the difference between man and the creatures is as essential for a proper understanding of his condition as the recognition of what he shares with them:

> Heark, how the birds do sing,
> > And woods do ring.
> All creatures have their joy: and man hath his.

Yet if we rightly measure,
            Mans joy and pleasure
Rather hereafter, then in present, is.

To this life things of sense
            Make their pretence:
In th' other Angels have a right by birth:
            Man ties them both alone,
            And makes them one,
With th' one hand touching heav'n, with th' other earth.

In soul he mounts and flies,
            In flesh he dies.
He wears a stuffe whose thread is course and round,
            But trimm'd with curious lace,
            And should take place
After the trimming, not the stuffe and ground.

                                        (1–18)

This contrast between the ascent of the soul and the descent of the
flesh defines the proper mode of aspiration and confirms the right-
ness of Herbert's wish in "The Search" to pierce both earth and sky
in his longing for God. The soul is indeed designed to "mount and
flie" toward its Maker or, as Herbert puts it in "The Storm," to quit
the earth and, "mounting more and more," dare to "assault thee, and
besiege thy doore." The aspiring soul figured in these poems retains
the essence of courtly aspiration, but now redirects it to the realm of
the spirit.

"Mans medley" also transposes the imagery of exterior and
interior which has, since *The Church-porch,* designated the false
braveries of worldly show and the emptiness of virtue within. Here
the "stuffe and ground" represent man's fleshly nature, which Herbert dismisses in courtly disdain as "course and round" material,[20]
while the trimming now represents the soul, whose "curious lace"
appropriately adorns a creature who touches heaven as well as earth.
It is a wonderful transformation of the mere "shreds of holinesse"
which were all he could claim in "The Sinner." This inversion of
relationships between outer and inner appearance, outer and inner
value, and this choice of courtly dress as vehicle for Herbert's
recognition that the soul rightfully aspires to mount toward heaven,
begin to create the image of God's courtier, whose will toward the
good is now directed to its proper end.[21]

The action of the will in "Mans medley" traces a reciprocal

relation between God and man which, as "The Holdfast" puts it, teaches man that "all things were more ours by being his." But as this poem also points out, "We must confesse that nothing is our own."[22] Both statements are simultaneously true. Insofar as man would reserve his will to himself in worldly self-assertion, he is bound to dust and all his mortal "power & might" are insufficient to save him. Yet the recognition that nothing is our own is just the knowledge that restores the efficacy of man's will by harmonizing it with that of God: "What Adam had, and forfeited for all, / Christ keepeth now, who cannot fail or fall." Thus all things become at last "more ours."

In the opening stanza of "Clasping of Hands," Herbert shows how this reciprocity gives man the advantage, for the loss of the self, when it is given over to God, restores a wholeness of identity that, in the absence of God's presence within, man has never really possessed:[23]

> Lord, thou art mine, and I am thine,
> If mine I am: and thine much more,
> Then I or ought, or can be mine.
> Yet to be thine, doth me restore;
> So that again I now am mine,
> And with advantage mine the more,
> Since this being mine, brings with it thine,
> And thou with me dost thee restore.
>   If I without thee would be mine,
>   I neither should be mine nor thine.
>   (1–10)

The chiastic transpositions of the second stanza restate this insight, but now explain it by reference to Christ's exemplary relinquishment of His divine identity in the Incarnation and Passion:

> Lord, I am thine, and thou art mine:
> So mine thou art, that something more
> I may presume thee mine, then thine.
> For thou didst suffer to restore
> Not thee, but me, and to be mine,
> And with advantage mine the more,
> Since thou in death wast none of thine,
> Yet then as mine didst me restore.
>   O be mine still! still make me thine!
>   Or rather make no Thine and Mine!
>   (11–20)

"Clasping of Hands" and "The Holdfast" suggest the necessary doubleness of man's experience. The submission of his capacities to God restores their efficacy, just as Christ's submission of His divinity to endure the death of the flesh restores man to the state of future immortality. Herbert is here working out the interior and spiritual meaning of the recognition more simply stated in "Charms and Knots," that only "on ground" can the humble soul "find himself" and "seek to rise": only an acceptance of lowliness can initiate the ascent.

This insight marks the crucial difference between the celebration of man's ability to will himself to virtue in the sixteenth-century courtesy books and this seventeenth-century courtier's attempt to do so in a courtly world from which virtue seems to be rapidly departing. Faith in the power of man's will to acquire virtue gives place to an increasing preoccupation with the need for God's grace to make up man's defects. The reciprocity figured in these poems attempts to harmonize the contradictory demands of acquired and infused virtue which are built into the courtly ideal. If Herbert's will to virtue is directed toward God rather than great place in the world, and if he takes Christ as his exemplar, the virtue that he can acquire becomes his own efficacious contribution to the transformation of his stony heart into a fit habitation for Christ. His will then in truth becomes "more his" in its accordance with God's will for him. But, though the virtue Herbert acquires in this way represents a necessary striving on his part, he also needs "thy blessed Spirit" to bear His part and make up his defects.

This is the role of grace, the infused virtue that, as La Primaudaye had pointed out in *The French Academie*, provides the courtier with the ultimate sufficiency that his acquired virtue lacks. But just as man's will and God's will are shaped into unity in *The Temple* in the exercise of Herbert's "utmost art" to harmonize these differences, so also the grace of the courtly artist plays a necessary part in figuring God's courtier. His courtly references clearly expose the falsity and emptiness of merely surface "graces." Even the graceful art of poetry, if directed exclusively to mortal love, serves only to "parcel out" the "glorious name" of immortal love and throw it on the "dust which thou hast made." "Love I" points out the destructive role of beauty and wit when they are limited to the ends of mortality:

> siding with invention, they together
> Bear all the sway, possessing heart and brain,

(Thy workmanship) and give thee share in neither.
Wit fancies beautie, beautie raiseth wit:
   The world is theirs; they two play out the game,
   Thou standing by: and though thy glorious name
Wrought our deliverance from th' infernall pit,
   Who sings thy praise? onely a skarf or glove
   Doth warm our hands, and make them write of love.

(6–14)

The courtier's worldly grace is apparently robbed of all value when his verse is dismissed as a duty "not to a true, but painted chair" and when the groves and arbors of pastoral are shadowed in what Herbert derides as "course-spunne lines" in "Jordan" (I). Yet in "Christmas," he redresses the image of the pastoral poet in accordance with a long tradition of Christ as shepherd which transvalues the secular by raising it to the level of the sacred:

   The shepherds sing: and shall I silent be?
      My God, no hymne for thee?
My soul's a shepherd too; a flock it feeds
      Of thoughts, and words, and deeds.
   The pasture is thy word: the streams, thy grace
      Enriching all the place.
Shepherd and flock shall sing, and all my powers
      Out-sing the day-light houres.
Then we will chide the sunne for letting night
      Take up his place and right:
We sing one common Lord; wherefore he should
      Himself the candle hold.

(15–26)

There is just as much courtly grace in the figure of God's pastoral poet here as there is in the worldly pastorals whose place Herbert somewhat scornfully grants in "Jordan" (I) – "Shepherds are honest people; let them sing" – but whose subject matter he rejects so plainly in the close of that poem. In "Christmas" the grace of the poet is transmuted into the spiritual activity of the soul. Here the matter of poetry is no worldly scarf or glove, nightingale or spring, but rather the material of a lifetime of service, a flock of "thoughts, and words, and deeds" ranging in the rich meadow of the holy scriptures watered by God's grace.

The diction and intonation of Herbert's courteous request to Christ in the final lines of the first part of "Christmas" also reflect a

very courtly grace: "Furnish & deck my soul, that thou mayst
have / A better lodging then a rack or grave." This is a transvalued
image of the worldly courtier in "The Thanksgiving" who asks in
bewilderment, "Shall thy strokes be my stroking? thorns, my flower? / Thy rod, my posie? crosse, my bower?" and who confesses in
"The Reprisall" that he is as yet unable to "give a disentangled state
and free." In becoming God's servant, Herbert does not abandon his
courtly identity but rather transfers it to the court and king of
heaven; indeed, in "The Glimpse" he asserts that he himself "by thy
coming may be made a court."[24]

"Discipline" transforms the action of courtly grace as well as its
language. Here Herbert celebrates the bestowal of God's grace upon
him with an answering grace which raises the *sprezzatura* of Castiglione's courtier to those heights that Pietro Bembo had urged him to
gain in the Fourth Book.[25] The poem is paradigmatic of the effortless
simplicity which Herbert masters as fully as any Renaissance courtier, yet at the same time it incorporates the experience of humility
that has transformed him into God's courtier:

> Throw away thy rod,
> Throw away thy wrath:
> > O my God,
> Take the gentle path.
>
> For my hearts desire
> Unto thine is bent:
> > I aspire
> To a full consent.
>
> Not a word or look
> I affect to own,
> > But by book,
> And thy book alone.
>
> Though I fail, I weep:
> Though I halt in pace,
> > Yet I creep
> To the throne of grace.
>
> Then let wrath remove;
> Love will do the deed:
> > For with love
> Stonie hearts will bleed.

Love is swift of foot;
Love's a man of warre,
                    And can shoot,
And can hit from farre.

Who can scape his bow?
That which wrought on thee,
                    Brought thee low,
Needs must work on me.

Throw away thy rod;
Though man frailties hath,
                    Thou art God:
Throw away thy wrath.

Just as the "curious lace" of the soul is a proper adornment in "Mans medley," so in "Discipline" the grace of the worldly courtier now adorns Herbert's language in a perfectly fitting invocation of divine grace. There is no lack of either the grace or the willfulness of the courtier in this simple, direct assertion that Herbert aspires to God's "full consent." Yet there is a humility more complete and composed than the outcries of "Longing" or "Complaining" in his relinquishment of any word or look that is not "by thy book" and in the hesitancy with which he approaches the throne of grace. Here his lack of advance is mitigated by the lesson of affliction in a harmonizing "though — yet" pattern which balances Herbert's tears against his failures and the movement of ascent against the slow pace of his progress.[26] He is no longer fragmented into broken parts of grief, as in "Deniall," nor is his language fragmented syntactically here, even in recounting his own insufficiencies. Now the plain dignity of his speech accepts failure and admits to sorrow.

The courtier of the early poems in *The Church* attempted to vie with God in holiness, though he found himself unequal to the task. As he put it in "The Reprisall," "was it not enough that thou / By thy eternall glorie didst outgo me?" In "Discipline," on the other hand, Herbert engages in a courteous contest with God as he will again in "Love" (III). His claims are moderated and his words are restricted to the single condition which joins man with God on the same level: "That which wrought on thee, / Brought thee low, / Needs must work on me." Love is this single force, the sufficient discipline which can accomplish what wrath cannot. Herbert's epithets for love unite the Cupid figure of courtly poetry, wielding the bow which, even "from farre," none can escape, with the higher love whose blood, shed in His passion for man, enables even man's stony heart to bleed as a sign that it has become "an heart of flesh."

There is a nice reciprocity in Herbert's courteous reminder to God that the same gentle love which led to Christ's incarnation must work on His creature as well. In the final stanza, both the measure of his language and the politic qualifier, "Though man frailties hath," sound the authentic note of God's courtier.[27] Here he even fulfills the traditional courtly role of leading his ruler to virtue. In concluding "Thou art God: / Throw away thy wrath," he implies that God, as the occupant of the throne of grace, has no need of the wrath that a lesser ruler might be tempted to display and, furthermore, that the gentle path is more suited to His divine nature.

"Discipline" also incorporates the principle of reciprocity in its structure. Herbert's "advice" to God in the opening stanza is followed by an account of his own offering in the next three, while the fifth stanza, once more invoking God's mercy, echoes Christ's desire in "The Sacrifice" to prove "with patience . . . / If stonie hearts will melt with gentle love" in reminding God that "with love / Stonie hearts will bleed." This hinge links Herbert's evidence for the transformation of his own stony heart, given in the preceding stanzas, to the transformation of God's wrath by the force of His own doctrine of love which Herbert will invoke in the following stanzas. These final three stanzas after the hinge establish a balance, as Herbert now seeks to bring God's actions into harmony with his own desire and aspiration as it has been expressed in the first half of the poem.

This patterning creates a structural analogue to the relation of interchange between divine and human which the figure of the Temple embodies. The earliest comparisons between Christ and Herbert in *The Church*, in "The Thanksgiving" and "The Reprisall," detailed an imbalance so great that no structural articulation of the relationship was even possible. "The Thanksgiving" in particular stressed the disproportion between the thorns and cross of Christ and the courtly flowers and bowers which Herbert would give up in exchange, while it concluded with a radical break in continuity: "Then for thy passion – I will do for that – / Alas, my God, I know not what."

Midway in *The Church*, the structure of "Dialogue" represents a midpoint in Herbert's continuing analysis of the relationship be-

tween himself and God. Here, alternate human and divine voices
present both sides of the case, stanza by stanza. Herbert opens by
protesting his inadequacy and unworthiness to receive God's love:

> But when all my care and pains
> Cannot give the name of gains
> To thy wretch so full of stains,
> What delight or hope remains?
>
> (5–8)

Christ's reply takes over the balance in the second stanza:

> *What, Child, is the ballance thine,*
> *Thine the poise and measure?*
> *If I say, Thou shalt be mine;*
> *Finger not my treasure.*
>
> (9–12)

The third and fourth stanzas repeat the pattern, but the vision of
reciprocity between divine and human is still beyond Herbert at this
point. Equilibrium fails in the radical disjunction between Christ's
act of freely parting with his "glorie and desert" for man and Herbert's inability to follow that "resigning"; Christ's words break off in
mid-sentence as Herbert interrupts in the concluding line, "Ah! no
more: thou break'st my heart."

In "Discipline," however, human and divine roles intertwine
harmoniously as the poet's grace in composing his poem matches the
grace of the "gentle path" of love which he is persuading his Maker
to take. This attainment of "poise and measure" is reflected again in
the contest of courtesy[28] in "Love" (III), the final poem in *The
Church*, which exhibits the courtly grace that we have seen in "Discipline." Its form and even its subject resemble "Dialogue" still more
closely, but here the exchange between Christ as Love, the host, and
Herbert as the unworthy guest is neither divided into alternating
stanzas nor broken off in discontinuity in the conclusion.

> Love bade me welcome: yet my soul drew back,
> Guiltie of dust and sinne.
> But quick-ey'd Love, observing me grow slack
> From my first entrance in,
> Drew nearer to me, sweetly questioning,
> If I lack'd any thing.

A guest, I answer'd, worthy to be here:
        Love said, You shall be he.
I the unkinde, ungratefull? Ah my deare,
        I cannot look on thee.
Love took my hand, and smiling did reply,
        Who made the eyes but I?

Truth Lord, but I have marr'd them: let my shame
        Go where it doth deserve.
And know you not, sayes Love, who bore the blame?
        My deare, then I will serve.
You must sit down, sayes Love, and taste my meat:
        So I did sit and eat.

Once more Herbert protests his lack of merit, and once more Christ points out that He "bore the blame" for man's fall into sin; but here, rather than presenting discrete speeches of the two participants, each stanza figures a complete exchange, in a movement forward and back as elegantly patterned as steps in a dance. The poem opens with Love's welcoming gesture, balanced in the same line by the drawing back of the soul, while Love, responding to this diffidence, draws nearer in concern. The second stanza traces a similar movement of doubt, then reassurance, then a gesture of turning away – "I cannot look on thee" – followed by a reciprocating act of response that draws host and guest still closer, as Love takes his guest's hand.

The final stanza again evokes by anticipation a movement away, as the soul begs, "let my shame / Go where it doth deserve," but that movement too gives way to the union of the concluding lines, as Love urges His guest to sit and, in the grace of offering His service, finally persuades him to partake of His feast. Here the speeches of the participants chime together within each stanza. Each movement away is equilibrated by a counter-movement towards, in a smooth progression from the hesitation appropriate to one "guiltie of dust and sinne" to the smiling grace of Love taking the hand of His unkind and ungrateful guest to the culmination, which accomplishes a wonderful reversal of roles in the Host's gracious service of Himself to His guest.

"Love" (III) harmonizes the grace which man can attain with the grace which only God can confer. The courtliness of its conception articulates the different grace which not only belongs to, but derives from, the heavenly King. Courtesy marks the entire exchange, defining the actions of both host and guest just as Herbert defines the essence – the *quidditas* – of Communion by evoking the setting of an earthly feast given by a noble host for an equally gentle guest. The graciousness of Love's behavior, quick to observe and smilingly taking His guest's hand, like the intimacy and warmth of His speech as He "sweetly questions" this dear visitor, transvalues to the highest plane the precept of courtly conversation which Herbert had recommended to the sweet youth of *The Church-porch* at the very beginning of *The Temple:*

> Be calm in arguing: for fiercenesse makes
> Errour a fault, and truth discourtesie.
> Why should I feel another mans mistakes
> More then his sicknesses or povertie?
>   In love I should: but anger is not love,
>   Nor wisdome neither: therefore gently move.
>   (stanza 52)

The guest in "Love" (III) is also calm in arguing, gently moving his objections as he was unable to do in "Dialogue," while the host is equally gentle in moving His guest to sit at the feast that is offered. The poem enacts as drama the "gentle path" which Herbert has recommended to his Lord in "Discipline."

The essential difference between this grace and the grace of the worldly courtier is that it is humble. This humility emulates the model set by the divine ruler to whom Herbert, as God's courtier, offers his service.[29] In "Love" (III), the host becomes the servant, matching the humility of His guest but also setting a standard for service by defining His own office as a humble giving of Himself to others. The act is accomplished with fully effortless ease and simplicity, at once courtly and holy.[30] The service of Christ to man is as much a work of art as the construction of Herbert's poems. In this sense the poem embodies the music that Herbert had called for in "Easter": "O let thy blessed Spirit bear a part, / And make up our defects with his sweet art."

iv

The Temple is a composition of parts whose wholeness validates
the spiritual force of "divisions" and "partitions" rather than constructing an undivided unity. In "An Offering," Herbert contrasts
this equivocally united soul with Christ's willing and exemplary
assumption of the divided state of man in the Incarnation: "one pure
heart is nothing to bestow: / In Christ two natures met to be thy
cure." "Love" (III) constitutes a moment of recovery in the harmony
and felicity of its communion with Christ, but the poem concludes
only the central section of *The Temple*. The interior transformations
of *The Church* must be configured with *The Church Militant* if we
are to understand the work's largest design. Here, both the comprehensive picture of England's moral state in Herbert's own time,
and the expansive temporal and spatial history, refigure the meaning
of a Temple whose frame and fabric are within.

The Church Militant traces a double progress of the Church and
Sin from their earliest beginnings to present time, prophesying their
course into the future all the way to the end of human time, when
"Judgment may meet them both & search them round." Each historical segment detailing the progress of the pilgrim, Religion, from east
to west through time and the continual overtaking of the pilgrim by
Sin closes with the refrain: "*How deare to me, O God, thy counsels
are! / Who may with thee compare?*" The apparent confidence of this
refrain is poised equivocally against the events traced in the body of
the poem.

Herbert's praise of God's counsels is difficult to accept when it
follows accounts of Greece and Egypt "given over . . . / To such
Mahometan stupidities, / As the old heathen would deem prodigies"
or of "new and old Rome" become "both together . . . one Anti-
christ," for what Herbert traces is in fact the progress of Sin:

> Yet as the Church shall thither westward flie,
> So Sinne shall trace and dog her instantly:
> They have their period also and set times
> Both for their vertuous actions and their crimes.
> (259–62)

Yet the huge scope of *The Church Militant* finally explains a refrain
that celebrates God's counsels even as it demonstrates Religion's
unsuccessful attempt to outrun Sin. The flight of the Church, by

going west, still proceeds eastward, drawing always "more neare /
To time and place, where judgement shall appeare." In the fullness of
time, God's judgment will finally vindicate the Church.[31]

The course of worldly events before that moment is reached,
however, suggests why the frame and fabric of the Temple must now,
in Herbert's own time, be erected within the individual heart. The
poem is structured as two parallel progresses. The first hundred lines
trace the journey of Religion westward from Abraham's time to
England's recent "higher victorie" — "Giving the Church a crown to
keep her state" — in a pattern, familiar to us from the lyrics within
The Church, which reveals the miracle of God's counsels through a
sequence of transformations and inversions. The "wonders of anger"
in Egypt now prove to be marvels of love, when "Nilus for monsters
brought forth Israelites," a transformation whose language recalls
Herbert's recognition in "The Priesthood" that God often makes
vessels "Of lowly matter for high uses meet": "Such power hath
mightie Baptisme to produce / For things misshapen, things of highest use." Plato and Aristotle are "wheel'd about again to spell *Christ-
Crosse,*" and the warrior celebrated in classical epic gives place to the
higher heroism of Christ:

> The Warrier his deere skarres no more resounds,
> But seems to yeeld Christ hath the greater wounds,
> Wounds willingly endur'd to work his blisse,
> Who by an ambush lost his Paradise.
> The great heart stoops, and taketh from the dust
> A sad repentance, not the spoils of lust:
> Quitting his spear, lest it should pierce again
> Him in his members, who for him was slain.
> The Shepherds hook grew to a scepter here,
> Giving new names and numbers to the yeare.
>
> (63–72)

This is the exemplary acceptance of lowly place to which Herbert
has alluded in "Faith," and which he has extended to the position of
the humble soul in "Charms and Knots." The image of Christ as
shepherd and king recalls the transformations of "Jordan" (I) and
"Christmas," which replaced the shepherd of worldly pastoral and
the worldly king to whom the shepherd-poet offers allegiance with
the heavenly King served by the true pastoral poet. Christ's action
distinguishes between the two modes of descent to dust which are
available to man, the one leading to a "sad repentance" that enables

the humble soul to rise – the progress we have traced in Chapter 5 in relation to Herbert's search for a calling – and the other yielding only the "spoils of lust," the inexorable entanglement in mortality which, as we have seen in Chapter 4, leads only to disintegration and dissolution.

The pattern of disintegration is also traced in the vast historical perspective of lines 101 to 210 of *The Church Militant*, which return over the same ground traversed in the first hundred lines but now follow the action of Sin:

> Much about one and the same time and place,
> Both where and when the Church began her race,
> Sinne did set out of Eastern *Babylon*,
> And travell'd westward also: journeying on
> He chid the Church away, where e're he came,
> Breaking her peace, and tainting her good name.
>
> (101–6)

The worship of false gods in Egypt spells out the difference between a humility that unites man with divinity, because it follows that exemplary model, and the delusive and false humility which binds him within the circumference of earth and separates him from the divine:

> Ah, what a thing is man devoid of grace,
> Adoring garlick with an humble face,
> Begging his food of that which he may eat,
> Starving the while he worshippeth his meat!
> Who makes a root his god, how low is he,
> If God and man be sever'd infinitely!
> What wretchednesse can give him any room,
> Whose house is foul, while he adores his broom?
>
> (111–18)

But here, too, Herbert shifts from the past to the present in which he writes in order to point out that man has still not freed himself from the bonds of earth:

> None will beleeve this now, though money be
> In us the same transplanted foolerie.
>
> (119–20)

The undertone of contemporary reference that marks *The Church Militant* as a prophetic warning to its own time is noticeable particularly in Herbert's figure of Sin as a gallant who "would needs foretell / As well what should befall, as what befell" in the "Rich shrines and oracles" of Greece, and as a poet who "would serve / His pills of sublimate in that conserve." The machinations of Sin are set forth in the same terms that have depicted the empty show of worth and service and the deceitful simulation of virtue in speech and action in *The Church-porch:*

> The world came in with hands and purses full
> To this great lotterie, and all would pull.
> But all was glorious cheating, brave deceit,
> Where some poore truths were shuffled for a bait
> To credit him, and to discredit those
> Who after him should braver truths disclose.
>
> (133–8)

The entanglements of Glory and Pleasure that have corrupted the Roman empire are no mere phenomena of the historical past, if we recall Herbert's rejection of the "wayes of Pleasure" in "The Pearl" or of "brave Glorie puffing by / In silks that whistled" in "The Quip."

The double progress of the Church and Sin come together in the final third of *The Church Militant,* which focuses Herbert's concern clearly in the present. The tracing of Sin's course has concluded with a powerful denunciation of Rome, but the Church's inability as institution to counter the inroads of Sin extends significantly beyond Rome to "the late reformation" and to the sins of present-day England:

> But as in vice the copie still exceeds
> The pattern, but not so in vertuous deeds;
> So though Sinne made his latter seat the better,
> The latter Church is to the first a debter.
> The second Temple could not reach the first:
> And the late reformation never durst
> Compare with ancient times and purer yeares;
> But in the Jews and us deserveth tears.
> Nay, it shall ev'ry yeare decrease and fade;
> Till such a darknesse do the world invade

At Christs last coming, as his first did finde:
Yet must there such proportion be assign'd
To these diminishings, as is between
The spacious world and *Jurie* to be seen.
Religion stands on tip-toe in our land,
Readie to passe to the *American* strand.
When height of malice, and prodigious lusts,
Impudent sinning, witchcrafts, and distrusts
(The marks of future bane) shall fill our cup
Unto the brimme, and make our measure up;
When *Sein* shall swallow *Tiber,* and the *Thames*
By letting in them both pollutes her streams:
When *Italie* of us shall have her will,
And all her calender of sinnes fulfill;
Whereby one may foretell, what sinnes next yeare
Shall both in *France* and *England* domineer;
Then shall Religion to *America* flee:
They have their times of Gospel, ev'n as we.
My God, thou dost prepare for them a way
By carrying first their gold from them away:
For gold and grace did never yet agree:
Religion alwaies sides with povertie.
We think we rob them, but we think amisse:
We are more poore, and they more rich by this.
Thou wilt revenge their quarrell, making grace
To pay our debts, and leave her ancient place
To go to them, while that which now their nation
But lends to us, shall be our desolation.

(221–58)

According to Walton, the couplet "Religion stands on tip-toe in our land, / Readie to passe to the *American* strand" was questioned by the Cambridge licensers of *The Temple* and delayed its approval for publication. Walton's unsupported evidence cannot be absolutely accepted, yet not very many years later, a Puritan clergyman was imprisoned for making a statement so similar that he may well have been alluding to Herbert's poem.[32] The full passage is more important than this single couplet, however. Herbert's anxiety concerning the future in the face of man's susceptibility to malice, lusts, greed, and distrust reflects the lamentation for his divided church that we have seen in "Church-rents and schismes," rather than the assured definition of the *via media* in the far more frequently quoted "The British Church." The latter poem details the orderly beauty of the

Anglican *ecclesia* as an ideal structure which Herbert poises against the bedizened falsities of Rome or the bare sparsity of Geneva. But the former poem, like this passage in *The Church Militant,* addresses the ecclesiastical actualities and personal vices of the world in which the poem is written, to which the poet speaks.

Herbert sees "our desolation" ahead for his own nation and church. He presents that vision in language that recalls the dissolutions of the court and disintegrations of the courtly ideal in the *Church* lyrics. It is the bleakness of his vision of England's present and immediate future which enables us to interpret the enormous temporal reach of *The Church Militant* and the placement of its only mitigating balance at the end of time, on the day of judgment. Only then shall the wisdom of God's counsels search out evidence of goodness in the Church and punish the depredations of Sin that have weakened its power to compel Common-weals to

> acknowledge thee,
> And wrap their policies in thy decree,
> Complying with thy counsels, doing nought
> Which doth not meet with an eternall thought.
>
> (5–8)

The parallel courses of Sin and Religion throughout *The Church Militant* point out the insufficiency of the Church, as an institution, to countervail the state of sin in mankind. The single real force for earthly good in the poem, the sole exemplar not outrun by Sin, is Christ, turning His shepherd's hook into a scepter of rule. In its account of the Church's limitations in the city of man, the seemingly expansive reach of *The Church Militant* turns back upon itself toward the Temple within, the transformation of the stony heart of man, modeled after the example of Christ, that fits it for His habitation – the endless making and mending detailed in the central portion of *The Temple*.[33]

Purification of the institution will occur only in the fullness of time, at the end of the entire span of earthly history. Herbert's concluding poem in *The Temple,* then, constitutes no naive paean to the perfection or the power of the Anglican church in the moment it is most deeply entangled in division and dissent. On the contrary, *The Church Militant* envisions continual encroachments of man's sinful nature, which not only weaken the institution but, as Herbert writes, are about to enmesh it in a civil war as much religious as political. In the largest perspective, Herbert projects God's vindication of the church's virtue. But in the perspective of his immediate moment, Herbert's despairing judgment on the state of the church in the last section of *The Temple* matches his despairing judgment on the state of the aristocracy in the first section.

Now we see why the Temple can neither be built solely by the hands of man nor associated with past earthly power and glory, as "Sion" has plainly declared in stating that such a structure was not God's aim. It is not God's aim in the present either, as *The Church Militant* makes equally plain in stating that God shall make "grace / To pay our debts, and leave her ancient place / To go to them. . . ." America rightfully will possess her "time of Gospel," since, although England may have her gold, "Religion alwaies sides with povertie." The world of secular power, dominated by gold, is defined unequivocally as "our desolation." The agency which pays our debts is Christ, the exemplary ruler whom alone a courtier in Herbert's time can serve virtuously. The workings of that grace are only to be found in the Temple whose frame and fabric are within the individual heart. And as the *Church* lyrics show, that Temple must be continually remade, rewritten, amended over a lifetime.

The Temple comprises "many gifts in one," making good Herbert's perception in "An Offering" that the broken parts of his own hard heart might be recovered by Christ's all-healing "balsome, or indeed a bloud, / Dropping from heav'n which doth both cleanse and close / All sorts of wounds." *The Temple* celebrates a wholeness that is always – and only – in the making, and earns its authority by confessing the worldliness that its exemplary speaker shares with his audience. It promises only a hope: faith in God's counsels. This inspired work of art ends with a question that both assures and warns us. Christ as exemplar is *in*comparable; the "holy Mr. Herbert" we would like to discover in *The Temple* is a fiction of our own assumptions. The human heart so agonistically building a Temple within which Christ might dwell is as marred and mortal a self at the end of *The Church*, in "Love" (III), as it was in "The Altar" where we first discover the parts of this hard heart. At the close of *The Temple*, human history has been parceled out in the deconstructions and disintegrations of sin. If Herbert is, through the making of these poems, a pattern or more for his age, that pattern is one that limns God's courtier, vivid and real in his worldly will and grace, humble in his longing for God's will and grace – one who fully shares with us the need for rewriting the self, reconstructing, ever mending our relation to the Christ so precariously lodged within any human heart.

Notes

Introduction

1. This count is not universally accepted; see especially John T. Shawcross, "Herbert's Double Poems: A Problem in the Text of *The Temple*," in Claude J. Summers and Ted-Larry Pebworth, eds., *"Too Rich to Clothe the Sunne": Essays on George Herbert* (Pittsburgh, 1980), pp. 211–28.

2. I follow the customary practice of designating MS. Jones B 62 (the Williams manuscript) as *W* and MS. Tanner 307 (the Bodleian manuscript) as *B*. The extensive alterations and additions from *W* to *B* suggest that Herbert greatly expanded his concept of *The Temple* as structure and sequence.

3. For structural interpretations of *The Temple*, see note 6 to Chapter 5. Too-neat patterns are minimally persuasive; the *Church* lyrics, in particular, seem to set up expectations of sequence that are repeatedly undermined when partial sequences are left open or interrupted.

4. All quotations of Herbert's poetry and prose, unless otherwise noted, are taken from F. E. Hutchinson, ed., *The Works of George Herbert* (1941; corr. reprint, Oxford, 1970). Line numbers for poems cited in part are identified in my text; cited parts of *The Church-porch* are identified by stanza numbers.

5. Wolfgang Iser, in *The Implied Reader: Patterns of Prose Communication from Bunyan to Beckett* (Baltimore, 1974), p. 282, also applies the constellation figure to the interpretive process of different readers. But Herbert's perception – as both writer and reader of his own text (and life) – of "configurations" and "constellations" has been far more productive for my reading of *The Temple;* for Herbert, these are, clearly, essential rather than incidental figures of interpretation.

6. See Hutchinson's note, p. 496, on the puzzling use of "watch."

7. I have gratefully borrowed my title from Maurice Hussey, who speaks of Herbert as "the Cavalier with high social connections, 'God's courtier' whose verse has the care for tone that one is tempted to call Caroline or Cavalier" in *Jonson and the Cavaliers* (London, 1964), p. 3.

8. Nicholas Ferrar, "The Printers to the Reader" of *The Temple*, in

Hutchinson, p. 3. Herbert's friend Nicholas Ferrar is generally accepted as the author of this preface, but see Edmund Miller's comments on the issue in *Drudgerie Divine: The Rhetoric of God and Man in George Herbert* (Salzburg, Austria, 1979), p. 127.

9.　Both secular and sacred sonnet cycles of the late sixteenth century bind their diversities of mood and tone within the repeated lyrical form. Although the lyric experimentation of the psalm translations by Philip and Mary Sidney may have been a model for Herbert, even these formally varied poems are bound to their single source. Much of *The Temple*'s artistic power derives from its discontinuities, multiplicities, and interwoven patterns. In this sense, the text is extraordinarily open, unbounded, and fluid – far more so than its many imitators later in the seventeenth century. Barbara K. Lewalski's magisterial *Protestant Poetics and the Seventeenth-Century Religious Lyric* (Princeton, 1979) shows how extensively the Bible served as a source for Herbert; Lewalski also points out that *The Temple* "moves beyond an imitative and derivative to a genuinely creative conception and use of biblical poetics" (p. 316).

10.　Stanley Fish, *The Living Temple: George Herbert and Catechizing* (Berkeley, 1978); Richard Strier, *Love Known: Theology and Experience in George Herbert's Poetry* (Chicago, 1983); Barbara Leah Harman, *Costly Monuments: Representations of the Self in George Herbert's Poetry* (Cambridge, Mass., 1982). Other recent configurations of the speaker in *The Temple* are by Heather A. R. Asals, *Equivocal Predication: George Herbert's Way to God* (Toronto, 1981); Diana Benet, *Secretary of Praise: The Poetic Vocation of George Herbert* (Columbia, Mo., 1984); Leah Sinanoglou Marcus, *Childhood and Cultural Despair: A Theme and Variations in Seventeenth-Century Literature* (Pittsburgh, 1978); and Camille Wells Slights, *The Casuistical Tradition in Shakespeare, Donne, Herbert, and Milton* (Princeton, 1981). I have learned much from these sensitive and illuminating readings, as from Herbert's earlier critics; my notes can only begin to acknowledge my debt to such a collective wealth of scholarship.

11.　This "Conclusion In Which It May Appear That Everything Is Taken Back" in Fish's *Living Temple* has served me as both challenge and invitation, just as Fish's *Self-Consuming Artifacts: The Experience of Seventeenth-Century Literature* (Berkeley, 1972) did in my earliest wrestling with the complex marvels of Herbert's poetry.

12.　Not all recent critics acquiesce in Roland Barthes' proclamation that "the author" is now dead, though. Lawrence Lipking, "Life, Death, and Other Theories," in *Historical Studies and Literary Criticism*, ed. Jerome J. McGann (Madison, Wis., 1985), pp. 180–98, offers a witty corrective to such absolutes. My emphasis here on Herbert's biography as a means of "authorizing" his text is disingenuous; I don't consider "the author," "authorizing," or even "authority" in literary texts as exact equivalents of, say, "authoritarianism." We need not – I would argue, should not – automatically prejudice the issue of biography before a given text is studied.

13. I am, of course, echoing Herbert's letter to his stepfather on the possibility that the Oratorship may "divert me too much from Divinity" (Hutchinson, p. 370).

14. See especially Alfred Alvarez, *The School of Donne* (London, 1961), p. 75 and George Williamson, *The Donne Tradition* (1930; reprinted New York, 1958), p. 100 on courtly elements of Herbert's style. Elizabeth Stambler, in "The Unity of Herbert's 'Temple,' " *Cross Currents*, 10 (1960), 251–66 and George Watson, "The Fabric of Herbert's *Temple*," *Journal of the Warburg and Courtauld Institutes*, 22 (1959), 354–8 discuss Herbert's sacred parody of secular love lyrics, though see also Rosemond Tuve's persuasive objections to this view in "George Herbert and *Caritas*," *Journal of the Warburg and Courtauld Institutes*, 22 (1959), 303–31, and "Sacred 'Parody' of Love Poetry, and Herbert," *Studies in the Renaissance*, 8 (1961), 249–90. Malcolm Ross, in "George Herbert and the Humanist Tradition," *University of Toronto Quarterly*, 16 (1947), 169–82 (reprinted with minor changes in *Poetry and Dogma* [New Brunswick, N.J., 1954]), relates Herbert to the court of his time rather than to the poetry of courtly love; I have learned much from this perspective and from Ross's remarks on Herbert's negative use of the royalist symbol. Helen Vendler, *The Poetry of George Herbert* (Cambridge, Mass., 1975), is continually sensitive to Herbert's courtesy as a quality of spirit, especially in "The Call," where she links his "exquisite apprehension of the metaphor of courtesy" to his religious relationship with God (p. 206; see also pp. 248–58). R. S. Thomas, in his introduction to *A Choice of George Herbert's Verse* (1948; reprinted London, 1967), stresses Herbert's service to God as "the transference of the courtier's allegiance" (p. 12).

15. Barnabas Oley, *Herbert's Remains. 1652* (facsimile reprinted New York, 1970), sigs. a 11ᵛ–a 12ʳ.

16. Izaak Walton, *The Lives of John Donne, Sir Henry Wotton, Richard Hooker, George Herbert, & Robert Sanderson*, introd. George Saintsbury (1927; reprinted Cambridge, 1950). See Chapter 2 in the present work for further problems in Walton's version of Herbert's life. C. A. Patrides, ed., *The English Poems of George Herbert* (London, 1975), asks in his introduction: "But did the poet ever fully subordinate the way of the world to his spiritual aspirations? Did he absolutely deny his parts and parentage which, alike impressive, appeared to promise a public career vastly different from his eventual translation to Bemerton's 'pittiful little chappel'?" (p. 7).

17.   Thomas Greene, "The Flexibility of the Self in Renaissance Literature," in *The Disciplines of Criticism: Essays in Literary Theory, Interpretation, and History*, ed. Peter Demetz, Thomas Greene, and Lowry Nelson, Jr. (New Haven, 1968), pp. 241–64; and Stephen J. Greenblatt, *Renaissance Self-fashioning: From More to Shakespeare* (Chicago, 1980) and *Sir Walter Raleigh: The Renaissance Man and His Roles* (New Haven, 1973). Frank Whigham, *Ambition and Privilege: The Social Tropes of Elizabethan Courtesy Theory* (Berkeley, 1984), provides a rich analysis of relations between self-construction and tropes of hierarchy, promotion, and rivalry in the courtesy literature.

18.   Chapter 1 will show how variously courtesy books confronted disparities in an ideal exerting both sacred and secular demands. Even in theory the "ideal courtier" was never a unitary design, but rather a figure – not unlike Herbert's – uneasily conjoining divisive and contradictory elements. Leah Marcus, in *Childhood and Cultural Despair*, notes that in his term as Public Orator, Herbert "clearly shared the assumption of sixteenth-century humanists that the English state mirrored the divine order, that faithful service to the King was at the same time service to the Lord who had anointed him"; quoting the same stanza of "Submission" that I cite (p. 4), she adds: "By the time he wrote '*Submission*' Herbert had clearly given up his earlier implicit belief that English state and church were part of single unity: the Kingdom of God and the kingdom of James I and Charles I were not one organic whole, but two distinct realms serving contradictory ends" (p. 99).

19.   As with theories of the rise of the middle class, dates marking the failure of courtiership tend to be located in whatever period concerns any given scholar. Yet it is also true that, however fictive or delusory, the courtly ideal enticed Elizabethan self-presenters to claims of their courtly virtue. These claims are increasingly acknowledged *as* fictions in the seventeenth century, notably by such representative Cavaliers as Carew and Suckling, whose lives and lyrics so radically redefine the image of the courtier. Not accidentally, I think, it's the elaborately fictive Caroline masque that promotes the claims of courtly ideality as England moves toward civil war; the war itself testified that the court had lost its power to represent an ideal worth preserving – at least for a large number of the crown's previously loyal subjects.

20.   See, for example, "Content," "The Temper" (II), "The Familie," and "Frailtie."

21.   Louis Martz, *The Poetry of Meditation* (1954; rev. 1962; reprinted New Haven, 1971), and *The Wit of Love* (Notre Dame, Ind., 1969). Martz compares Carew and Herbert: "Both were, in their own ways, courtiers: one, the courtier of the Queen of Love and Beauty, the earthly Venus; and the other, the courtier of Heavenly Love, addressing to his Lord the art that the Cavalier world addressed to Mortal Love" (*The Wit of Love*, p. 151). I would instead define Herbert's courtly God in terms of the relationship between a courtier and his king (thus implicating God's courtier in the politics of service to a ruler); "Love I" and "Love II" seem to me exceptional rather than typical of Herbert's reference to courtly poetics. Nevertheless, Martz's remarks initially helped me to associate Herbert with a line of courtly, rather than religious, poets. Of course Martz is not the only critic addressing the issue of Herbert's sacred parody of secular love lyrics; but, particularly in *The Wit of Love*, he enables us to recognize wider dimensions of the "courtliness" Herbert shares with other courtier poets.

22. Although Donne says in Holy Sonnet 18, "Let myne amorous soule court thy mild Dove," and in Holy Sonnet 19, "In prayers, and flattering speaches I court God," I've deliberately omitted Donne from my choice of courtly poets as contexts for Herbert. These two holy sonnets by no means typify Donne's self-figuration in his religious poems (compare, for instance, the far more characteristic drama and extremity of "Batter my heart"), and Donne's various roles in the secular poetry seldom play on conflicts between courtly ideal and actuality. Donne, I'd argue, does not configure the roles of worldly courtier and God's courtier together over the body of his poetry. Another way to put it: I'm not convinced that the courtly ideal *as* an ideal – either to aspire toward, resist, reject, or reshape – exerted power over Donne as it did for Sidney, or Herbert, or Carew.

23. Barbara Harman, in *Costly Monuments*, gives the best analysis I know of rewriting within the structure of individual lyrics. My interest is rather in the way one poem rewrites another and how such cross-poem rewritings accumulate throughout the whole structure of *The Temple*. Since my concern is with parts of poems in dynamic and ever-shifting relations, I seldom read individual poems – except in Chapter 4 – in order to elucidate their meaning as discrete, self-contained structures.

Chapter 1: The Ideal of the Courtier

1. I shall cite a wide range of texts to show a common core of characteristics. For changing emphases in seventeenth-century courtesy books, see especially Ruth Kelso, *The Doctrine of the English Gentleman in the Sixteenth Century* (Urbana, Ill., 1929); John E. Mason, *Gentlefolk in the Making: Studies in the History of English Courtesy Literature and Related Topics from 1531 to 1774* (1935; reprinted New York, 1971); and E. N. S. Thompson, "Books of Courtesy," in *Literary Bypaths of the Renaissance* (New Haven, 1924), pp. 127–71. My brief discussion has been much helped by these three seminal studies of the courtesy literature. Kelso includes an excellent bibliography, but Gertrude E. Noyes, *Bibliography of Courtesy and Conduct Books in Seventeenth-Century England* (New Haven, 1937), and Virgil B. Heltzel, comp., *A Check List of Courtesy Books in the Newberry Library* (Chicago, 1942), should also be consulted. See also Diane Bornstein, *Mirrors of Courtesy* ([Hamden, Conn.], 1975), which deals primarily with medieval courtesy literature.

2.   Daniel Javitch, *Poetry and Courtliness in Renaissance England* (Princeton, 1978); and Wayne A. Rebhorn, *Courtly Performances: Masking and Festivity in Castiglione's "Book of the Courtier"* (Detroit, 1978). Javitch's oppositions between the ideals of classical orator and Castiglione's courtier, and Rebhorn's demonstration of theatricality in the dialogues at Urbino, are not, generally, applicable to the courtly model developed by English and French humanists. See also Alfredo Bonadeo, "The Function and Purpose of the Courtier in *The Book of the Courtier* by Castiglione," *Philological Quarterly,* 50 (1971), 36–46; O. B. Hardison, Jr., "The Orator and the Poet: The Dilemma of Humanist Literature," *Journal of Medieval and Renaissance Studies,* 1 (1971), 33–44; Richard A. Lanham, *The Motives of Eloquence: Literary Rhetoric in the Renaissance* (New Haven, 1976), especially his chapter on Castiglione, "The Self as Middle Style"; Marianne Shapiro, "Mirror and Portrait: The Structure of *Il libro del Cortegiano,*" *Journal of Medieval and Renaissance Studies,* 5 (1975), 37–61; W. Lee Ustick, "Changing Ideals of Aristocratic Character and Conduct in Seventeenth-Century England," *Modern Philology,* 30 (1932), 147–66; and J. R. Woodhouse, *Baldesar Castiglione: A Reassessment of "The Courtier"* (Edinburgh, 1978).

3.   Thomas Elyot, *The Boke Named the Governour,* ed. H. H. Croft (1883; reprinted New York, 1967), II, 2. Here and throughout this study, i/j and u/v are normalized.

4.   King James I, *Basilicon Doron* (1599; reprinted Menston, England, 1969), sigs. B2^v, K4^r–K4^v. Jonathan Goldberg, *James I and the Politics of Literature* (Baltimore, 1983), amply details the contradictions and concealments built into *Basilicon Doron* as well as in James' life and the literature of his reign.

5.   Pierre de la Primaudaye, *The French Academie* (1586; reprinted Hildesheim, W. Ger., 1972), sig. Tt 8^r.

6.   See the discussion of this point in Kelso, p. 106.

7.   John Cleland, *The Scottish Academy, or the Institution of a Young Noble-Man* (London, 1611), p. 271.

8.   Elyot, II, 27–8. The nature of nobility is continually debated in the courtesy books. *Nennio,* for example, is entirely devoted to the question of whether birth and fortune, on the one hand, or honorable deeds, on the

other, constitute the basis of true nobility. Here the question is resolved, as it customarily is, by asserting the primacy of morally virtuous deeds after the manner of Elyot, while simultaneously recognizing the claims and superior advantages afforded by noble birth and fortune. (Giovanni Battista Nenna, *Nennio, or a Treatise of Nobility*, trans. William Jones [1595]; reprinted, introd. Alice Shalvi [Jerusalem, 1967]). Elyot's chapter "What very nobilitie is" in the second book of *The Governour* is particularly interesting, and Croft's notes (II, 26–38) provide instructive parallels, especially from Erasmus, Ferne's *Blazon of Gentrie*, and Patrizi.

9. George Meriton, *Sermon of Nobilitie* (London, 1607), sigs. C2^v, C3^v.

10. Baldesar Castiglione, *The Book of the Courtier*, trans. Sir Thomas Hoby (1561); reprinted, introd. Walter Raleigh, London, 1900). But even in Castiglione, there is an almost religious intensity in the imperative of worldly service: "I will have our courtyer therfore . . . to turne al his thoughtes and force of minde to love, and (as it were) to reverence the Prince he serveth above al other thinges, and in his wil, maners and facions, to be altogether pliable to please him" (p. 123). Castiglione also claims that the primary role of the courtier's service is leading his prince toward virtue:

> And so shall the Courtier, if he have the goodnesse In him that these Lordes have geven him accompanied with readinesse of witt, pleasantnesse, wisedome, knowleage in letters and so many other thinges, understande how to beehave himself readilye in all occurrentes to drive into his Princis heade what honour and profit shall ensue to him and to his by justice, liberalitie, valiauntnesse of courage, meekenesse and by the other vertues that beelong to a good Prince, and contrariwise what sclaunder and damage commeth of the vices contrarie to them.
>
> (pp. 297–8)

11. But see Javitch, *Poetry and Courtliness*, pp. 23–49, for a counter emphasis: "The prime function of the courtier is to delight. . . . It can be said that *delectare* assumes the functional priority in courtiership that *movere* is granted in oratory" (p. 40). Although Javitch acknowledges a shift toward the courtier's "didactic and persuasive functions" in the Fourth Book, he argues that "It becomes progressively evident in Castiglione's book that the political pressures of despotism shape and require an artful behavior quite foreign to Cicero's ideal of the civilized man" (p. 46).

12. The simplicity of the sub-title balances nicely against the elevated main title, although it may be Barnabas Oley's addition, as Amy Charles claims in *A Life of George Herbert* (Ithaca, N.Y., 1977), p. 157. Herbert's preface to the reader, however, could certainly have inspired the full subtitle, "The Countrey Parson His Character, and Rule of Holy Life": "That the way to please him, is to feed my Flocke diligently and faithfully, since our Saviour

hath made that the argument of a Pastour's love, I have resolved to set down the Form and Character of a true Pastour, that I may have a Mark to aim at . . ." (Hutchinson, p. 224).

13. The opening sentence of *The Country Parson* defines his role: "A Pastour is the Deputy of Christ for the reducing of man to the Obedience of God" (p. 225).

14. For thorough discussions of this process, see Rosemond Tuve, *Allegorical Imagery: Some Mediaeval Books and Their Posterity* (Princeton, 1966), pp. 57–143; and William O. Harris, *Skelton's Magnyfycence and the Cardinal Virtue Tradition* (Chapel Hill, N.C., 1965), pp. 67–126. I am greatly indebted to both works for my brief sketch of the virtue tradition, especially to Harris' well-documented account of its role in the courtesy books. The cardinal virtues, deriving from Cicero's *De Officiis* – an essential source for Renaissance courtesy books, as well as for the virtue tradition – were assimilated to Christian thought as early as St. Ambrose and St. Augustine, codified by Macrobius in the commentary *In Somnium Scipionis,* and systematized further by St. Thomas Aquinas in the *Summa Theologiae.* By the sixteenth century, Sir Thomas Elyot, Pierre de la Primaudaye, Spenser's friend Lodowick Bryskett, and a host of other courtesy writers were using the four cardinal virtues as structural principles in their treatises.

15. St. Thomas Aquinas, *Summa Theologiae,* trans. W. D. Hughes et al. (London, 1964), I-II, Q63, and I-II, Q109.

16. Harris traces the "Christianizing" of Cicero's original reference to equanimity in military and political adversity, pp. 101–14.

17. See Arnold Stein, *George Herbert's Lyrics* (Baltimore, 1968), pp. 85–100, and Vendler, *The Poetry of George Herbert,* pp. 231–76, who stresses Herbert's impatience in adversity rather more than his development of patience.

18. See, for example, Cleland, p. 177, and Thomas Aquinas, I-II, Q66, especially the discussion of fortitude in II-II, Q123–140.

19. See particularly Anthony Esler, *The Aspiring Mind of the Elizabethan Younger Generation* (Durham, N.C., 1966), and Chapter 2 below.

20. Books stressing manners and civility, treatises concerned with management of the domestic economy, and guides to travel abroad become as numerous as earlier works on statecraft, advice to princes, or debates on the source of nobility. E. N. S. Thompson observes that in the early seventeenth century, "the old-time, comprehensive books of courtesy were thus disintegrating and filtering through into newer types of literature . . ." (p. 154; see also pp. 152–71).

21. Daniel Tuvill, *The Dove and the Serpent* (London, 1614), p. 8; Henry Peacham, *The Compleat Gentleman* (1622; reprinted New York, 1968), sig. D 3ᵛ.

22.   Mason, p. 220. The tendency appeared still earlier, however. As Felix Gilbert, *History: Choice and Commitment* (Cambridge, Mass., 1977), has pointed out, "all trace of the idealized human personality as such has vanished from Machiavelli's portrait of the prince" (p. 105), and this radical shift had been preceded by an increasing emphasis on the prince's exterior image. Thus, Gilbert notes, Pontano

> maintains that the prince's gestures, his way of speaking, the sound of his voice, and even his dress and table manners – the whole of his life, in fact – must be subject to exact rules which are stated in minute detail. Pontano's view amounts to the claim that the respect accorded to the prince is determined by his outer bearing and deportment. (p. 102)

23.   E. N. S. Thompson points out that even sixteenth-century treatises depicted the "unfavorable side of the courtier's life and character." He cites Thomas North's translation of Guevara's *Diall of Princes:* "If I fetched as many sighes for my sinnes, as Courtyers doe for their mishaps and disgraces, what a number would they come to?" (p. 145).

24.   In his translation of a still unidentified French source, the *Politique Discourses, treating of the differences and inequalities of Vocations, as well Publique, as Private . . .* ([London], 1578), Aegremont Ratcliffe stresses that the "action, use, and handling of all affairs" are to be directed to "the Common profite and Service of men" (sig. 31ᵛ); indeed, "each one is called, not by Fortune, but by the assured providence of God, to the conservation of order, policie, and government of the life, and societie of men . . ." (sig. 10ʳ).

25.   Stefano Guazzo, *The Civile Conversation of M. Steeven Guazzo,* trans. George Pettie and Bartholomew Young (1581 and 1586), introd. Sir Edward Sullivan, Bart. (London, 1925) I, 24 and 31–32. Herbert's possible "withdrawal" to a contemplative life – or a melancholic one, perhaps, if we were to accept the evidence of his poems – in the country during the late 1620s should be noted in relation to Guazzo's argument and counterargument.

26.   Although I by no means wish to claim Guazzo in any specific sense as a "source" for Herbert in respect to the issue of vocation, it is interesting that Herbert was almost certainly familiar with *The Civile Conversation,* since he borrowed a substantial number of his Outlandish Proverbs from this Italian source. See John Lievsay, *Stefano Guazzo and the English Renaissance 1575–1675* (Chapel Hill, N.C., 1961), pp. 141–3.

27.   But of course, Guazzo was Italian, not English, and furthermore, much of his book is devoted to the development of "personal perfection." Simple dichotomies such as "English versus Italian" are not really adequate to account for the complexity with which the two ideas are interwoven in both English and Italian texts.

28. Sigs. 44^r, 57^v. Ratcliffe does, however, commend St. Ambrose for serving initially in the political realm, having been assigned to "the government of bodies" by God and finally serving in the ecclesiastical realm when called to "the government and charge of soules" (sig. 44^r).

29. Kelso, pp. 54–5. As Archbishop Sandys put it, "the ministers of the Word; the messengers of Christ . . . are esteemed *tamquam excrementa mundi.*"

30. Oley, sigs. a 11^v–a 12^r. I shall weave this powerful recollection by a contemporary of Herbert's at Cambridge into my text at several key points. It is likely to be accurate and it helps to characterize *some* of Herbert's first readers; it also characterizes the speaker in *The Temple* who so often confesses his own troubling complicity with their values.

Chapter 2: Actualizing the Ideal

1. Like Barnabas Oley's recollection, this claim by Nicholas Ferrar is woven into my text at several points. Neither what Ferrar means by "pattern," nor how a pattern "for his age" helps define the speaker in *The Temple,* has been explored as questions to guide readers in our age. Each rewriting of Ferrar's statement will mark stages in my interpretation of his claim.

2. David Novarr, *The Making of Walton's "Lives"* (Ithaca, N.Y., 1958), p. 319.

3. Oley exclaims, "Lo, the humility of this gracious man!" Though God "magnified him with extraordinary Gifts," Herbert had "little esteem of this Book [*The Country Parson*], and but very little of his Poems. . . . And even this lowlinesse in his own eyes, doth more advance their worth, and his vertues" (sigs. c 5^v–c 6^r). To Oley, Herbert is a "signe of contradiction."

4. Walton, p. 314. Henry Fairfax, contemporary and Cambridge colleague of Herbert, was commended by his father in similar terms: "I pray God bless you and your studies to the service of his Church which is the happiest profession that can be. All other services be bondage, but this is perfect freedom. If it be honour to serve a King, it is more to serve the King of Kings, and after his reward there is no wants" (George W. Johnson, ed., *The Fairfax Correspondence: Memoirs of the Reign of Charles the First* [London, 1848], I, xxxiii). A brief account in the Fairfax MSS. stresses the exemplary pattern that he shares with Herbert: "Mr. Henry Fairfax had his education in Trinity College, Cambridge. . . . He was Fellow of the College at the same time that Mr. George Herbert, of the same college, was Orator of the University, with whom he was familiarly acquainted: their dispositions were much alike, and both very exemplary for learning and piety" (I,

64–65). Amy Charles notes that this nineteenth-century editorial comment appears to be the only evidence for the "otherwise unverified legend" that Herbert and Henry Fairfax were friends (*Life of Herbert*, p. 70). As in the case of Walton's claims, the desire to articulate the exemplary pattern predominates over strict documentation.

In *British Autobiography in the Seventeenth Century* (London, 1969), Paul Delany suggests that Herbert's account of spiritual conflicts in *The Temple* reflects his preference for the medium of lyric poetry over prose autobiography. Delany speculates that the "dearth of spiritual auto-biographies by Anglicans in the period" may be partly a matter of generic and social selection: "the leading spirits of Anglicanism were highly edu-cated and gentlemen; this combination of qualities usually ensured that their desires for creative self-expression found issue in more recognized and respected literary genres than autobiography" (p. 54).

5.   Novarr's study is the most complete, but see also John Butt, "Izaak Walton's Methods in Biography," *Essays and Studies*, 19 (1933), 67–84; and the excellent overview by Robert E. Reiter of the general biographical practice, "George Herbert and His Biographers," *Cithara*, 9 (1970), 18–31.

6.   As F. E. Hutchinson points out, Barnabas Oley was a student at Clare Hall, Cambridge, from 1617 and a Fellow from 1623 through 1644: "he was, therefore, living in Cambridge for a large part of Herbert's years of residence and must have known him well by repute, if not personally" (p. 556).

7.   Donald Stauffer, *English Biography Before 1700* (1930; reprinted New York, 1964), pp. 64–90; and Richard Altick, *Lives and Letters: A History of Literary Biography in England and America* (New York, 1965), pp. 19–23.

8.   See, for example, the biographies of Donne and Wotton in Izaak Walton, *The Lives of John Donne . . .* ; P. Peckard, *Memoirs of Mr. Nicholas Ferrar* (Cambridge, 1790); and the editorial comment in Bernard Blackstone, ed., *The Ferrar Papers* (Cambridge, 1938).

9.   This confluence of value blends the two major medieval traditions of English biography, which as Stauffer shows were both opposite and com-plementary. Although the saint's life "makes clear the fruits of moral living," while the royal biography stresses "the uncertainty of worldly riches and worldly power," Stauffer remarks that "The single aim of teaching the good life by example is common to them both; but where the method of the saint's life is 'the commendation of virtue,' that of the *Mirror for Magis-trates* is ordinarily 'the detestation of vice' " (p. 53). The fall-of-princes theme inherently argues the inadequacy or insufficiency of virtue in the court of the world, though as Stauffer notes, John Copgrave's fifteenth-century *Liber de Illustribus Henricis,* by making the royal biography "a

vehicle for presenting virtuous precepts" (p. 30), prefigures the sixteenth-century treatises *de regimine principum,* which concentrate on inculcating princely virtue rather than emphasizing the fall from worldly eminence.

Sir Thomas More's dedication to his life of Pico della Mirandola blends classical and Christian virtues in his hope that it may be "profitable to th' achyvynge of temperaunce in prosperite, . . . to the purchasynge of pacience in adversite . . . to the dyspysinge of worldly vanyte . . . to the desyrings of hevenly felycyte" (*Life of Pico della Mirandola,* cited in Stauffer, p. 37). In an interesting parallel to Edward Herbert's praise of his brother George (see p. 54 in the present work), More observes that Pico was "bothe reputed and was indede bothe a perfyte philosophre and a perfyte devyne" (cited in Stauffer, p. 36). More's exemplary purpose reflects the two parts of forti-tude discussed in Chapter 1, and would not be inappropriate as a preface to *Scrinia Reserata* or *The Temple.* Although he does not explicitly draw the connection with seventeenth-century biographies, Stauffer's examples pro-vide a basis for my suggestion that these later works combine the purpose of both saints' lives and royal biographies.

10.   But see Steuart A. Pears, ed. and trans., *The Correspondence of Sir Philip Sidney and Hubert Languet* (1845; reprinted Farnborough, England, 1971), for possible doubts on Sidney's part at some periods in his life. Sidney argues to Languet that "while the mind is thus, as it were, drawn out of itself [in public service], it cannot turn its powers inward for thorough self-examination; to which employment no labour that men can undertake, is anyway to be compared." He adds a light disclaimer – "Do you not see that I am cleverly playing the stoic?" – but Languet takes him seriously enough to reply, "I am especially sorry to hear you say that you are weary of the life to which I have no doubt God has called you, and desire to fly from the light of your court and betake yourself to the privacy of secluded places to escape the tempest of affairs by which statesmen are generally harassed . . ." (pp. 143, 155). See also Languet's stricture two years later, that some of Sidney's friends

> are astonished that you find pleasure in your long retirement; and though they readily believe that it is made most delightful to you by the society of your dearest friends, still they think you ought very carefully to reflect whether it is consistent with your character to remain so long concealed. They fear that those who do not so well know your con-stancy may suspect that you are tired of that toilsome path which leads to virtue, which you formerly pursued with so much earnestness. They are fearful too, that the sweetness of your lengthened retirements may somewhat relax the vigorous energy with which you used to rise to noble undertakings, and a love of ease, which you once despised, creep by degrees over your spirit. (pp. 182–3)

Compare Languet's comments here with Hacket's contrast between "the pleasure of Ease, and the Guerdon of Virtue" (p. 38, in Chapter 2 above) in relation to Bishop Williams.

11.   Thomas Moffet, *Nobilis,* ed. and trans. Virgil B. Heltzel and Hoyt H. Hudson (San Marino, Calif., 1940), p. xii.

12.   Walton reminds us of the rise to worldly power enjoyed by Herbert's two immediate predecessors in the Oratorship (p. 270). In 1619 Nethersole became secretary to the Queen of Bohemia, to whom Herbert wrote two poems of consolation during her exile in "late 1621 or early 1622, . . . at a time when Herbert still entertained political ambitions" (Ted-Larry Pebworth and Claude J. Summers, "Recovering an Important Seventeenth-Century Poetical Miscellany: Cambridge Add. MS 4138," *Transactions of the Cambridge Bibliographical Society,* 7 [1978], 163.) Walton says that Herbert learned Italian, French, and Spanish as preparation for public service, a claim also made by the biographers of Sidney and Williams in respect to their linguistic training.

13.   Fulke Greville, *The Life of the Renowned Sir Philip Sidney . . .* (London, 1906), pp. 3–4. Greville's *Life of Sidney,* first published in 1652, was written during the early 1600s, before his return to office under James.

14.   John Hacket, *Scrinia Reserata: A Memorial Offer'd to the Great Deservings of John Williams, D. D. . . .* (London, 1693), I, 4.

15.   See, for example, Warren Chernaik, "Waller's 'Panegyric to my Lord Protector' and the Poetry of Praise," *Studies in English Literature, 1500–1900,* 4 (1964), 109–24; O. B. Hardison, Jr., *The Enduring Monument: A Study of the Idea of Praise in Renaissance Literary Theory and Practice* (Chapel Hill, N.C., 1962); Barbara K. Lewalski, *Donne's Anniversaries and the Poetry of Praise* (Princeton, 1973), pp. 11–41; and Ruth Nevo, *The Dial of Virtue: A Study of Poems on Affairs of State in the Seventeenth Century* (Princeton, 1963).

16.   Sir Philip Sidney, *An Apology for Poetry,* ed. Geoffrey Shepherd (New York, 1973), p. 101.

17.   Hacket's reference to the traditional choice of Hercules again stresses his point that actual lives can exemplify an ideal of behavior. Since his primary interest is to show that the ideal can be actualized, he transforms his exemplary subject in this way into a moral figure.

18.   See note 10. The Languet correspondence reveals pressures of actuality on Sidney with special authenticity, since Languet hoped to mold Sidney into an exemplary courtier.

19.   Hacket, I, 73; see also I, 34–6. There is an excellent discussion of Williams' appointment and its significance in Elizabeth Dew Roberts, *Mitre and Musket: John Williams, Lord Keeper, Archbishop of York, 1582–1650*

(London, 1938), pp. 37–51. Although Williams was, according to Ivor Bowen, "the only Protestant prelate who ever held the Great Seal of England," nevertheless Roberts points out that "he can also be regarded as the last of a line of medieval prelate-statesmen to hold office under the English crown" (p. 44). Roberts tells us that by the time of Williams' appointment, "It had become unusual for a churchman to hold high office in the State, and his promotion was considered – as indeed it was – a flagrant example of royal favouritism." But she also notes that Williams justified his appointment "by his own ability and industry. If not a great Chancellor, he filled the office competently and with dignity" (p. 50).

20.   Anthony Weldon, *The Court and Character of King James . . .* ([London], 1651); Arthur Wilson, *The History of Great Britain, Being the Life and Reign of King James the First . . .* (London, 1653).

21.   Hacket has ample reason to attack them. Weldon, for instance, compares Williams with his predecessor in order to stress his even greater iniquity: "In *Bacons* place comes *Williams,* a man on purpose brought in at first to serve turnes, but in this place to doe that which none of the Layity could be found bad enough to undertake. . . . This *Williams,* though he wanted much of his Predecessors abilities for the law yet did he equall him for learning and pride, and beyond him in the way of bribery . . ." (pp. 129–30).

22.   Daniel Javitch, *Poetry and Courtliness,* pp. 107–38, shows that the courtly ideal begins its reductive alteration in the 1590s.

23.   Herbert's letter to Sir John Danvers, October 6, 1619 (cited in Hutchinson, p. 370).

24.   See the excellent discussion of this point in Joseph Summers, *George Herbert: His Religion and Art* (1954; reprinted Cambridge, Mass., 1968), pp. 28–48. Ferrar, in "The Printers to the Reader," asserts that there were no "outward enforcements" to Herbert's choice.

25.   Lawrence Stone cites the Marquis of Newcastle's view of the "chain of causation" in which the loss of virtue in the aristocracy brought about the fall of the monarchy: "Once 'Noble-men weare pullde doune, which is the foundation off monarkeye – monarkeye soone affter fell' " (*The Crisis of the Aristocracy 1558–1641* [Oxford, 1965], p. 120). Stone says of the early seventeenth century, "Even now the call of duty and the pricking of ambition remained, though in many cases the sense of vocation was gone" (p. 401).

26.   J. M. Shuttleworth, ed., *The Life of Edward, First Lord Herbert of Cherbury written by himself* (London, 1976), pp. 1, 19. Sidney Lee's earlier edition of the *Autobiography* (London, 1892) is a less reliable text, but should be consulted for its informative editorial material, including Lee's

"Continuation" of Lord Herbert's life after 1624, and for its selections from his correspondence.

27.   Shuttleworth, p. 19. This contrast between knowledge and manners betrays a disturbing disjunction between actual court life and ideal courtly aspirations, especially because Edward Herbert seems completely unaware of it.

28.   Shuttleworth, p. 44. The courtesy books included frequent discussions of dueling and debated the fine points of honor at issue in specific circumstances. Much of Edward Herbert's detailed accounting of his own duels seems to be directed to a similar end, to establish that they were honorably based and honorably conducted. It is interesting that, in advising "That discreete Civillity which is to bee observed in Communication either with friends or strangers," he specifically recommends the study of two widely read courtesy books, Della Casa's *Galateo* and Guazzo's *Civile Conversation*.

29.   Hacket, II, 81, emphasizes these qualities of Buckingham above all else. "Gallantry" takes on increasingly pejorative connotations in criticisms of courtly corruption under James and Charles written in the 1650s, and is often associated with frivolity and triviality. The French sense of the term, stressing pleasing manners and skill in amorous byplay, came into use in England during the seventeenth century (*Oxford English Dictionary*, s.v. "gallant").

30.   See Thomas Clayton, ed., *The Works of Sir John Suckling: The Non-Dramatic Works* (Oxford, 1971). The religious poems, dated by Clayton as "c. 1626 or before," are on pp. 9–13; the letter to Jermyn, pp. 163–7; "An Account of Religion by Reason," pp. 169–80. See also Lester Beaurline, "New Poems by Sir John Suckling," *Studies in Philology*, 59 (1962), 651–7.

31.   According to John Aubrey, cited in Clayton, p. xlvii.

32.   Cited in Clayton, p. 208. Clayton gives three versions of the mock-ballad attack on Suckling's adventures in war. They share not only their scurrility but also the implication that courtliness is debased by a figure like Suckling.

33.   Stone, pp. 494 and 122. In these years, Stone notes, "religious beliefs, tastes in interior decoration, painting, architecture, sculpture, poetry, and music, attitudes towards sex, drink, and gambling, all differed widely from those prevalent in the country at large" (p. 62).

34.   Thomas Carew, "To my worthy friend Master *Geo. Sands*, on his translation of the Psalmes," in Rhodes Dunlap, ed., *The Poems of Thomas Carew* (1949; reprinted Oxford, 1970), pp. 93–4. See also pp. 77–8 in the present work.

35. From an anonymous memoir (1845 edition of Carew), cited in Dunlap, p. xl.

36. Alan Maycock, in *Nicholas Ferrar of Little Gidding* (London, 1938), points out that in this period the decision to become a deacon would not automatically imply an intention to enter the priesthood:

> At that time, of course, there was a much sharper line of division than there is nowadays between the diaconate and the priesthood. The idea of the former as primarily a preparation for the latter is comparatively modern. Throughout the Middle Ages the two orders stood quite distinct, and we may recall that St. Thomas of Canterbury was only in deacon's orders when he was elected archbishop. Many men, in the ordinary course, entered the diaconate without any intention of becoming priests; and that tradition endured until at least the latter part of the seventeenth century. (pp. 119–20)

37. Whether, as Walton avers, they never saw each other in later years, but only corresponded by letters, is scarcely crucial to determine (Walton, p. 312). But since Ferrar and Herbert served together in Parliament and both Ferrar and Herbert's stepfather were officials of the Virginia Company at this time, Walton's statement seems unlikely to be accurate.

38. *Reliquiae Wottonianae* (London, 1672), pp. 327–9. Walton edited the *Reliquiae;* as Logan Pearsall Smith notes in his *Life and Letters of Sir Henry Wotton* (1907; reprinted Oxford, 1966), Walton's revision of his life of Wotton for the second edition of his collected *Lives* reports that Wotton associated his own retirement to the contemplative life with the exemplary model set by Charles V (I, 202–3).

39. I rely chiefly on Hutchinson's short but responsible account and on Amy Charles' recent, very full biography (*Life of Herbert*) for this chronological summary. Hutchinson speculates that Herbert may have begun *The Church-porch* early in the 1620s while he was still at Cambridge (p. xxvi), and suggests that during the last three years at Bemerton, Herbert revised "many of the earlier poems and [wrote] . . . perhaps the larger half of *The Temple*" (p. xxxviii). This assumption that the poems in W pre-date Bemerton, whereas those added in B belong to the years in the priesthood, rests entirely upon the fact that specific references to Herbert as priest in the poems are limited to the latter group. Amy Charles believes that the poems in W may have been composed before the 1620s and even suggests that *The Church-porch* might be dated "at least as early as 1614," having perhaps been written partly for the instruction of his younger brother, Henry (pp. 78–87). J. B. Leishman's caution in *The Metaphysical Poets* (1934, reprinted New York, 1963) still makes good sense:

A comparison of the two manuscripts teaches us much about Herbert's careful artistry, but it tells us nothing about the date of the poems or of the order in which they were written; for while it is obvious that many of the 73 poems in the Williams MS. are earlier than the corresponding versions in the Bodleian, it is impossible to decide *how much* earlier, and it is also impossible to decide whether the remaining 96 poems in the Bodleian MS. were written earlier or later than those of which we possess two versions. (pp. 118–19)

40. Two College appointments preceded the Orator's post: as Sublector Quartae Classis at Trinity in 1617 and as Praelector in Rhetoric, 1618 (Amy Charles, *Life of Herbert*, pp. 71–2).

41. Hutchinson, p. xxx. Amy Charles, in "George Herbert, Deacon" (*Modern Philology*, 72 [1975], 272–6), claims that "There is no question that Herbert was the orator referred to" (in the report of the speech, which simply names the giver of it as "the orator"). But as is sometimes the case in discussing the fuzzy details of Herbert's life, she may be inclined to affirm the identification because it fits the argument she is making – at this point, that it was Herbert's preparation for Buckingham's installation which kept him from attending his own installation as prebendary eight days previously (p. 276). This interpretation supports her major claim that Herbert decided for the priesthood at the end of 1624, much earlier than has usually been thought, when he applied for dispensation to be made deacon "at any time."

42. His brother Henry succeeded him in 1626.

43. Amy Charles, "George Herbert, Deacon," pp. 272–3. But the six years that follow Herbert's appointment as comportioner argue that the record of doubt and hesitation concerning the priesthood in the poems may in truth mirror such emotions in the life.

44. Ibid., p. 276. Herbert's installation as deacon should be viewed in the light of Nicholas Ferrar's attitude toward the office, discussed above, p. 47.

45. The best treatment of the question is in Novarr, pp. 516–20.

46. Summers, *George Herbert*, p. 441. Since this is a large amount of money for the time, it is clear that Herbert had sufficient resources to have maintained himself in the household of other members of either his or his wife's family, a not uncommon practice in the period. His decision to enter holy orders was certainly not, as has sometimes been suggested, simply a means of supporting his family.

47. See Amy Charles, *Life of Herbert*, pp. 90, 198; and Leicester Bradner, "New Poems by George Herbert: The Cambridge Latin Gratulatory of 1613," *Renaissance News*, 15 (1962), 208–11.

48. See W. Hilton Kelliher, "The Latin Poems of George Herbert," in *The Latin Poetry of English Poets,* ed. J. W. Binns (London, 1974), pp. 134–45, and the discussion in Charles' *Life of Herbert,* pp. 90–4. G. M. Story, "George Herbert's *Inventa Bellica:* A New Manuscript," *Modern Philology,* 59 (1962), 270–2, gives a different version of the "Triumphus Mortis," Herbert's important antiwar poem included in *Lucus* which, as Charles points out, is related in attitude if not in date of composition (which is unknown) to Herbert's undiplomatic attack on war in his oration welcoming Prince Charles on his return from Spain in 1623.

49. Pebworth and Summers, "Recovering an Important Seventeenth-Century Poetical Miscellany," pp. 162–4. See also Ted-Larry Pebworth, "George Herbert's Poems to the Queen of Bohemia: A Rediscovered Text and a New Edition," *English Literary Renaissance,* 9 (1979), 108–20.

50. As late as 1632, in *The Country Parson,* Herbert describes an aristocrat's proper activity in terms that suggest the civic conscientiousness he might once himself have possessed:

> When there is a Parliament, he is to endeavor by all means to be a Knight or Burgess there; for there is no School to a Parliament. And when he is there, he must not only be a morning man, but at Committees also; for there the particulars are exactly discussed, which are brought from thence to the House but in generall. (p. 277)

This sensible advice to young men in search of a calling – the subject of this chapter of *The Country Parson* – does not reflect either the disillusionment with worldly pursuits or the decisive rejection of their value which Walton is so concerned to show as exemplary in Herbert's life choices.

Herbert recommends here the proper and virtuous conduct of *any* calling. The only choice rejected as worthless is that of "the Gallant, who is witty enough to abuse both others, and himself, and who is ready to ask, if he shall mend shoos, or what shall he do?" (p. 275). In this same chapter, Herbert describes the court as "the eminent place both of good and ill" (p. 277). These attitudes, even after Herbert had become the holy parson of Bemerton, show that he continued to accept the value of worldly service and the need for virtuous conduct in such offices – for others, if not for himself.

51. See especially Earl Miner, *The Cavalier Mode from Jonson to Cotton* (Princeton, 1971), pp. 43–99.

52. Anthony Weldon remarks that King James "did much love Mountgomery, and trusted him more at the very last gaspe, then at the first minute of his Favoriteship" (p. 167).

53. See Benjamin Farrington's discussion of this point in "Francis Bacon after His Fall," *Studies in the Literary Imagination,* 4 (1971), 157–78. Farrington notes Bacon's view in Book Seven of the *De Augmentis* that "the moral philosophers have succeeded well in describing the virtues, but have failed in teaching how to cultivate them. This branch of knowledge, which he calls the *Georgics of the Mind,* requires a much richer knowledge of the permanent characters and transient dispositions and affections of men than the moralists provide" (p. 154). This concern is not unlike Herbert's attention to the actual ways of men in *The Country Parson,* or the demonstration of virtues in actual persons found in exemplary biographies.

The most interesting recent discussion of Herbert's relation to Bacon is by William A. Sessions, "Bacon and Herbert and an Image of Chalk" in Summers and Pebworth, eds., *"Too Rich to Clothe the Sunne,"* pp. 165–78. See also Summers, *George Herbert,* pp. 195–7; and Marchette Chute, *Two Gentle Men* (1959; reprinted New York, 1966), pp. 59–65. Chute's biography, too often dismissed as merely "popular," speculates intelligently about Herbert's own attitudes in the light of his friendship with Bacon.

54. *De Veritate* was first issued in 1624; see Sidney Lee's edition of Edward Herbert's *Autobiography,* pp. 246–50.

55. Hutchinson, p. 370. The three letters to Danvers on the Orator's post span five months; texts are in Hutchinson, pp. 369–71.

56. G. E. Aylmer, *The King's Servants: The Civil Service of Charles I, 1625–1642* (New York, 1961), pp. 372–9; and Perez Zagorin, *The Court and the Country: The Beginning of the English Revolution* (New York, 1970), pp. 96–7. Summers is exceptionally sound in weighing "inward" and "outward" enforcements bearing on Herbert's decision.

57. See [Hyde] Edward Earl of Clarendon, *The History of the Rebellion and Civil Wars in England . . .* (Oxford, 1826), VI, 234–5, for the "scorn and detestation" in which Danvers was held by the Royalists for this action. But as Chute points out, Danvers "had opposed the King on the hotly contested issue of ship money" as early as 1628 – during Herbert's lifetime – as well as serving as colonel for the Parliamentary forces during the civil wars (pp. 259–60).

58. Robert Ray, "George Herbert in the Seventeenth Century: Allusions to Him, Collected and Annotated" (Ph.D. diss., U. of Texas [Austin], 1967), quotes Puritan praise of Herbert's prophetic acuity by Samuel Ward, pp. 31–2; by Richard Baxter, pp. 72–3; and by others *passim.*

59. But see Heather Asals, *Equivocal Predication,* pp. 5, 13–14, for a different viewpoint.

60. A prayer of Charles in the *Eikon Basilike: The Portraiture of His*

Sacred Majesty in His Solitudes and Sufferings, ed. Philip A. Knachel (Ithaca, N.Y., 1966) opens, *"For Thou, O God, infinitely good and great, art with me, Whose presence is better than life and Whose service is perfect freedom"* (p. 139). Another prayer suggests that Charles, or Gauden if indeed he ghost-wrote the *Eikon,* may have been reading Herbert as well as his Bible: *"The broken and contrite heart, I know, Thou wilt not despise. Thou, O Lord, canst at once make me Thy temple, Thy priest, Thy sacrifice, and Thine altar; while from an humble heart I (alone) daily offer up in holy meditations, fervent prayers, and unfeigned tears myself to Thee, Who preparest me for Thee, dwellest in me, and acceptest of me"* (pp. 147–8).

61. So claims Sir Thomas Herbert, who attended Charles in his last imprisonment. But note also C. A. Patrides' comments in the introduction to his *George Herbert: The Critical Heritage* (London, 1983), p. 11.

Chapter 3: A Failing Equilibrium

1. Javitch, *Poetry and Courtliness,* pp. 141–62, is helpful on this point.

2. Patricia Thomson, *Sir Thomas Wyatt and His Background* (Stanford, Calif., 1964), shows how "Service to God and Service to the King are found in perfect harmony" in Wyatt's letter to his son, 1537 (p. 3), and associates Wyatt's dedication to "court and government" with Herbert's line from "Affliction" (I): "Like George Herbert's his 'birth and spirit rather took, The way that takes the town'" (p. 8). Raymond Southall, *The Courtly Maker: An Essay on the Poetry of Wyatt and His Contemporaries* (Oxford, 1964), notes that in Wyatt's poetry – in distinction to the biographical attitudes cited by Thomson – "nowhere . . . is there a commendation of court life" (p. 92). Wyatt's life, of course, records how little harmony his service to the state could bring.

3. Thomson shows that "Myne owne John Poynz" owes much to Alamanni's tenth satire but adds a more stringent moral note when Wyatt depicts himself in retirement "To will and lust lerning to set a lawe" (p. 250).

4. Thomas Wyatt, *Collected Poems,* ed. Kenneth Muir and Patricia Thomson (Liverpool, 1969), p. 95. All citations of Wyatt's poetry are to this edition.

5. George Gascoigne, *Complete Works,* ed. John W. Cunliffe (1907; reprinted New York, 1969), I, 349. All citations of Gascoigne's poetry are to this edition.

6. Gascoigne's references here to Aristotle and Cicero counter Javitch's view of oppositions between ideals of orator and courtier, thus pointing out a crucial difference between Castiglione and the English humanists. Yet the

ironic force of the allusions does validate Javitch's perception of strain between the two models.

7.   Gascoigne, II, 148–9. Gascoigne's play with mirror reflections of what is and what ought to be should be compared to Herbert's play with inversed perspectives on the great and humble; see Chapter 4 in the present work.

8.   See Roger Howells, *Sir Philip Sidney: The Shepherd Knight* (London, 1968), and "The Sidney Circle and the Protestant Cause in Elizabethan Foreign Policy," *Renaissance and Modern Studies,* 19 (1975), 31–46, on Sidney's efforts to establish a Protestant League. For another valuable perspective on Sidney's Protestantism, see Andrew D. Weiner, "Moving and Teaching: Sidney's *Defence of Poesie* as a Protestant Poetic," *Journal of Medieval and Renaissance Studies,* 2 (1972), 259–78, and *Sir Philip Sidney and the Poetics of Protestantism: A Study of Contexts* (Minneapolis, 1978). Kenneth Alan Hovey, in "George Herbert's Authorship of 'To the Queene of Bohemia,' " *Renaissance Studies,* 30 (1977), 43–50, provides information that might suggest affinities between this "Protestant" poem and the Sidneyan model of the Protestant courtier.

9.   Franco Marenco, *Arcadia Puritana* (Bari, Italy, 1968). The changes are given added point by Greville's remark in the *Life of Sidney* concerning Sidney's purpose in writing the *Arcadia:* "not vanishing pleasure alone, but morall Images, and Examples (as directing threds) to guide everyman through the confused *Labyrinth* of his own desires, and life" (pp. 164–5). See also Chapter 2, note 10, above on the Sidney–Languet correspondence for a less assured view of Sidney's struggles with the demands of action and contemplation.

10.   Marenco, pp. 192, 119; cf. La Primaudaye's emphasis on Christian nobility in Chapter 1, p. 17 of the present work.

11.   I am indebted to William O. Harris for his encouragement and assistance with this approach to Sidney's revisions.

12.   Sir Philip Sidney, *The Countesse of Pembrokes Arcadia,* in *The Complete Works,* ed. Albert Feuillerat (1912; reprinted Cambridge, 1939), I, 388. All citations of the *Arcadia* are to this edition.

13.   The term is Neil Rudenstine's, in *Sidney's Poetic Development* (Cambridge, Mass., 1967).

14.   See Louis Martz, *The Poetry of Meditation,* especially pp. 260–82.

15.   Sir Philip Sidney, *The Poems,* ed. William A. Ringler, Jr. (Oxford, 1962), p. 224. All citations of Sidney's poetry are to this edition.

16.   David Kalstone, *Sidney's Poetry: Contexts and Interpretations* (Cambridge, Mass., 1965), p. 180.

17.   Rudenstine points out that in the *Certain Sonnets* Sidney developed "a

poetic version of courtly conversation. . . . the mode of a courtier writing *in propria persona* for an audience of friends and acquaintances" (p. 122). This mode enables Sidney to emphasize claims of actual experience over ideal expectations in *Astrophil and Stella*.

18.   See Martz' comparisons between Sidney and Herbert in *The Poetry of Meditation*, especially his discussion of Herbert's debt to Sidney's psalm translations (pp. 273–8). Martz also notes echoes of *Astrophil and Stella* in "Jordan" (I). See Rosemary Freeman, "Parody as a Literary Form: George Herbert and Wilfred Owen," *Essays in Criticism*, 13 (1963), 307–22, for further parallels between Sidney and Herbert; and D. M. Hill, "Allusion and Meaning in Herbert's *Jordan I*," *Neophilologus*, 56 (1962), 344–52, for an interesting connection between the idea of embellishment in this poem and Sidney's term "Courtesanlike painted affectation" in the *Apology*; Hill reads these allusions in Herbert as a castigation of contemporary love poetry.

19.   Yet even here in "Affliction" (I), God is far more kingly ruler than sacred love object; the nature of courtly service is as much at issue as the courtier's ability to love rightly.

20.   Carew's collected poems play the sharp and wry statement in such lyrics as "A divine Mistris," "A prayer to the Wind," or "Ingratefull beauty threatned" in illuminating counterpoint to such sweet phrases and curling metaphors as we find in, say, "Aske me no more." The claims of the new courtly image – as so often in Sidney or Herbert – gain authority because Carew masters the old image so well.

21.   Cf. Hugh Richmond on qualities linking the Cavaliers to Herbert: "Renaissance lyrics offer thus a kind of systematic 'meteorology' of the spiritual climate of sexual love, analogous to Herbert's exposition of that of religious feeling" (*The School of Love: The Evolution of the Stuart Love Lyric* [Princeton, N.J., 1964], p. 146).

22.   A. J. Smith, "The Failure of Love: Love Lyrics After Donne," in *Metaphysical Poetry*, ed. Malcolm Bradbury and David Palmer (London, 1970), pp. 41–3.

23.   Smith defines the Caroline mode as enactment of "a celebration of love in the midst of questioning the point and dignity of life altogether, . . . [letting] the contrary motives stand as balancing opposites, gracefully posing a basic human question" (p. 48). As my examples suggest, I find Carew and Suckling to be concerned more with imbalances between aspiration and experience in love.

24.   Cf. Rebhorn, *Courtly Performances*, especially pp. 11–21.

25.   Since they appeared in the second edition of Sandys' *Paraphrase upon the Divine Poems* (1638), there is at least no chronological barrier to such speculations.

26. Carew did "strive to gaine . . . one Thorne" from the "dry leaveless Trunke on *Golgotha*" in a belated death-bed repentance, according to the apocryphal story, and made some verse paraphrases of the psalms. They lack, for the most part, the lively speaking voice of his secular poetry, though in Psalm 114 the characteristic tone of immediacy flashes out:

> What oh Sea, hath thee dismaide?
>   Why did Jourdane backwards make?
> Mountaines, why like Ramms affraide
>   Skipt yee, wherefore did yee shake
> Hillocks, like the Lambes that quake?

27. As cited in L. A. Beaurline, "New Poems by Sir John Suckling," p. 653. Beaurline meticulously reviews the evidence for attributing these lyrics from the Sackville manuscript to Suckling. Since they were probably written in the early 1620s, they could either reflect an acquaintance with Herbert's work – Latin or English – or simply confirm suggestive similarities of tone and language in the work of the two poets.

28. According to Beaurline,

> It might be argued that the best poem in this collection, "Upon Stephen stoned," is more characteristic of George Herbert than of Suckling, and we would not expect this kind of ingenuity from the young Cavalier. However we should notice that this is the one poem that breaks away from the crude couplets of the other religious verses and tries a stanza with varying line lengths, similar to Suckling's more successful songs: The writer exploits the paradoxes of Stephen's martyrdom, setting the literal against the metaphorical meanings of fire and stone, in order to show how the gentleness of Stephen's words was unable to penetrate the hard hearts of his persecutors. The words, turned to stones by the fire in the Jews' hearts, were hurled back at him and became his monument. Such an elaborate metaphysical conceit is not foreign to Suckling's powers. (p. 653)

29. Marc McCloskey and Paul R. Murphy, trans., *The Latin Poetry of George Herbert* (Athens, Ohio, 1965), p. 83. The original reads, "Qui silicem tundit, (mirum tamen) elicit ignem: / At Caelum è saxis elicuit Stephanus." These modern, often free translations of the Latin poetry may be compared with the selected translations by Edmund Blunden in "George Herbert's Latin Poems," *Essays and Studies*, 19 (1933), 29–39. See Robert Wickenheiser, "*Poetae Responsoriae:* A Study of George Herbert's Latin Poems and Their Relationship to His English Poems" (Ph.D. diss., U. of Minnesota, 1970), for an account of the considerable parallels in imagery between the two groups; and Edmund Miller, *Drudgerie Divine*, pp. 207–18, on the "Baroque Voice" of *Passio discerpta*.

30.   These are Beaurline's terms; he suggests that Suckling's "public image" – as "the prototype of an irreverent and fast living dilettante, the virtuoso gentleman of the earlier seventeenth century" – may obscure other, more serious qualities that the actual historical person also possessed. I have noted some of these in Chapter 2.

Chapter 4: Shreds of Holiness

1.   Similar inversions of perspective appear in two poems listed as doubtful by Hutchinson. "A Paradoxe. That the Sicke are in Better State then the Whole" urges, "Cease then to judge calamityes / By outward forme and showe, / But veywe yourselves, & inward turn your eyes." "To the Queene of Bohemia" plays on the figure of the perspective glass in relation to Elizabeth's exile in Holland – "Mee thinkes, in that Dutch optick I doe see / Thy curious vertues much more visibly: / There is thy best Throne" – and, as in "The Foil," argues the value of affliction in the heavenly perspective: "For afflictions are / A foile to sett of worth, & make it rare. / Through that black tiffany thy vertues shine / Fairer & richer" (pp. 210–11). "The Foil" is now generally accepted as Herbert's and an important addition to the canon: see Pebworth and Summers, "Recovering an Important Seventeenth-Century Poetical Miscellany"; Pebworth, "George Herbert's Poems to the Queen of Bohemia"; and Hovey, "George Herbert's Authorship of 'To the Queene of Bohemia.' " See John M. Steadman, "Herbert's Platonic Lapidary: A Note on 'The Foil,' " *Seventeenth-Century News,* 30 (1972), 59–62, for an excellent discussion of Herbert's perspectival inversions in that poem and the sources of the concept in classical tradition.

2.   This image of division and dissolution contrasts sharply with the lucidities and balances of "The British Church." In its limited and local application to England it anticipates the larger cycle of growth and decay traced in *The Church Militant,* where another personification, Sin, successfully dogs the true Christian church clear across the globe through all the ages of human time. In *B* the poem was entitled "Church-rents or schismes," a rather more equivocal way of putting it. In the *editio princeps,* published in the year Archbishop Laud came to power and schisms indeed began literally to rend apart the "Anglican compromise," the equivocal "or" is replaced by the more definite "and." No other title was altered from *B* to 1633; if J. Max Patrick's hypothesis in "Critical Problems in Editing George Herbert's *The Temple*" (J. M. Patrick and Alan Roper, *The Editor as Critic and the Critic as Editor* [Los Angeles, 1973], pp. 33–40) is correct, this alteration might represent Herbert's despairing judgment on the increased pace of division at this time. The poem itself, however, testifies sufficiently to Herbert's concern. See also Richard Strier, "George Herbert and the World," *Journal of Medieval and Renaissance Studies,* 11 (1981), especially pp. 232–6.

3. Hutchinson's note points out that the traditional (though mistaken) etymological association of the sycamore with the fig tree identifies the subject of the third stanza as the original fall of man (p. 505).

4. It would be overstating to speak of an apocalyptic vision in the lyrics preceding those on the Four Last Things, in spite of the temporal breadth of these images of destruction. Yet the perception of a world in pieces, "all cohaerence gone," without ever being an explicit and extended subject in the manner of *The Anniversaries,* shows how much Herbert shares the "Jacobean world view" of Donne in those poems.

5. For example, from an Elizabethan *Sermon of Obedience:* "Take awaie Kynges, Princes, Rulers, Magistrates, Judges, and suche states of God's ordre, no man shall ride or go by the high way unrobbed . . . , no man shall kepe his wife, children, and possessions in quietnesse, all thynges shall be common, and there muste nedes folowe all mischief and utter destruccion, bothe of soules, bodies, goodes, and common wealthes." Cited in Ernest W. Talbert, *The Problem of Order: Elizabethan Political Commonplaces and an Example of Shakespeare's Art* (Chapel Hill, N.C., 1962), p. 9. See also Talbert's discussion of this point (pp. 7–20) and his exposition of disorder in the state in the chapters on Sidney (pp. 89–118) and Richard II (pp. 146–200).

6. It is all the more interesting that Herbert calls on God in this poem to "turn out these wranglers" – rejecting both parts of the self and voices of others whom he would disown.

7. See Fish, *Self-Consuming Artifacts,* pp. 179–82: "Every withdrawal from a prideful claim only reconstitutes it on the other side of a gesture" (p. 182). In *The Living Temple,* Fish notes "the never-ending process of self-examination" recorded by the *Church* lyrics (p. 125), and I would argue that "Miserie" marks an advance – a moment of self-discovery – whose reconstitution of pride is only in later poems recognized as a retreat.

8. See Diana Benet, *Secretary of Praise,* pp. 55–63. Benet reads "The Bag," immediately following "Longing," as a corrective to the fragmentation and despair that "Longing" records.

9. "Jesu" also recovers the whole by assembling fragments:

> Jesu is in my heart, his sacred name
> Is deeply carved there: but th' other week
> A great affliction broke the little frame

> Ev'n all to pieces: which I went to seek:
> And first I found the corner, where was *J*,
> After, where *E S*, and next where *U* was graved.
> When I had got these parcels, instantly
> I sat me down to spell them, and perceived
> That to my broken heart he was *I ease you*,
>   And to my whole is *J E S U*.

"Spelling" the fragments – learning to recover a whole out of them – echoes Herbert's similar use of the term in "Church-monuments," another poem of fragmentation: "Therefore I gladly trust / My bodie to this school, that it may learn / To spell his elements, and finde his birth / Written in dustie heraldrie and lines" (6–9).

10.   The title of the poem, insofar as it refers to the scholastic sense of *quidditas* as essence or true substance, also supports such an interpretation. If the sacred verse that joins Herbert with God is the true substance, then courtly verse and, by extension, the courtly world as well consist merely of accidents, nonessentials possessing neither significance nor intrinsic worth. See *Oxford English Dictionary*, s.v. "quiddity," 1, and "accident," 6 and 7. Burton's *Anatomy of Melancholy* is cited for extension of the meaning of "accident" to "nonessential" or "accessory."

11.   See the information from Charles Cotton's *Compleat Gamester* on this term in Jess Cloud's note, *The Explicator*, 34 (1975), item 32, which also makes an ingenious argument for parallel Christian allusions as submerged references in each item of the courtly catalogue. Helen Vendler remarks that "The Quidditie" "finally shows the world to be only a sequential procession of single nouns and verbs," while "the final definition . . . limits the secular world suddenly to its own now impoverished inventory, which until this moment had seemed the spirited sum of all things and all doings" (p. 183). Although Vendler does not analyze this poem in terms of fragmentation, see her excellent discussion of the "almost surrealistic images of fragmentation and disconnection" in "Deniall" and "Longing," pp. 259–65.

12.   See, for instance, Mary Ellen Rickey, *Utmost Art: Complexity in the Verse of George Herbert* ([Lexington, Ky.], 1966), pp. 31–3; and Rosemond Tuve, *A Reading of George Herbert*, (1952; reprinted Chicago, 1969), pp. 187–8. Rickey makes a persuasive connection between "Jordan" (I) and sonnet 15 of *Astrophil and Stella*.

13.   Anthony Low, "Herbert's 'Jordan (I)' and the Court Masque," *Criticism*, 14 (1972), 109–18.

14.   See, for example, Summers, *George Herbert*, pp. 108–9. But there is still little agreement on this point; Low briefly summarizes the range of supposed allusions.

15. Since "The Temper" (II) did not precede "Jordan" (I) in W, we can suppose that their juxtaposition in B and 1633 represents Herbert's deliberate reordering. I would suggest also (as did D. M. Hill earlier) that line 3 – "Is all good structure in a winding stair?" – alludes both to poetry that winds about rather than plainly stating, and to the "winding stair" to court preferment described by Bacon:

> The rising unto place is laborious; and by pains men come to greater pains; and it is sometimes base; and by indignities men come to dignities. The standing is slippery, and the regress is either a downfall, or at least an eclipse, which is a melancholy thing. . . . All rising to great place is by a winding stair; and if there be factions, it is good to side a man's self whilst he is in the rising, and to balance himself when he is placed.

("Of Great Place," in Francis Bacon, Works, ed. James Spedding, Robert Ellis, and Douglas Heath [London, 1889], VI, 398–9, 401. All citations of Bacon are to this edition.)

As "The Quidditie" shows, the world of the court often lies behind Herbert's allusions to court verse. Low makes other connections with Bacon, on the suggestion of J. Max Patrick, in respect to the falsity of the masque ("Of Masques and Triumphs") and to the "winding and crooked courses" of falsity in general ("Of Truth"). Patrick also suggested to Low an association between the painted chair of "Jordan" (I) and the "chair of grace" in "The Temper" (II) which is similar to that which I propose, though Low sees it as the state chair in which the king is seated at a masque performance, while I believe it signifies the throne of the king to whom any courtly poet owes duty.

16. Harman, in Costly Monuments, notes that "Jordan" (I) "gives elaborate expression to the very tradition it would have us reject" (p. 45) and thus considers the final statement "reduced or minimal." But Herbert's claim that his King is God empowers his rejection of poetry that serves worldly kings just as, I think, his elaborate appropriation of the courtly poets' language does.

17. Harman calls this, like "Jordan" (I), a "collapsing" poem – "more successful in recording a dilemma than in solving one" (p. 48). As a rewriting of "Jordan" (II), "The Forerunners" affirms her position. Yet the echo of Sidney in "Jordan" (II) complicates Harman's claim that the "possibility of a new kind of writing is indicated in the final lines, but it has no representation in them": Astrophil did not inscribe Christ's "sweetnesse" in his love sonnets, but Herbert inscribes Sidney's language here.

18. See Strier's excellent analysis of "The Forerunners" in Love Known, pp. 208–17.

19. See, for instance, "The Quip," "A true Hymne," "The Sinner," "The Banquet," and "The Collar."

20. Fredson Bowers, "Herbert's Sequential Imagery: 'The Temper,' " *Modern Philology*, 59 (1962), 202–13, gives a valuable introduction to thematic clusters in *The Temple*; Bill Smithson, "Herbert's 'Affliction' Poems," *Studies in English Literature, 1500–1900*, 15 (1975), 125–40, offers what might be called a revisionist view of the matter. More recently, Sidney Gottlieb, "How Shall We Read Herbert? A Look at 'Prayer' (I)," *George Herbert Journal*, 1 (1977), 26–38; and Daniel Rubey, "The Poet and the Christian Community: Herbert's Affliction Poems and the Structure of *The Temple*," *Studies in English Literature, 1500–1900*, 20 (1980), 106–23 present two remarkably interesting and suggestively varied approaches; Gottlieb's "Linking Techniques in Herbert & Vaughan," *George Herbert Journal*, 2 (1978), 38–53, catalogues an extraordinary range of interconnective strategies.

Chapter 5: The Circumference of Earth

1. "Sion": "And now thy Architecture meets with sinne; / For all thy frame and fabrick is within" (11–12). In "The Search," Herbert asks: "Lord, dost thou some new fabrick mould, / Which favour winnes . . ." (25–6). Since the preceding stanza has referred to Herbert's groans, the image calls back to the insight in "Sion" that the "frame and fabrick" of the heart's Temple must be built of groans, "musick for a King." In "The Search," however, all Herbert's sighs and groans seem – once more – to be unheard by that King. In this poem he fears that *his* heart cannot constitute the new fabric molded by God.

2. These assertions relate *The Temple* to exemplary biographies and auto-biographies of its time by claiming a value for it that rests upon similar premises. If in our time a biographical reading of the work can be called "critically simplistic" (Roger B. Rollin, "Self-Created Artifact: The Speaker and the Reader in *The Temple*," in Summers and Pebworth, eds., "*Too Rich to Clothe the Sunne*," p. 160), Herbert's seventeenth-century audience saw the matter very differently. Hacket casts *Scrinia Reserata* into "the figure of a Moral Example" and claims that it is the "true Image" of Williams' life because "A right History is a System of Exemplary, or Practick Philosophy." His description of Williams closely resembles Ferrar's image of Herbert: "he was a man as like Vertue it self, as could be pattern'd in Flesh and Blood." As I pointed out in Chapter 2, Edward Herbert's autobiography shares a common pattern and purpose with exemplary biographies of the period. Of course Herbert's use of his own life in *The Temple* would associate his work with spiritual autobiography, but I stress the likeness to exemplary biography here because Ferrar's preface and, I believe, Herbert's

practice suggest a significant difference from the former genre: Ferrar views Herbert, and Herbert depicts himself, as a figure of the worldly courtier exemplary in his transformation to the holy priest.

3. For this view, see Martz, *The Poetry of Meditation,* pp. 288–320; Heather Asals, "The Voice of George Herbert's 'The Church'," *ELH,* 36 (1969), 511–28; and Hermine J. Van Nuis, "Herbert's 'Affliction' Poems: A Pilgrim's Progress," *Concerning Poetry,* 8 (1975), 7–16.

4. Helen C. White, in *The Metaphysical Poets: A Study in Religious Experience* (1936; reprinted Cambridge, 1964), refers to the seeming disorder of the sequence but suggests that the poems "tend . . . to gravitate into little centers and to form, as it were, beads of verse, sometimes loosely strung along the thread of a central procedure, more often not" (p. 160). See her fine brief discussion of the problem of order in *The Temple,* pp. 158–65. In *Secretary of Praise,* Diana Benet traces a vocation sequence somewhat different from mine (though our sequences often overlap), primarily because her reading generalizes the speaker of *The Temple* as "the Christian": she describes her sequence of twenty-three poems as Herbert's "partial and depersonalized autobiography" (p. 104). Our readings are perhaps both opposite and complementary, since I am attempting to "repersonalize" the voice of the "I" in Herbert's poems.

5. See Fredson Bowers, "Herbert's Sequential Imagery," for the first detailed tracing of sequence in these poems, though he deals only with the imagery of tempering. Bowers argues that the order is "planned according to developing sequences that work out major themes":

> within these sequential poems Herbert develops clusters of images that are appropriate not only for the poem in which they appear but also – in some sense – exist coincidentally with the individual poems and apply independently to the great central theme of the section and then of *The Temple.* I take it that Herbert . . . intended any separate poem to be read as a sufficient unit; but in addition, that he planned large sections of *The Temple* for a cumulative effect that could be gained only by reading a sequence in order and understanding its larger theme. (p. 202)

Bowers also notes "the occasional linking of poems by reference in first lines to the last lines of the preceding poem" (p. 203) that I call "juxtaposition." He does not mention "The H. Scriptures. II" in connection with the interrelated patterns of reference from poem to poem, perhaps because he stresses far more than I do the orderliness of the sequence. See also Amy Charles, "The Williams Manuscript and *The Temple,*" *Renaissance Papers* (1971), pp. 59–77, for a discussion of structural development from *W* to *B.*

6. These poems are interspersed among other first-person lyrics possessing

no overt biographical reference and still other, relatively impersonal lyrics concerning the liturgy, holy days, and architecture of the church or the state of humanity in general. Echoing figures create webs of cross-reference, constellations which enable us to read the person in the impersonal and to recognize the circumference that surrounds and informs the issues of vocation. Roger B. Rollin's "Self-Created Artifact: The Speaker and the Reader in *The Temple*" designates "Sacred Poems," "Private Ejaculations," and "Mixed Poems," each representing "three distinctive but related devotional modes, modes that necessitate [Herbert's] adoption of three somewhat different poetic voices or speakers" (pp. 148–9 in "*Too Rich to Clothe the Sunne*"). Benet, in *Secretary of Praise,* and Gottlieb, in "How Shall We Read Herbert?" and "Linking Techniques in Herbert and Vaughan," cross-cut freely to create their configurations, as I do. For earlier analyses of structure in *The Temple,* see Valerie Carnes, "The Unity of George Herbert's *The Temple:* A Reconsideration," *ELH,* 35 (1968), 505–26; Annabel Endicott, "The Structure of George Herbert's *The Temple:* A Reconsideration," *University of Toronto Quarterly,* 34 (1965), 226–37; Elizabeth McLaughlin and Gail Thomas, "Communion in *The Temple,*" *Studies in English Literature, 1500–1900,* 15 (1975), 111–24; Florence Sandler, " 'Solomon vbique regnet': Herbert's Use of the Images of the New Covenant," *Papers on Language and Literature,* 8 (1972), 147–58; Stanley Stewart, "Time and *The Temple,*" *Studies in English Literature, 1500–1900,* 6 (1966), 97–110; Joseph Summers, *George Herbert,* pp. 73–94; and J. D. Walker, "The Architectonics of George Herbert's *The Temple,*" *ELH,* 29 (1962), 289–305. The relation of experience to the design of *The Temple* is discussed by John R. Mulder, "George Herbert's *The Temple:* Design and Methodology," *Seventeenth-Century News,* 31 (1963), 37–45; and by A. L. Clements, "Theme, Tone, and Tradition in George Herbert's Poetry," *English Literary Renaissance,* 3 (1973), 264–83, though Clements is not primarily concerned to offer a structural theory of the work.

7.   William Perkins, "A Treatise of the Vocations or Callings of Men," in *The Work of William Perkins,* ed. Ian Breward (Abingdon, England, 1970), pp. 459–60. Elisions are Breward's. Perkins is an important source of Reformation "covenant theology" for Strier in *Love Known;* Robert Shaw, in "The Call of God: The Theme of Vocation in the Poetry of Donne and Herbert" ([n.p.], 1981), argues that Perkins attempted "to accommodate humanist ideas within a system bounded by Calvinist definitions" (p. 19).

8.   Ratcliffe, Cleland, and La Primaudaye especially make this point. Robert Shaw, in "The Call of God: The Theme of Vocation in Donne, Herbert, and Milton" (Ph.D. diss., Yale University, 1974), accepts the argument advanced by Richard M. Douglas, in "*Genus Vitae* and *Vocatio:*

Ideas of Work and Vocation in Humanist and Protestant Usage," Comité International des Sciences Historiques, XIIe Congrès International des Sciences Historiques, *Rapports,* III (Vienna, 1965), that there is a "diametric discrepancy between the humanist and early protestant views" of vocation arising from the humanist emphasis upon man's choice versus the Protestant stress upon God's disposing (Shaw, p. 24). Douglas' point, though, is that the humanist concern with "gifts and affections" as an index to one's proper vocation possessed "no relevance" for Luther and Calvin. But by Herbert's time the two views were blended, as Perkins' own Protestant treatise amply shows. According to Douglas, the question of choice "did not appear in Protestant thought until it was added by English Puritans of the seventeenth century" (p. 76). Perkins is thus a significant example of such a collocation.

Aside from this point, Shaw's dissertation and later book are essentially unrelated to my own study of vocation in Herbert, since he is primarily concerned with the larger concept of the term also discussed by Calvin, vocation as election by God to salvation, in distinction to vocation as the particular calling on earth designed by God for each person.

9.   Perkins, pp. 461–2. St. Ambrose, an important exemplar of the transition from a worldly to a heavenly vocation, was untrained for sacred service and bitterly resisted the calling *of the people* that drew him from the magistracy to the episcopacy. The experience of this Church Father, and the warnings in Perkins' Renaissance treatise, suggest the importance which the judgment of others might have held for Herbert.

10.   See Thomas Greene's valuable discussion of "transformation" as both possibility and problem in the Renaissance, "Flexibility of the Self," pp. 25–57.

11.   Two reasons are usually given: first, Walton's argument that Herbert was for a time enticed away from his purpose by the temptation to worldly glory provided by his office as Orator and the favorable notice of King James as well as several noblemen highly placed at court; second, the "argument of unworthiness" – that his own conviction of sin, and the additional burden of repeated illness, made Herbert question his capacity to undertake the duties of a priest. As I noted in Chapter 2, both Ferrar and Wotton offered the argument of unworthiness in their decision to remain deacons.

12.   It would seem most likely that Herbert is referring to his position as Orator, though he might, of course, be alluding to the academic posts he held before the Oratorship, which perhaps would have led to a calling as Fellow at Cambridge. Yet the emphasis on "Academick praise" and the half-serious threat to "go seek / Some other master out" suggest the shift from University Orator to servant of the crown made by his two predecessors in the Oratorship. Whether we accept Walton's version of the

circumstances or Ferrar's, "Some other master" certainly evokes kings and courts more than universities.

13.   W has an even more worldly term – "graces perquisites" – evoking courtly honors legitimized by God's bestowal of them as, indeed, Herbert suggests in "The Thanksgiving" – "If thou dost give me honour, men shall see, / The honour doth belong to thee."

14.   This complaint introduces the struggle alternatively to use his wit in God's service and to recognize its worldly insufficiency that we have seen worked out in the poems on poetry. Wit is implicated in Herbert's courtly vanity, but at the same time its loss is sorely regretted.

15.   Harman's brilliant analysis of "Affliction" (I), in *Costly Monuments,* pp. 89–105, shows how "God's restrictions . . . threaten the permanence and coherence of the self and frustrate the making of meaning upon which autobiography depends" (p. 105). I agree with her reading, yet I also see this poem as a deliberate dissolution of the self and its story, performed because the self's worldly identity – in Herbert's configuration over the entire *Church* sequence – entangles him in "the circumference of earth." This version of the self must be (repeatedly) unmade as a preliminary to re-making.

16.   In *Love Known,* Strier suggests that "Employment" (I) in its final stanza "undermines the traditional great chain conception" (p. 173). Herbert does, as Strier says, invoke "the possibility of being the object of a decisive action," becoming one of God's consort and thus transcending the "static hierarchy." But that transcendence is *only* possibility: the same stanza opens with a declaration of status – "I am no link of thy great chain, / . . . all my companie is a weed" – that locates Herbert, if anywhere, *below* the chain, not above in the consort.

17.   If no context were given in the poetic sequence, the interpretive problem would be entirely different. My point is that Herbert does provide his spiritual conflicts with a context; therefore he expects us to make these connections. The scriptures serve as exemplary text for Herbert's own work, just as his reading of scripture serves as model for our interpretation of *The Temple.* The rich variety of critical approaches to the work demonstrates that Herbert's readers recognize the principle even though it is not always explicitly stated. The great value of Tuve's *Reading of George Herbert* was her emphasis upon this heuristic source – thus opening the way for many other studies of interaction between the forms of scripture and *The Temple.*

18.   This pattern of interpretation is well known to all critics of Herbert, of course, and is not unlike the similar process of cross-reading pursued by any student of the sonnet sequences. But the contours of the narrative are far less

discernible in *The Temple:* the variety of metrical and stanzaic forms interrupts continuity and sets up new patterns of cross-connection, while the continual alternation of "personal" and "impersonal" lyrics emphasizes the fragmentation of attention – a double consideration not only of the poet's own state, but also the condition of the external world – that functions ultimately to incorporate disorder on every level before order either within or without can be achieved. Such incorporation, furthermore, qualifies the possibilities of a fully-realized sense of order.

19. The placement of "The H. Scriptures. II" immediately after "Employment" (I) invites the reader to begin "constellating" figures which have already set up echoes of earlier poems.

20. A canceled stanza of "Grace," just preceding, also emphasized delay in an accusation similar to Herbert's attack on God's cross-biasing in "Affliction" (I):

> What if I say thou seek'st delayes;
> Wilt thou not then my fault reprove?
> Prevent my Sinn to thine owne praise,
> > Drop from above.

But the juxtaposition of images here is new in *B;* in *W,* "Grace" appeared two poems after "Praise" (I).

21. Hutchinson glosses "let loose to" as "to aim at," but the association of crown and cloister with Charles V suggests relinquishment of the crown, not aspiration towards it. Yet "complies and suits with all estates" seems to define Herbert's meaning as that kind of acceptance even of kingship which values it rightly – i.e., not too much, and in the context of eternity, rather than temporality – a fleeting good, like all earthly goods in the poem.

22. For the Sidney–Languet correspondence, see Chapter 2, note 10, in the present work. If Walton's unsupported statements are correct, Herbert did retire to the country in the late 1620s. His lines in *Memoriae Matris Sacrum,* VII, offer a partial confirmation: "Out in the country / I have a tiny house with a panelled ceiling, / Ten roof beams in it; I have / A little garden too, where space / Fights it out with flowers' fleece; still, it is / The kind a tasteful owner wants" (trans. McCloskey and Murphy, *The Latin Poetry,* p. 139). Since Herbert shared in the proceedings of sale of the manor at Ribbesford at this time, such a life would have been possible.

23. See John B. Gleason, "Dr. Donne in the Courts of Kings: A Glimpse from Marginalia," *Journal of English and Germanic Philology,* 69 (1970), 599–612, for the "pressure of the actual" which Donne perhaps experienced in the role. Gleason makes a persuasive case for the compromises entailed by the position of one of James' favored preachers, and offers

interesting information about Donne's ironic references to current governmental abuses in the margins of his copy of More's *Lucubrationes*.

24. And it was described as the "Arminian Nunnery" in a scurrilous pamphlet so entitled.

25. See especially the full discussions in Earl Miner, *The Cavalier Mode from Jonson to Cotton* (Princeton, 1971), pp. 43–99, and Maren-Sofie Røstvig, *The Happy Man,* 2nd ed., rev. (Oslo, 1962), I, *passim.*

26. A similar contrast of perspectives is found in "Coloss. 3.3" and "The Wreath." "Coloss. 3.3" defines the straight line as that which ties us to earth, while an oblique motion tends upward to God. But "The Wreath," much later in *The Church,* contrasts Herbert's "crooked winding wayes" with the directness of God's path for man. Arnold Stein, in *George Herbert's Lyrics* (Baltimore, 1968), pp. 33–37, discusses Herbert's reshaping of the traditional "plot" of "rejecting the ways of the world, the flesh, and the devil, each in a stanza," though I am not sure that Herbert's three rejections fit this traditional list quite as neatly as Stein believes. Barbara Harman reads the "silk twist" as a loss of mutuality (*Costly Monuments,* p. 91) and Stanley Fish suggests there must be "yet a yet to the speaker's fourth 'Yet' " (*Self-Consuming Artifacts: The Experience of Seventeenth-Century Literature* [Berkeley, 1972], p. 179). I'd agree that later lyrics in the sequence recognize the "yet" still to come, but argue that Herbert's earlier uses of labyrinth and entanglement figures mark this ending as an enabling (if momentary) insight about *reciprocal* roles for God and Herbert.

27. Sharon Seelig, in *The Shadow of Eternity: Belief and Structure in Herbert, Vaughan, and Traherne* (Lexington, Ky., 1981) sees "spiritual naïveté" in ll. 15–16 of "Submission"; I think there's also a somewhat begrudging relinquishment of the spiritual pride which is immediately uncovered in "Justice" (I).

28. Many poems earlier, in "Mattens," Herbert hoped that "this new light, which now I see, / May both the work and workman show: / Then by a sunne-beam I will climbe to thee" (18–20).

29. "Miserie" ends by figuring Herbert *into* the design he has castigated in others; in constructing an exemplary pattern, his participation in human sinfulness might also draw his readers to figure themselves into his efforts to overcome his condition.

30. As, of course, "The Altar" had pointed out from the beginning. But the lyrics we have been examining trace the constructions of the worldly self that, in its pride, would do without God's hand.

31. St. Ambrose, *On the Duties of the Clergy,* trans. Rev. H. de Romestin, in Philip Schaff and Henry Wace, eds., *A Select Library of the Nicene and Post-Nicene Fathers of the Christian Church,* Second Series, vol. X (Grand

Rapids, Mich., 1955), p. 31. The translator gives "experience" for Ambrose's *probatio,* a term far more expressive of the testing process that Herbert speaks of in "The Flower" as not only "finding" but "proving."

32. See the portrait of Herbert, from the drawing by Robert White, reproduced as frontispiece to Amy Charles' *Life of Herbert;* the image wonderfully illustrates Herbert's text.

33. Again St. Ambrose provides the best gloss on the process of *probatio* that is now beginning to work patience and hope rather than outcries and despair:

> In these two points, then, consists the excellency of the soul: so that thy soul, trained in good thoughts, and with a pure heart, first, may see what is true and virtuous . . . , and may decide that only to be good which is virtuous; and, next, may never be disturbed by business of any kind, nor get tossed about by any desires.
>
> Not that this is an easy thing for any one. For what is so difficult as to discern, as though from some watch-tower, the resources of wisdom and all those other things, which to most seem so great and noble? Again, what so difficult as to place one's decision on fixed grounds, and to despise what one has decided to be worthless, as of no good? Or, once more, what so difficult, when some misfortune has happened, and it is looked on as something serious and grieving, as to bear it in such a way that one considers it nothing beyond what is natural. (p. 32)

The perspective of "The Size" is indeed "as though from some watch-tower": the equanimity of Herbert's self-assessment reflects his growth in fortitude.

34. I won't even try to acknowledge the wealth of interpretations of "The Collar," nor am I offering in any sense a reading of the poem: what I do want to stress is how its referents vary according to the poems with which we configure it. "The Collar" not only contains a retrospective narrative, but is itself a retrospective gathering of images from earlier lyrics in the sequence.

35. Although the child figure suggests submission, perhaps abdication of the will, the restoration of rhyme in the closing lines *enacts* reciprocity.

36. This statement signifies in reverse, too: the meek Christ flatters Herbert's power to welcome Him within Herbert's stony heart, to give Him the creative joy of turning Herbert's rough and inanimate clay into something of rare life and beauty.

37. Here, as in "Jesu" and "Church-monuments," "spelling the elements" recovers the wholeness that man's limited perspective prevents him from recognizing.

38. St. Ambrose says of the clerical calling: "I think, then, that one should strive to win preferment, especially in the Church, only by good actions and with a right aim; so that there may be no proud conceit, no idle carelessness, no shameful disposition of mind, no unseemly ambition. A plain simplicity of mind is enough for everything, and commends itself quite sufficiently" (p. 61).

39. Herbert's transformation thus resembles that of Red Crosse in Book I of *The Faerie Queene,* noted by Greene, "Flexibility of the Self." But because in Herbert's vision the transformed self does *not* transcend human limitations, *The Temple* in a sense offers a solution to the dilemma of limits to transformation posed by Montaigne and other late Renaissance writers. See Greene, pp. 359–64.

Chapter 6: All The Frame and Fabric Is Within

1. While most critics concentrate entirely upon *The Church,* some uneasily try to account for *The Church-porch* and *The Church Militant* by apologizing for the former and disjoining the latter altogether from *The Church.* On *The Church Militant,* see especially Endicott, "The Structure of George Herbert's *Temple*"; and Lee Ann Johnson, "The Relationship of 'The Church Militant' to *The Temple,*" *Studies in Philology,* 68 (1971), 200–6. J. E. Mason, associating *The Church-porch* with seventeenth-century books of parental advice, stresses its attention to surface manners. Such a view, common also in recent criticism, does not differentiate between a preoccupation with mere surface and the measurement of habitual virtue by the evidence of behavior. Joseph Summers calls *The Church-porch* "a long didactic poem which wittily appeals to a semi-worldly common sense" (*George Herbert,* p. 103). Barbara Lewalski refers to its "dry, didactic prescriptions regarding the externals of a Christian life and the behavior fitting a Christian profession which constantly echo classical moral philosophy and ethics" ("Typology and Poetry: A Consideration of Herbert, Vaughan, and Marvell" in *Illustrious Evidence: Approaches to English Literature of the Early Seventeenth Century,* ed. Earl Miner [Berkeley, 1975], p. 52), and C. A. Patrides, in his introduction to *The English Poems of George Herbert,* speaks of both *The Church-porch* and *The Church Militant* as "brutally moralistic" (p. 15). See also the generic study by Sheridan D. Blau, "The Poet as Casuist: Herbert's 'Church-Porch,' " *Genre,* 4 (1971), 142–52.

Amy Charles cautions us about attributing the work's title and its epigraph, "In his Temple doth every man speake of his honour," to Herbert (*Life of Herbert,* pp. 185–6). Since neither title nor epigraph appear in W or

B, we have no firm evidence that Herbert himself rather than, possibly, Nicholas Ferrar designated this overarching title for his three-part structure. Nevertheless, the figure of the temple of the spirit is so pervasive within the work as to perfectly reflect Herbert's conception. Although Charles finds the title less appropriate than *The Church,* she does not consider figurative uses of the temple in scripture and commentary.

2.   See especially 1 Cor. 6:19, "know ye not that your body is the temple of the Holy Ghost which is in you, which ye have of God, and ye are not your own?" and 2 Cor. 6:16, "for ye are the temple of the living God." See also Summers, *George Herbert,* p. 85; Fish, *The Living Temple,* pp. 54–89; Lewalski, "Typology and Poetry," pp. 49–53; and Patrides, *The English Poems of George Herbert,* pp. 16–17, who cites Acts 17:24 – "God that made the world and all things therein, seeing that he is Lord of heaven and earth, dwelleth not in temples made with hands" – a text stressing the crucial distinction Herbert makes in "Sion" between the work of man and the work of God. Patrides also cites Donne's application of the figure to the Church, though as "Sion" implies and as my discussion of *The Church Militant* will attempt to show, I do not believe that the Temple primarily represents *ecclesia* to Herbert.

3.   Only stanza 71 ("Let vain or busie thoughts have there no part: / Bring not thy plough, thy plots, thy pleasures hither"), which is also directed to behavior in church, suggests the "intended audience of modest intelligence for the most part probably rustic" assumed by Arnold Stein for *The Church-porch* (p. 13). But of course even "thy plough" might refer to the lord of the country estate as well as to his tenants. Such stanzas as 47 – "Yet be not surety, if thou be a father" – do not limit Herbert's advice to a sweet youth just entering adulthood but, like that in stanza 15 – "Art thou a Magistrate?" – address his activities in the world and his place in society throughout adult life. See Robert B. Hinman's persuasive configuration of the Verser in "The 'Verser' at the *Temple* Door: Herbert's 'The Church-porch'," in Summers and Pebworth, *"Too Rich to Clothe the Sunne,"* pp. 55–75, and Stephenie Yearwood, "The Rhetoric of Form in *The Temple,*" *Studies in English Literature, 1500–1900,* 23 (1983), 131–44.

4.   This negative image of "sheepishnesse" contrasts with the transvalued pastoral imagery in "Christmas," 17–22, and *The Church Militant,* 71–2.

5.   See p. 44 in the present work for Herbert's clear distinction between true and false "braverie" in "great deeds" (stanza 37) and the marked contrast to Edward Herbert's preoccupation with the show of honor in respect to dueling: "do them not" invokes a wisdom that undoes his brother's active and choleric pride. The figure of the web in stanza 38 resembles Bacon's citation of Guicciardini in *De Augmentis Scientiarum:* "the resolution of men truly moral ought to be such as the same Gonsalvo

required in a soldier, 'whose honour,' he said, 'should be of a stouter web, and not so fine as that everything should catch in it, and rend it' " (V, 10). See Hutchinson's note on the passage, p. 480, for other uses of the figure in Bacon.

6. Stanza 11 also metaphorically contrasts exterior and interior, though here it is the vice of excess which ought to be "pared away" down to the virtuous substance of true wit:

> When thou dost tell anothers jest, therein
> Omit the oathes, which true wit cannot need:
> Pick out of tales the mirth, but not the sinne.
> He pares his apple, that will cleanly feed.
>   Play not away the vertue of that name,
>   Which is thy best stake, when griefs make thee tame.

7. The sixteenth-century courtesy books considered the vice of intemperance a particular danger to the young, and notably include linguistic excess in this category. See, for example, Lodowick Bryskett's denunciation of extreme merriment, "quips and biting speeches," and the preference for "pleasant conceits" rather than "grave sayings" – all, he says, special failings of youth – in his *Discourse of a Civill Life* (1594), ed. Thomas E. Wright (Northridge, Calif., 1970), pp. 78–9.

8. This procedure of condensing much into little has already been noted in Chapter 4, in reference to such brief lyrics as "The Quidditie" and "Dotage," and is not sufficiently stressed in studies of *The Temple*. Despite the personal emphasis of many of the lyrics in *The Church* and the single-minded focus on social behavior in *The Church-porch*, Herbert's scope of reference incorporates the entire world of his time with remarkable economy and consequent force. It is like looking through a perspective glass turned the wrong way around; everything in Herbert's world is clear, sharp, but reduced in size to its essential parts. See Rosalie Colie, *The Resources of Kind: Genre-Theory in the Renaissance*, ed. Barbara K. Lewalski (Berkeley, 1973) for a productive series of speculations on the significance of "small forms" in the later Renaissance, especially her key chapter on the topic, "*Multum in parvo*." Herbert's reflections of the contemporary world incorporate both his society and his criticism of that society into even his most personal lyrics in a way not unlike the inclusion, noted by Colie, of social elements in such "psychological" forms as the love sonnet.

9. La Primaudaye's chapter, "Of Speech and Speaking," in *The French Academie* is particularly interesting in relation to Herbert's attitudes toward conversation and the use of wit in *The Church-porch*. La Primaudaye argues

that "All talke ought to have reason for a foundation, and the love of our neighbor for a marke to aime at." He quotes Agapetus, *"That the toong is a slipperie instrument, and bringeth great danger to those that neglect it,"* and adds, "but if we direct it with a religious understanding, it will sing us a song tuned with the concords of a true harmony of vertue." Like Herbert in stanza 52, La Primaudaye also stresses that

> bicause in every action of our life, the perturbations of the soule are to be eschewed, we must be carefull that our speech be voide thereof: namely, that it be without choler, without extreame affections, also without carelesnes, and other such like imperfection. Especially we must strive to make it knowne, that we love & reverence those with whom we speake. (sig. K iii^r)

Herbert's recurrent references to language in a poem primarily concerned with behavior reflect an estimate of its importance similar to La Primaudaye's: "talke being the messenger of thought discloseth our maners a great deal more than the lines & draughts of our face do" (sig. K iv^v).

10. This association of magnanimity and humility reflects Cicero's warning in *De Officiis*, "the higher we are placed, the more humbly should we walk" (trans. Walter Miller [1913; reprinted London, 1951], i.26.90). Hutchinson's note cites the *Arcadia*, II.vi.2: "Who shootes at the mid-day Sunne, though he be sure he shall never hit the marke; yet as sure he is, he shall shoote higher, then who aymes but at a bush" – an interesting reference since these words of Pamela to Musidorus, encouraging his suit, also praise his modeling himself upon Pyrocles, whom Musidorus has just described as the ideal courtier: "so could not you . . . finde in the world a fitter subject of commendation; as noble, as a long succession of royall ancestors, famous, and famous of victories could make him: of shape most lovely, and yet of mind more lovely; valiant, curteous, wise, what should I say more?" (Feuillerat, I, 184). See Barbara Lewalski, *Protestant Poetics*, pp. 284–92, on the multiple generic sources of *The Church-porch*.

11. This reflection of the randomness of experience, and the difficulties of attaining to virtue given man's actual failings, resembles Bacon's argument in *De Augmentis*, calling for a "Georgics of the Mind," that the most "noble and effectual" means of "reducing the mind unto virtue" is

> *"the electing and propounding unto a man's self good and virtuous ends of his life and actions; such as may be in a reasonable sort within his compass to attain.* For if these two things be supposed, that a man set before him honest and good ends, and again that his mind be resolute and constant to pursue and obtain them, it will follow that his mind shall address and mould itself to all virtues at once."

Bacon's recommendations for "obtaining virtue by habit" describe a process much like that worked out by Herbert. In both *Church-porch* and *Church,* rather than postulating a sequential pattern of progress in virtue, Herbert works on "rudiments" of all the parts at once. This process conforms to Bacon's recommendation that the Georgics of the Mind seek to account for the hindrances men actually experience within themselves, as well as for the ideal toward which they are striving. He calls for

> *knowledge touching the affections and perturbations,* which are, as I have said, the diseases of the mind. . . . But to speak the real truth, the poets and writers of history are the best doctors of this knowledge, where we may find painted forth with great life and dissected, how affections are kindled and excited, and how pacified and restrained, and how again contained from act and further degree; how they disclose themselves, though repressed and concealed; how they work; how they vary; how they are enwrapped one within another; how they fight and encounter one with another. (V, 23–4)

Herbert's lyrics evidently work in this way, particularly when he is concerned with the internal government of his unruly faculties and discovering the worldly entanglements which separate him from God.

12.   As in stanza 21, Herbert appeals to the courtier's sense of decorum and natural response to the worldly hierarchy in order to raise his sights to the higher King to whom, all the more, he *should* owe allegiance. Strier remarks that the "ideal is the supremely flexible and uninhibited opportunist" ("George Herbert and the World," p. 232, referring particularly to stanza 59). But the opportunism betrayed in such stanzas is that classical, humanist aspiration which seeks the "goods" of *both* earth and heaven. The insufficiency of such a harmonious ascent from the one state to the other is exactly the problem that the assured Verser, safely distanced from his *own* worldliness in the second-person address of the *Porch,* will only uncover in the first-person failures of *The Church* to rhyme *himself* to good.

13.   La Primaudaye shows how worldly and heavenly prudence are interrelated. Prudence, he says, flows from

> that true and perfect Idea of Good, . . . that she may governe their actions according to Gods will, and to the profit of humane societie. Therefore it is from knowledge and reason gotten in the studie of wisedome by the grace of God, from whence the vertue of Prudence proceedeth, which is that rule of all the actions of man, whereby through good and sage advice he discerneth and chooseth good from bad, that which is profitable from the contrarie, to the end he may shun the one and practice the other. . . . But Prudence is a beame proceeding

from that true sunne, which doth not only illuminate and lighten the understanding, but also warmeth and kindleth the affection. . . . To be short, Prudence causeth a man to refer all his actions both private and publike to the best end, which is, to serve God, and to profit his neighbor. (sigs. H iv^v–iv^r, H v^r)

La Primaudaye here uses the same figure of clarity and light to denote Christ's instructions for heavenly wisdom that Herbert employs in "Divinitie." The passage and its emphasis recall Herbert's comment in *The Church-porch*: "Man is but a shop of rules."

14. J. Hutchison, cited in Alexander Grosart, *The Complete Works in Verse and Prose of George Herbert* (London, 1874), II, xcii.

15. Josephine W. Bennett, in *The Evolution of "The Faerie Queene"* (1942; reprinted New York, 1960), notes an interesting precedent to Herbert's substitution of Mansuetude for one of the four cardinals: "The Bible of 1569 has on its title-page a picture of the Queen with Justice and Mercy (in place of Temperance) supporting her crown, and Fortitude and Prudence supporting the throne" (p. 224).

16. Hutchinson, p. 501. Hutchinson's assumption that the beasts are the passions seems to rest entirely on a comparable use in *The Church-porch* (263–4), but a consideration of sources in Christian iconography suggests a more specific relationship between these particular beasts and the vices contrary to the cardinal virtues.

17. Another level of meaning may be operating simultaneously, since in Christian iconography the peacock also represented the Resurrection. By showing the Virtues beholding and coveting "the grace / Of that brave gift," Herbert is surely referring to the plume as a sign of worldly pride, an exterior show ("bravery" as he uses it in *The Church-porch*); yet if the plume, when rightly understood in its spiritual significance, symbolizes the Resurrection, the action of Humilitie in giving it to all, as an echo of Christ's humble sacrifice, translates the gift to a spiritual one which rightly strengthens rather than divides the harmonious rule of the Virtues.

Louis Réau points out the peacock's double significance: "Quant au symbole de la Résurrection, il a été tout naturellement suggéré par la mue annuelle de cet oiseau qui perd chaque hiver son magnifique plumage pour le retrouver au printemps. Les théologiens en ont tiré cette conclusion que, comme le paon, 'notre corps rejettera un jour les plumes de la mortalité pour revêtir celles de l'immortalité.'" Furthermore, the peacock doubly signifies vice and virtue, since it is "Emblème de l'orgueil quand il fait la roue, il se 'pavane' en étalant son plumage. Mais s'il regard la laideur de ses pattes, il se sent humilité et laisse retomber sa queue" (*Iconographie de l'Art Chrétien* [Paris, 1955], I, 83, 130). See also George Ferguson, *Signs and*

Symbols in Christian Art (New York, 1959), p. 9. Since the peacock refuses to offer up his plume in Herbert's poem, we cannot suppose that he has developed humility through the regard of his ugly paws rather than his beautiful tail, but it is Humilitie who offers this gift which restores rule to the Virtues and renews the harmony destroyed by their wrangling. As the gift of humility, the peacock's plume clearly does not represent only worldly pride. In the turn of the fable, it may indeed symbolize the gift of Christ to man.

18. See William A. Ringler's valuable commentary and notes on the poem, pp. 112–15. "Humilitie" may be further associated with Philisides' pastoral eclogue since it raises to a higher level of application a tale whose overtones were originally worldly and political, a process which accords with the poetic principle attributed to Languet (Sidney's mentor and the teacher of this song to Philisides) in an early stanza of the poem:

> He said, the Musique best thilke powers pleasd
> Was jump concorde between our wit and will:
> Where highest notes to godlines are raisd
> And lowest sinke not downe to jote of ill. . . .
>   (29–32)

Herbert's retelling accomplishes this purpose as Sidney's poem does not, since Humilitie's conciliatory act of relinquishment rescues the virtues from their descent to "jote of ill" by following the example set by "godlines." See Richard Strier, "Ironic Humanism in *The Temple*," in Summers and Pebworth, eds., *"Too Rich to Clothe the Sunne,"* pp. 45–50, for another view of the poem's critique of Christian humanism.

19. The poem has been criticized as a lapse into un-Christian stoicism by Clark L. Chalifour ("Genre and Didactic Purpose in George Herbert's *The Temple*" [Ph.D. diss, Brown University, 1970]) who finds the " 'honest man' of *Constancie*" to be

> more stoic than Christian. . . . There is no mention of faith, hope, or charity, but the cardinal virtues are all present in the character. . . . This man suffers from the taint of prigishness [sic] common to all paragons of natural virtue. . . . Humility, the religious virtue that redeems the cardinal virtues, is certainly not characteristic of Herbert's honest man. The placement of the third *Affliction* immediately after *Constancie* poses another reason for qualifying the stoic ideal. (p. 141)

Chalifour's interesting discussion of this group of poems also sets them in the virtues tradition, and we share many common readings of their significance, though his emphasis upon their stoicism rather than their Christian humanism leads him to somewhat different conclusions from mine.

20. The tone as well as the substance of this figure are wonderfully appropriate to the legend, propagated by Walton, of Herbert's worldly concern with elegant attire.

21. These images remind us of the celestial court in which Herbert envisions himself in "The Starre," which as Elizabeth Stambler notes is a "very courtly heaven" ("The Unity of Herbert's 'Temple'," p. 259).

22. Not all Herbert's critics would agree that such poems as "The Holdfast" and "Mans medley" allow any efficacy remaining to man's will once it harmonizes with God's will. But if all things are *more ours* "by being his," the self is at the very least reified and, I think Herbert claims, enlarged rather than diminished by its harmonizing.

23. William A. Nestrick, " 'Mine and Thine' in *The Temple*," in Summers and Pebworth, eds., *"Too Rich to Clothe the Sunne,"* pp. 115–27, shows how the reciprocities of "Clasping of Hands" work both to separate and to unify.

24. In the graceful conceit of "To All Angels and Saints," heaven is a court and its inhabitants are not only courtly but regal. Here, "ev'ry one is king, and hath his crown, / If not upon his head, yet in his hands." Yet Herbert "dare not" worship these heavenly beings,

> for our King,
> Whom we do all joyntly adore and praise,
> Bids no such thing:
> And where his pleasure no injunction layes,
> ('Tis your own case) ye never move a wing.
>
> All worship is prerogative, and a flower
> Of his rich crown, from whom lyes no appeal
> At the last houre:
> Therefore we dare not from his garland steal,
> To make a posie for inferiour power.
>
> Although then others court you, if ye know
> What's done on earth, we shall not fare the worse;
> Who do not so;
> Since we are ever ready to disburse,
> If any one our Masters hand can show.
>
> (16–30)

In " 'To all Angels and Saints': Herbert's Puritan Poem," *Modern Philology,* 77 (1979), 132–45, Richard Strier notes the poem's shift from its opening vision of a "democratic" heaven – "Where ev'ry one is king, and hath his crown" – to a "vision of a single absolute monarch reigning equally over both heaven and earth" (p. 135).

25. Though Herbert's pattern of ascent is of course Christian, not Platonic.

26. On this point, see Strier, "Herbert and Tears," *ELH*, 46 (1979), 221–47.

27. This is only a more subtle but, in tone at least, more humble version of Herbert's conclusion to "The Priesthood":

> There will I lie, untill my Maker seek
> For some mean stuffe whereon to show his skill:
> Then is my time. The distance of the meek
> Doth flatter power. Lest good come short of ill
> In praising might, the poore do by submission
>   What pride by opposition.
>   (37–42)

28. Helen Vendler also uses this phrase in relation to "Love" (III). See her excellent discussion of the poem (*Poetry of George Herbert*, pp. 274–6).

29. Cf. "Longing": "Thy board is full, yet humble guests / Finde nests."

30. Of course Castiglione prescribes an appearance of ease cloaking artfulness. This sense of *sprezzatura* is appropriate to Herbert's poetic art in "Love" (III). But the simplicity of act presented in the poem is, I think, earthly *sprezzatura* itself transfigured.

31. See Stanley Stewart, "Time and *The Temple*," for a judicious interpretation of the "deliberate 'distancing' " of *The Church Militant* from *The Church* as a transition from the temporal to the timeless in contrast to the temporal and spatial transition from *Church-porch* to *Church;* and G. J. Weinberger, "George Herbert's 'The Church Militant,' " *Connecticut Review*, 4 (1971), 49–57, for an account of *The Church Militant* as "the historical equivalent of what we may call the public or popular experiences of 'The Church-Porch' and of the individual inner experiences of 'The Church' " (p. 49).

32. See Dwight Levang, "George Herbert's 'The Church Militant' and the Chances of History," *Philological Quarterly*, 36 (1957), 265–8. In 1635, according to William Prynne in *Canterburies Doome*, Samuel Ward of Ipswich was imprisoned for remarking in the course of a sermon that "*Religion and the gospel stood on tiptoes ready to be gone.*" The close resemblance of Ward's language to Herbert's lines justifies Levang's supposition that the Puritan preacher was deliberately alluding to them. Levang also suggests that

> A second conjecture may be made. May not the severity of Ward's
> punishment, when compared with the mild hesitation of the Vice-

Chancellor over Herbert's lines, indicate the increased political and religious tension that came with Laud's program of "Thorough"? Laud's systematic efforts to enforce conformity to orthodox ritual really began only in 1633 (the year *The Temple* was published), when he succeeded the Calvinistic Abbot as Archbishop of Canterbury. The "thoroughness" of Laud's program is perhaps illustrated by comparing the Vice-Chancellor's liberal action in 1633 toward Herbert's lines from "The Church Militant" with the severity of Laud toward the same words and sentiment in the year 1635. (pp. 267–8).

According to Walton's unsupported statement, the Vice-Chancellor finally accepted *The Temple* because, he is supposed to have said, "I knew Mr. Herbert well, and know that he had many heavenly speculations, and was a divine poet: but I hope the world will not take him to be an inspired prophet, and therefore I license the whole book." This remark suggests the complicated interrelationship between the roles of exemplar and of prophet. If Walton's reconstruction is not just the work of his own imaginative hindsight, the Vice-Chancellor's attitude witnesses both to Herbert's exemplary power in his time and to the Anglican establishment's ability to ignore even its own "inspired prophets." Herbert may have been expressing far more explicitly prophetic concerns than his Anglican and Royalist readers, drifting toward civil war, cared to heed, though it is also clear from later references to these lines in *The Temple* by Puritan readers that they, at least, read such allusions in this manner.

33.   The best gloss on Herbert's Temple is perhaps not scripture or commentary, but Martin Heidegger's chapter "Building Dwelling Thinking" in *Poetry, Language, Thought,* trans, and introd. Albert Hofstadter (New York, 1971), as my student Diane Riley has reminded me. Heidegger brings together structure and figure by tracing the relations between building and dwelling. He conjoins *Bauen,* building; Old English and High German *buan,* to dwell; and *bin,* to be:

> What then does *ich bin* mean? The old word *bauen,* to which the *bin* belongs, answers: *ich bin, du bist* mean: I dwell, you dwell. The way in which you are and I am, the manner in which we humans *are* on the earth, is *Buan,* dwelling. To be a human being means to be on the earth as a mortal. It means to dwell. . . . Building as dwelling, that is, as being on the earth . . . remains for man's everyday experience that which is from the outset "habitual" – we inhabit it. (p. 147)

"Dwelling," for Heidegger, *is* the state of our being: "on the earth," "under the sky," "remaining before the divinities," and "belonging to men's being with one another" (p. 149). So Herbert says in the last stanza of "Man":

Since then, my God, thou hast
So brave a Palace built; O dwell in it,
That it may dwell with thee at last!
Till then, afford us so much wit;
That, as the world serves us, we may serve thee,
And both thy servants be.

Index